Adrian McGregor is a feature writer with wide experience on Australian newspapers. He is currently employed with the *Sydney Morning Herald* where he began his career. He has worked on Fleet Street, the *Australian* and the *Courier-Mail*, and for five years was Queensland Bureau Chief of the *National Times*. He has a BA from the University of Queensland where he tutored in journalism for many years. He has won several journalism prizes, including a National Press Club award for best sporting feature. His biography of cricketer Greg Chappell has been acclaimed as one of the finest contemporary contributions to the history of cricket. His second biography *King Wally* was also a bestseller, and a pioneer in the field of quality football writing.

Wally and the Broncos

Adrian McGregor

University of Queensland Press

First published 1989 by University of Queensland Press,
Box 42, St Lucia, Queensland 4067 Australia
Reprinted 1989

Typeset by Savage Type, Brisbane
Printed in Australia by The Book Printer, Melbourne

Distributed in the USA and Canada by
International Specialized Book Services, Inc.,
5602 N.E. Hassalo Street, Portland, Oregon 97213-3640

Cataloguing in Publication Data

National Library of Australia

McGregor, Adrian.
    Wally and the Broncos.

    Includes index.

    1. Lewis, Wally, 1959- . 2. Rugby football players —
Australia — Biography. 3. Rugby League football — New
South Wales. 4. Broncos (Football team). I. Title.

796.33'3'0924

ISBN 0 7022 2182 1

CONTENTS

PREFACE

Over the past two years momentous events have transformed rugby league in Australia. Just when it seemed Wally Lewis's career had peaked, new horizons opened before him with the entry of the Brisbane Broncos into the Sydney premiership.

The Broncos became a sporting phenomenon. They gave Queenslanders another opportunity to express partisan loyalties in the ongoing, friendly, north-south sporting debate. And they proved themselves just as fascinating to Sydney fans, swelling crowd attendances wherever they played, from the Gold Coast to Wollongong.

Wally and the Broncos takes up where *King Wally* left off — when Wally returned from leading the victorious 1986 Kangaroos. With Wally's help I traced the Broncos from Queensland's historic decision in early 1987 to send a team to Sydney, through the Broncos' exciting first season. As usual Wally made his own history en route, through such incidents as the beer-can state-of-origin and his heroism in playing on with a broken arm during the World Cup final in New Zealand.

For the background of documented material included here I readily acknowledge the reports of Paul Malone, Steve Ricketts and Robert Craddock of the Brisbane *Courier-Mail* and the *Sun*'s Bernie Pramberg. Daily they wrote history from the battlefront at Lang Park. The *Sydney Morning Herald*'s John Mac-Donald and Paul Tait reported Wally and the Broncos' appearances in their bailiwick with sympathy and insight.

I am indebted to the *Courier-Mail* for the use of their cutting files and photographic libraries. Helen King proved invaluable as transcript typist and reader.

In *King Wally* I related the life of the master footballer. *Wally and the Broncos* ventures further along that intriguing, rock-strewn path while at the same time bringing us closer to history in the making.

1 HISTORY IN THE MAKING

The phone rang in Paul Vautin's comfortable hillside home a short jog from the northern beaches of Sydney. The STD beeps subsided. "Fatty?" asked Wally in an amiable voice. Yeah? replied Vautin. Wally: "We're going to bash you when you come up here!" Click! Giggling to himself Wally sat back, waiting for the return call, which duly came. Vautin laughed disarmingly, "Ah, good one mate. What's doing?" Not much said Wally, relaxed, you? "Not much," said Vautin. "Oh, except for this match against some low Brisbane cats who can't play." Wally laughed and the two good mates chatted about football, their families and work.

With theatrical staging the Brisbane Broncos, led by Wally, were cast for their historic debut in the Sydney premiership in 1988, against the 1987 premiers, Manly, captained by Vautin. Wally and Paul had played against each other as juniors in Brisbane's under-18 competition, and together for Brisbane, Queensland and Australia. They had toured, shared memories of victories and defeats that would last a lifetime. Their friendship went back 15 years and the Broncos' challenge to Sydney could not affect that, even temporarily. Those conversations were the closest thing to light relief Wally enjoyed in the tension-filled week leading up to the match.

Sunday 6 March 1988 loomed in Wally's mind as a challenge the equal of his titanic struggles against NSW in the state-of-origins. His Sydney critics conceded he had proved himself in that fierce furnace, but there were only three Origin matches a year. How would Wally go in the weekly grind of the Sydney premiership, touted as the world's toughest football competition? The last rallying cry of his detractors was that Wally had never made it to Sydney. Even though he had played 25 Tests, 17 as captain, the fear gnawed away. It was one thing to be confident, to know he had the right stuff, another to produce the performance to match. For months doubt had dogged his days, trying him mentally, preparing him for the trial ahead.

He was not battle fit. His gait barely concealed a knee operation seven weeks earlier. He had not played a serious match since late August, 1987. In truth he had not been fit since he tore the cartilage in his right knee in Australia's lacklustre loss to New Zealand in a Test at Lang Park in July 1987, seven months before. The surgery sidelined him for the Broncos' pre-season game against the Canberra Raiders and he played only half the Broncos' other practice match, against a New Zealand President's XIII. Indeed he came off after that game and confessed to being exhausted after only a few minutes play. "I did three tackles in a row and I really had my hands on my hips," he said.

Sydney, oh Sydney, the bane of Wally's life. Gene Miles was not encouraging. While Wally was recovering from his knee surgery Geno played for the Broncos in the Bicentennial Sevens tournament at Parramatta Stadium in February 1988. When Miles returned he warned Wally, "Gees mate, I'm not looking forward to playing in Sydney this year." The big Test centre shook his head warily. "Didn't the crowd give it to us! And you weren't even there. Can you imagine what it would have been like if you had been playing?"

Wally did not need to imagine. He knew. Seven days before the Manly match Wally and his wife Jacqueline flew to Sydney for the opening of the new Sydney Football Stadium. Afterwards the occasion transformed into a reunion of the 1986 Kangaroos with Wally, Geno, Royce Simmons, Steve Roach, Mick O'Connor plus Gary Belcher and Mal Meninga, all batting on. Black ties and silken wives never stopped Kangaroos from enjoying themselves but beneath the ribaldry there was an excitement, an anticipation about the Broncos, the new boys.

That week the cover of *Rugby League Week* was a photograph of Wally, regaled in blue and gold braided naval uniform and tricorn hat, at the helm of a tallmaster, under the headline, "Captain Wally and the Second Invasion of Sydney". The expectations of all Queensland weighed heavily on Wally, as did the poised pens of the Sydney media, ever ready to dismiss the Broncos as brumbies. When Wally and Jacqui went shopping near their home they were bailed up in supermarket lanes by well-meaning matrons wanting to chat about the coming game. By mid-week the media from two states had asked Wally 50 times, "Do you think you will make it in Sydney?" And 50 times Wally coolly replied, "There have been 44,000 other Queenslanders who have gone down there and done the job, why not one more?"

He wrote in his Brisbane newspaper column:

> Your tolerance gets low. The Sydney media have such an opinion of their competition it must be an embarrassment when these Queenslanders make it. Their players are all supposed to be 10ft tall and bullet proof but, like Fatty Vautin says, they all have the same number of arms and legs. The only big difference is the egos.

On Tuesday that week nerves began fraying. At training young ex-Easts lock, Terry Matterson, had a crisis of confidence about his goalkicking. Wayne Bennett ordered him to get the hell out and practice. Ex-Wallaby fullback Roger Gould, who had accepted Bennett's invitation to instruct the team kickers, took Matterson aside for an hour's coaching. Gould is possessed of the most powerful punt kick in any Australian football code. He kicked field goals from beyond half-way in Tests and at Ballymore his line kicks had to be fetched from a nearby creek. Wally liked Gould but found him of limited value. "You'd only see the ball for the first 50 yards," Wally joked. "After that it went out of sight." After two hours training in the rain Wally, wet through, slipped the media, jumped straight into his car without changing, turned the heater up full blast to ward off pneumonia and drove home.

Wednesday he had physiotherapy on his knee and Thursday survived a torturous session as coach Wayne Bennett put the Broncos through the hoops. It was wet underfoot, the footballs greasy. A dropped ball meant 30 pushups for the offender. Like everyone else, Wally fell victim.

Friday, Wally had a last chance to shed the cares of captaincy. His long-time friend and manager, Wayne Roberts, a morning radio announcer known as Waynee Poo, invited Wally and Broncos fullback Colin Scott on to his breakfast show. Roberts and his offsider, Ross Davie, capture good ratings with a blend of goonery, tricks, jokes, pranks and insanity. Roberts concluded the program with Scott, an Aborigine with a hilarious sense of humour, singing in soft, mock-Aboriginal English: "A white, sports coat, and a pink, carnation, eh!"

Saturday, match eve, the Broncos trained lightly for an hour and then fired a barbecue for lunch at their new club. The Broncos' wealthiest and most visible director — stockbroker and occasional philanthropist Paul Morgan — addressed the team in his cheerful, stonegravel voice. "If you blokes don't get out there and show some heart don't look for me at the end of the season for your bloody cheques. I won't be found." He paused and, with cauliflowered eloquence, concluded, "I hope you play the game in the right spirit, but I bloodywell hope each of you has a bit of bastardry in you as well!"

The team seemed relaxed but underneath there was an apprehension, particularly in the younger players, which Wally sought to defuse. He had watched the Broncos outpoint Canberra 22–16 in a pre-season trial. Sitting beside coach Wayne Bennett in the Lang Park grandstand, he had seen Allan Langer, the 160 cm imp from Ipswich, turn on the dazzling play which that season would lift him into the Australian Test team. Canberra had made the 1987 grand final against Manly with a team containing six former Queenslanders — Gary Belcher, Peter Jackson, Kevin Walters, Gary Coyne, Sam Backo and Steve Walters.

Wally could see a few of the players thinking, "Here they come, Manly, the premiers of Sydney, the rugby league capital of the world, where all the best football's played." Wally told them, "Hang on, have a look at those Canberra blokes. A season or so back they were playing beside you in Brisbane club football. They didn't play any better than you then and they didn't when you beat them. Why should Manly be any different?"

There was no denying the pressure. All that week Wally gradually withdrew into himself. It began with just isolated moments of distraction, when he didn't hear conversations, didn't notice action about him, didn't respond. In those seconds his mind moved ahead to the match, perhaps contemplating tactics, rehearsing his own role, storing calm, stacking psychological energy for the release to come. By Sunday morning he was well nigh unapproachable. He was like a prize-fighter on a hairtrigger. Late to rise, he ate breakfast wordlessly at 10 a.m. Jacqui kept the children away. "I've learnt by my mistakes," she told me. "When he gets like that I might as well talk to a brick wall." The match had been put back from 3 to 5 p.m. to avoid Queensland's heat. That upset Wally because the late start made the match unusual for both teams, diminishing Brisbane's home ground advantage.

The Broncos were so new they did not yet officially own their clubhouse, formerly a junior rugby league club, in Red Hill, an old inner-city suburb being restored like Sydney's Paddington. The club is spacious more than luxurious. One of the four Broncos directors is publican and restaurateur Gary Balkin, whose two paddlewheelers, the *Kookaburra Queens*, now ply the Brisbane River as major tourist attractions. As co-director Paul Morgan put it, "Gary can walk in, take one sniff and tell whether the beer is stale. He'll soon straighten this place out."

Sunday, match day, the club was packed for a supporters' lunch with the jokes supplied by Broncos general manager, John Ribot, and Manly's team conditioner, Terry Randall. The pair, ex-Kangaroos and former team-mates at Manly, were individually on edge but hid their tension on stage with the courtesy of diplomats. "Manly have always had the tag of silvertails," said Ribot. "But they are a fine club. Players who aren't paid a great deal still stay at the club for 12 to 15 years." Randall responded that at Manly club one day Wally Lewis had revealed that as a young bloke his pin-up player had been Terry Randall. "It made me feel proud, but it also made me feel old," said Randall. Ribot conceded that Manly had four to five key game breakers but predicted the Broncos would win 18-14. Randall said he would be glad if Manly won by a point and that was his prediction: "Manly by a point, for sure...I think."

As a favour Broncos chairman Barry Maranta drove to the airport to collect the parents of Manly's star winger, Dale Shearer, who were arriving from Mackay. Just then the Manly team streamed into the airport lounge from their Sydney flight. With only hours to kick-off Maranta was a suitable case for paranoia and, fearing Bob Fulton might think he had come to spy, hid behind posts to avoid recognition. And nearly missed Dale Shearer's parents.

At club headquarters Paul Morgan, three months without a smoke, oscillated between nicotine-starved elation and despair. Automobile sales magnate, Ron McConnell, long time and large scale banker of the perennially losing Queensland Sheffield Shield cricket team, happened by as Morgan was in the low mode. Morgan to McConnell: "We'd better bloodywell win. We've got the best player, the best coach, no injuries and three months to prepare. If they can't win their home matches they're bloody hopeless." His mental pendulum abruptly swung and he cheerfully told McConnell, "Win lose or draw come back to the club afterwards. It'll be a good night whatever."

Downstairs in the club offices, Broncos promotions officer Kev Keliher sat by himself fielding phone calls. He listened intently to one call. The champagne had not been delivered to the corporate boxes at Lang Park. They what! Another call. The entertainment might be late. Keliher heaved a sigh worthy of his large frame. "At least it's fine," he murmured.

Two kilometres away at Lang Park a line of tour coaches was spilling fans into queues outside the main gates. Children in Broncos jerseys skipped underfoot, Manly flags were safely furled. Australian coach Don Furner said he could choose an Australian side from the two teams. I bought a program and became another grandstand selector: Colin Scott at fullback, wingers Dale Shearer and Matthew Burke, centres Mick O'Connor and Gene Miles, Wally five-eighth, Des Hasler half, Paul Vautin lock, Bryan Niebling and Noel Cleal second row, props Greg Dowling and Phil Daley and Greg Conescu hooker. Twelve players — six Broncos and six Sea Eagles — had represented Australia and Matthew Burke had played rugby union for Australia. They were high powered personnel.

Upstairs in his Lang Park Trust boardroom, the former maestro of all Queensland rugby league, Ron McAuliffe, was holding court amid invited dignitaries. At 3 p.m., two hours to zero, he welcomed his old sparring partner and buddy, Australian Rugby League chairman Ken Arthurson and his wife Barbara. The Arthursons were about to witness their fourth Winfield Cup match, in four different cities, in three days. They watched Easts fall to St George at the new Sydney Football Stadium on Friday night, flew north to see Parramatta overwhelm the Knights at the Newcastle International Sports Centre on Saturday afternoon, and then sped by fast Fokker to Coolangatta for Gold Coast's loss to Canterbury that evening. On Sunday morning, along with their entourage of 50 officials and press, they had bussed to Brisbane. They had already seen two of the three freshman clubs in the Sydney premiership and now Arthurson was at the citadel of Queensland rugby league to observe the fate of the third. Arthurson's grand tour was testimony to the spread of rugby league along the Australian east coast.

Senator Ron, as the old Labor warhorse was still affectionately known, sidled to the window and peeped behind the blinds to gauge the crowd arriving at Lang Park. Relations between McAuliffe and the Broncos had soured since McAuliffe had backed a losing consortium in the skirmish to put a Brisbane team into the Sydney competition. To make matters worse McAuliffe, backroom boffin and managing hero of Queensland's state-of-origin renaissance, had allowed his pique to override his good judgment. He backed Manly to beat the Broncos and his treachery had been leaked to the media. In the boardroom Ron recanted. "I laid that weeks ago when I thought Wally would not be fit to play," he told me. "Now I wish I could get off the bet. You know my saying — any team that has Wally must start odds-on favourite." Even so Senator Ron could not resist a last dig at the Broncos consortium. He returned from reconnoitring at the window. "They were hoping for 25,000 but I'd be surprised if they top 20,000," he said.

Downstairs the Broncos were arrayed in their still unfamiliar jerseys: maroon, yellow and white in stripes, hoops and bands — a brassy combination of Queensland and Brisbane colours. The Broncos steed snorted on each player's left breast while the right bore the blue and white shield of the NSW Rugby League. Above that was a small sponsor logo, Peerless, and emblazoned right across the chest the Broncos' major sponsor, the then unknown "Power" beer company. Gene Miles, upon being presented with his jersey at a public launch months earlier, had held it to his chest and muttered, "Logos! Have a look at these things. Ought to be hanging off a Christmas tree." Wally was no more taken with the design than Gene but everything about this Broncos venture was so new, so recent — the name, the jerseys, their clubhouse, team songs, even the team itself — that all the usual psychological comforts of recognition and tradition had to be foregone. The Broncos had known each other for months but, with 30 minutes to zero and counting down, there was a disconcerting sense of unreality in the dressingroom.

Wayne Bennett entered, his mouth pursed in a half-grimace, his hypnotist gaze sweeping the room. Bennett believes he can smell a team's attitude when he walks into the dressingroom. He moved about, talking to one or two players and then, with 15 minutes to go, sent the team into an adjacent ante-room for their warmup. As they had in their previous two trials they began running through a series of drills and ballhandling skills in the cramped quarters.

What ensued was a catastrophe of dropped balls, missed calls, players being out of position or leaving the ball behind. For a minute everything went wrong and Wally suddenly shouted, "For Christ's sake, stop! This is ridiculous, let's start again!" Bennett heard Wally's angry yell and came to the door of the ante-room. Wally lectured the players, "We're starting again but this time we're getting everything right. Start thinking about the bloody game now and what you've got to do." The warmup proceeded with concentrated care. With five minutes left, the team moved back into the dressingroom. As Wally passed Bennett at the door the coach asked quietly, "How's the attitude? " Wally shook his head. "It's shithouse," he said.

He was wrong. The team was primed, about to hit Manly like grapeshot. But Wally is the first to admit that detecting team attitudes is an imprecise science. Bennett asked the assembled team, "Are you ready? Are you in the right frame of mind?" Yeah, yeah, came the responses, we're good, they said. Exactly the way we want to be, they said. As they lined up to run out Bennett gave his last instructions. "You don't want to drop the ball. We'll take it up for two rucks and kick the shit out of it." Wally, juggling a ball thoughtfully, turned quickly. "Mate do you mind if I change that plan?" Why, asked Bennett, his adam's apple bobbing, eyes piercing. Said Wally, "Well, it's our first game, they're the defending premiers. They're going to be pretty keen to get up and knock us over. Whether it's their fault for moving up too quickly or the ref is watching expecting them to do that, I reckon we'll be looking at a penalty in the first six tackles. Let's hold it a bit longer." Bennett nodded. OK.

Outside, a cowboy had been galloping his horse up and down the sidelines. Tiny bulbs, sewn into his uniform and in the horse's bridle, flashed in time to his song, "Rhinestone Cowboy". He shot a symbolic sea eagle, feathers flew everywhere and finally he galloped off. Wally and Fatty led their teams on. The Lord Mayor of Brisbane, Alderman Sallyanne Atkinson, was introduced to both teams but it was scarcely an unbiassed formality. Sallyanne, the Broncos number one ticketholder, was wearing her No 1 Broncos jersey. I joined Paul Morgan in one of the corporate boxes which have improved the archaic seating in the main grandstand at Lang Park. Morgan summoned general manager John Ribot. "Reebs you've given us a box with a post in front of it," he said. Ribot shot back, "Paul, every seat in this old stand has that." Morgan, agitated, scanned the field. "I hate to say this," he said worriedly. "But we look too well fed."

Manly kicked off, pulses quickened and Lang Park broke into an excited roar, witnessing football history in the making. Gene Miles caught the ball and ran at Manly with awesome intensity. On the fourth tackle the Sea Eagles, overanxious, moved up too quickly and — as Wally predicted — were penalised for encroaching inside the five metres. Sydney realities struck. Allan

Langer, the smallest man on the field, chased his own chip kick and was poleaxed by Manly prop, Phil Daley, probably the biggest man on the field. Langer's vision doubled. He packed as lock while Wally moved to halfback and then departed for five minutes respite in the headbin. Another 15 minutes into the match second-rower Brett Le Man was helped off with a serious eye injury that would keep him out half the season. Next moment Niebling fell to the ground writhing, clutching his knee. He limped off and Billy Noke, who had played a full reserve grade game, ran on.

Paul Morgan exclaimed, "Bloody hell! We're getting bashed up. These sleaze bags have put three of our blokes out already." Specialty replacements were becoming scarce. Wally's younger brother Scott, a halfback, had smashed his knee in the reserve grade match, an injury that put him on crutches for months. His Broncos career had lasted just 37 minutes.

The Broncos managed a 6–2 lead but it was a contradiction of play. Dale Shearer was doing as he pleased, doing his parents proud. The Broncos couldn't tackle him, couldn't put him to ground and couldn't stop him passing. Inevitably he put Manly five-eighth Cliff Lyons through a gap. Panic hit the Broncos. Lyons, his half Des Hasler screaming in support, raced towards Broncos fullback Colin Scott. Wally saw Hasler and thought, "Oh no! He's too fast." They wouldn't catch him. But Lyons, unaccountably, misjudged his run and propped as he closed on Scott. Hasler overran the play emptyhanded. Lyons was not yet finished. He twisted in Scott's tackle and tossed the ball wildly into the air from which it was plucked by the ubiquitous Dale Shearer who carried the movement over half-way. Shearer fed Michael O'Connor who stepped nimbly infield and raced past the Broncos quarterline before passing to Lyons who had rejoined the movement. Play had now swept 70 metres.

Lyons' original indecision had given the Broncos' three quickest men — wingers Michael Hancock and Joe Kilroy and centre Chris Johns — time to regroup and now they converged on Lyons. Incredibly, just 10 metres from the tryline, with the Broncos defenceless, Hasler once more materialised in support for Lyons and just as unbelievably Lyons missed him again.

Hasler ran past and pulled up, his face thrown to the sky. It was tragic football from the premiers. The number of breaks Lyons made which came to nothing. "He just runs out of ideas," said Wally. "He outthinks himself. Tries too hard."

The pace was punishing. Players, their shorts shiny with sweat, bent at the waist like rowers at the end of a race, searching for breath in Brisbane's humid evening air. It was too much for one Manly forward. While referee Mick Stone awarded a penalty to the Broncos, the Manly player calmly hitched one leg of his shorts aside and urinated on the field. Like the best magicians he acted so naturally his sleight of hand went unnoticed except by television's all-seeing eye. Several female viewers complained to Channel 10 that the stream was visible for five seconds on television.

The penalty which precipitated all of this was the third awarded to Wally for Manly players holding him down after a tackle. Wally is a master at this. Opponents like to hold him down. They know it irritates him and, because he has usually gained territory, delaying him is sound tactics. But with his great body strength Wally can lift several players lying over him by arching his back. And of course he exaggerates. The message to the referee becomes: if he can move why can't the tacklers? Wally eventually had Phil Daley sent to the sinbin for just that offence. In our private box Paul Morgan's father, Bill, a huge man and a pretty good footballer in his day, roared laughing. "Wally's going to become a member of the Light Opera Company if he keeps this up." Known as "The Colonel" from his army rank, commanding bearing and military moustache, Big Bill Morgan was leaning forward in his seat, once more a young footballer, eager to take the field himself.

The Broncos then showed Manly the meaning of opportunism. Play was near centre field, two metres from the Manly line. Langer, at dummy half, shaped to pass Wally. The marker moved to swamp Langer, Noel Cleal edged sideways to cover Wally. Langer saw that nothing would come of nothing. He hesitated, feigning to dart forward himself. Doubt delayed Cleal's assignation with Wally a fraction. In that same moment Langer sped the ball to Wally. Cleal and the crowd knew what was coming. Wally remembers, just before he dived over, hearing the crowd roar, a rare thing on field. The try was so telegraphed that all of Lang Park saw the opening. The Broncos led 14–2 but with 30 seconds to half-time Dale Shearer showed that if his team would not grasp their opportunities, he would. From a tap penalty 12 metres out he speared between tacklers for a surprise try. At oranges it was Broncos 14–6.

The Broncettes, 30 dancing cowgirls and five athletic cowboys, dashed on field to display their wares. I walked between the corporate boxes, dodging waiters serving corpulent customers. Small screens showed the privileged occupants the live television coverage going to Sydney. It was strange to see such sophistication at a working-class sport. Greg Chappell leaned forward and offered, "The boys might find it tough in the second half. That last try was very soft." Too right.

The Broncos were feeling the pinch. Dowling, Miles and Langer were all in some distress from knocks. Bennett walked around the dressingroom laying it on the line: they would all have to endure pain before this match was out. He praised the desperate defence of Scott and Miles but the team had to stifle Manly's clean breaks. On the other side of a dividing brick wall Bob Fulton was stating the obvious. Manly had made twice as many tackles as Brisbane, 73–38. Corollary: Brisbane had more of the ball. Manly had to cut down their mistake rate and use the chances they were creating. He didn't need to finger Cliff Lyons.

As the Broncos filed out for the second half Wally was cutting the air with his palms, explaining to Greg Dowling how he wanted the angles run. "Keep angling, keep angling," he told Dowling. "As soon as we catch them short on one side I'll give the boss call and we'll hit them there." Wally interpreted for me. He wanted Dowling to take the ball up in one direction for three or four rucks to draw Manly's defence to that side. Wally sought to catch Manly with too many players on one side and then he would give the "boss" call, the overriding code word which signalled to every Bronco that the ball had to go to Wally from the ruck. Wally would run where Manly's defence had thinned.

Six minutes into the second half the match belonged to no one. Then Wally made it his. The Broncos took play to Manly's quarterline, about 10 metres in from touch. Manly's defence spread to the open side with only the marker, Don McKinnon, and winger Matt Burke covering the blindside. Fullback Shearer had eased towards the centre of the field to cover a possible bomb or grubber kick.

Wally ran in to dummy half but gave way to Greg Conescu. "Go yourself Turtle," he said. Conescu ran to the open side, drew Manly's marker, McKinnon, and switched the ball back to Wally who had followed through on his shoulder. Matthew Burke was now the sole blindside defender. Wally stood Burke up by running at him but declined Burke's waiting embrace. Instead he straightened and ran slap bang into Manly's cover, Hasler and Daley. "Hasler went high, as he usually does," said Wally. "So I tried to fend him." Wally's straight-arm fend to Hasler's chest lifted the nuggety halfback off his feet and shot him backwards as if unsaddled by a jousting lance. Now a little luck. "Daley came for a big hit, he always tries to hit pretty hard," said Wally. "I sort of ducked and Daley slid over the top." Wally's legs kept pumping and amazingly he burst clear, still moving. If such television lens existed they would have detected a triumphant gleam light Wally's eye. The line was only 10 metres away.

Burke, having shadowed the action, expecting the Broncos captain to fall, frantically darted forward at Wally's ankles. But Wally, who had fended Hasler with his left palm, had now transferred the ball to that hand and with his other fended Burke ingloriously into the grass. Shearer, who had watched with increasing alarm, accelerated across field in a last ditch tackle. He barrelled in to get underneath Wally to turn him over. The other Manly wing, Stuart Davis, had arrived on the scene and together they tried to sandwich Wally and hold him up over the line. Said Wally, "I remember I had four yards to run when Shearer hit me." Wally had since transferred the ball back to his right hand to fend Shearer with his left. "I wanted to use the fend like a shock absorber, let him hit me but use his weight to go sideways and forward at the same time." This he did, crashing over in Shearer and Davis's dual tackle.

Lang Park reverberated to massed voices, a tuneless chant of Wagnerian dimensions, "WALL-LLY, WALL-LLY, WALL-LLY". All conversation ceased. It was impossible to hear. Though McAuliffe was correct in estimating it was not a state-of-origin sized crowd, the 17,451 fans were making an Origin sized commotion. Wally's team-mates crowded around him. If he had imagined he was carrying the cross of Sydney's judgments alone, the crowd and the players were telling him different.

David Wright, Channel 10's commentator, echoed everyone's thoughts:

> Can he handle Sydney football? I'll tell you he can...This guy's got every skill in the book, he's the best player in the world and that's why...What a fantastic try from the Emperor of Lang Park.

It wasn't Wally's first try in the Sydney premiership — that had come easily in the first half. It was the style of this try, starting 20 metres out where it seemed nothing existed. Wally had planned carefully, like a big cat setting up a kill which the victim does not even see until too late. Through five tackles, never able to gather more than half pace and yet moving implacably towards his goal. He had done it to England in the third Test in 1986 and he repeated it against NSW in 1987, a try to break the spirit, to sap the will, to win the match. The scoreboard blazed "Horsepower"; it should have been Wallypower. Brisbane led 20–6 and from here on it became a procession. Manly were gone.

It was 6 p.m. In his corporate box Paul Morgan's flow of adrenalin finally eased. He turned and said, "Now that we can relax Adrian, isn't that a lovely sunset." The pink and purple tropical sky was indeed a beauty to behold, but nothing could compare with the glorious pageant unfolding before us on Lang Park. As the score soared my arm grew tender from Morgan's pounding. Our coffee went cold, the roast beef sandwiches went limp and the beer spilled as we rose and cheered in concert with the rest of Lang Park.

The ground lights, assuming ascendancy over the setting sun, gave the field a surreal glow and the Broncos produced a performance to match. They raided remorselessly. Near Manly's line Wally fed Geno who smashed down the blindside straight into Test team-mates Vautin and Cleal who had read the move like a bus timetable. But they hadn't read the alterations. Geno swivelled in their grasp and one-handed a pass to Wally who had doubled around. Wally drew the remaining defence and slipped the ball to Billy Noke who galloped over. "Wally and Geno, what would we do without them!" rasped Morgan in ecstasy. With 14 minutes left it was 32–6.

David Fordham, on Channel 10, announced to two million television viewers, "I don't know whether I should make this public but last Saturday night I had a little bet with the former senator Ron McAuliffe where I backed the Broncos. I couldn't believe he'd back Manly but I think I have come up with $20." Another try to Matterson. 38–6. "This is a flogging," said Fordham.

The Broncos became outlandish. Wally called a move codenamed "outback", flicked an audacious pass behind his back which ended in Joe Kilroy dashing in for his first Sydney premiership try. Kilroy flashed his white teeth in a huge Islander grin all the way back into position, raising a finger to indicate his first. A diversion began on the sideline. Two buxom blondes resplendent in cowboy hats, red and white tops and shimmering gold shorts, were shaking their tails and pom-poms. Splitting them was a man shouting into a massive red funnel for a loudspeaker. It was Kilroy's personal cheer squad going into a minor frenzy. Horses whinnied over the ground loudspeakers. The scoreboard printed up, "And the crowd goes wild!" It was a carnival.

The score progressed to its eventual conclusion, 44–10, but not before Wally pulled one last unspeakable little trick. With Manly desperate for a score, any score, Paul Vautin charged to within five metres of the Broncos line. Wally told me, "I knew I was going to do it." He became Vautin's marker. As they rose Wally sniped. "I thought you were going to beat us Fatty," he said smiling. Vautin shook his head disconsolately. Having distracted his friend Wally struck with his foot and raked the ball back to the Broncos. "Oh you bastard, why couldn't you do it to someone else," Vautin groaned. "Bozo (Fulton) will think I let you do this now!" Wally laughed. Vautin was not to blame. Once every match, when the herd grazes most peacefully, Wally pounces. Don't watch for it. You won't have the patience. He only acts when you've lost concentration. Most memorably he once dispossessed the wily, match wizened, Ray Price himself in a state-of-origin match. That was sheer bliss. That was The Phantom, Wally's comic book hero, dispossessing the leader of the southern roughnecks. But to do it to Fatty, his mate!

At full-time I made my way earthwards past Lord Mayor Atkinson. She waved and called, "Your boy Wally, he's wonderful isn't he? He's the very essence of leadership." Greg Chappell overheard and seconded the sentiments, "A class act." A little further along two faces looked numbed. I tapped Ron McAuliffe's shoulder. He rolled his eyes and said, "He's amazing isn't he?" Next to him Ken Arthurson wore one of those confused smiles which come from intense personal disappointment combined with the recognition of an undeniable public good. A Manly man, he was shattered by his club's loss yet as the ARL president he knew rugby league must benefit. "The man is a genius," he said.

The era of Brisbane as rugby league second-class citizens was over. Now Brisbane shared the mantle so hard won by the Queensland state-of-origin teams. The Newcastle Knights may have been trounced on Saturday afternoon, the Gold Coast Giants overwhelmed on Saturday night, but this Sunday evening Wally and the Broncos had made the north-south rugby league dialogue a reality. Channel 10 director of marketing, Mike Lattin, watched the stands emptying and predicted good ratings. Any program opposing the Broncos was in trouble, he said. In fact the match rated 26, outscoring the previous Sunday evening champion, Channel 9's *60 Minutes*.

In the dressingroom Wayne Bennett delayed the media inquisition for several minutes to put the match in perspective. "Don't get carried away," he commanded. "Congratulations on the win, a fine game, but don't get overconfident. We can't live on one match. There are 23 others to come." Wally received the man-of-the-match award and, despite Bennett, allowed his emotions a little rein. "I didn't think we'd score that many points against Manly in three games this season let alone one," he enthused. " Everything we tried came off and conversely everything Manly tried went wrong."

Manly coach Bobby Fulton had the statistic to back that. His team dropped the ball 18 times on the first or second tackle. He told the media, "You can't give a man like Wally Lewis that much possession and get away with it." He offered this caution to the Broncos: "It's a hard school. If a team puts pressure on Wally and his team, it will be a different story." A further analysis showed that, for Manly, Vautin topped the tackle count with 22, followed by five-eighth Lyons and halfback Hasler with 17 each. It could be surmised that Manly's pack did not support Vautin but the truth was that the Broncos ran at the Manly halves, committing them to tackle. The Broncos did not attempt to run through the middle of Manly's forwards. The Broncos did not have the brawn for that. Thereby lay a lesson for those who would read it. Sydney took half a dozen matches to focus.

Wally sat in his shorts, fielding media questions, sipping a soft drink. He always winds down slowly, last to shower, last to get dressed. He shaved, cleaned up, exchanged the soft drink for a beer and prepared to leave for the revelry beginning back at the Broncos club. Wayne Bennett caught him at the door, looked him in the eye and said, for no other ears than Wally's, "We've got a hell of a football team here."

2 KING HIT

If the Broncos' defeat of Manly ranked among the high points
of Wally's football career, a year earlier he was embroiled in a
controversy he rates as close to the lowest in his life. The
launching of his biography, *King Wally*, should have been a
celebration but a few malevolent forces in the media turned the
occasion into a witchhunt enabling those who had envied or
criticised him to demand he be stripped of his Test captaincy.
It shocked Wally to discover how quickly factions in Sydney,
dormant since he made the national leadership indisputably his,
sought to exploit such an opportunity.

Apart from recording Wally's life story, *King Wally* exposed
the background to a number of controversial incidents in contemporary rugby league history, notably the 1982 Kangaroo
tour of Great Britain and the 1985 Australian tour of New
Zealand. Those involved included former Test coaches, Frank
Stanton and Terry Fearnley, and Test players, Ray Price,
Wayne Pearce, Peter Wynn and Michael O'Connor. Wally was
the centre of, or was closely associated with, these incidents.

The problems began even before the book was launched. The
now defunct Sydney afternoon tabloid, the *Sydney Sun*, had
bought the rights to serialise extracts from *King Wally*. I asked
the editor of the newspaper not to "gut" the book — that is not
to select the most controversial incidents and publish them out
of context. Unfortunately an author has limited control over
such editorial decisions, especially as that newspaper was involved in a cut-throat circulation war with its afternoon rival,

the *Daily Mirror*. Sensationalism sells papers and Wally was seen as fair game.

On Monday 4 May, the *Sydney Sun* published the first of its extracts in which its top sports writer, Steve Crawley, culled the book for its highlights including the sections where Wally clashed with Sydney coaches and players. Crawley's condensed version made the book sound as though it was largely an assault upon the integrity of Sydney rugby league, its officialdom and players. That was all many Sydney rugby league fans ever read of *King Wally* and they judged it accordingly. As well, the *Sun*'s advertising headline, "King Wally: My Amazing Life In League", conveyed the impression that the book was an auto-biography, not a biography. This crucial misrepresentation meant that facts and opinions in my book could be taken as Wally's, which was never intended.

So the rumour swept Sydney that *King Wally* was an unsporting autobiography. By the time we launched the book in Brisbane on 8 May, five days after the *Sun*'s first extracts appeared, *King Wally* was damned. As Lindy Chamberlain once observed, a rumour will circle the earth while the truth is still pulling on its shoes. Wally's erstwhile sparring partner, Ray Price, set the tone. In a radio interview he declared Wally a good, but not great, footballer. "Fair dinkum, he's the only person who thinks he's a king," said Price.

At the Brisbane media launch at Lang Park, headquarters of the Queensland Rugby League, scene of so many of his tri-umphs, Wally was put on the defensive as he has rarely been in his football career. Wally responded to Price's criticism of the title. "I've never called myself King Wally, ever," he said. "It's a title that's been put on me by sections of the media for the past five or six years." It was the media's constant use of the sobriquet which suggested the title. Only five months earlier, when Wally scored an amazing individual try to seal the third Test against Great Britain for the 1986 Kangaroos, Sydney league caller Peter Peters had shouted hoarsely over the air waves, "Wally Lewis! King Wally! What a player! What a try!"

At the launch Wally sought to separate his role in the book — relating his own experiences — from my role as author, commentator and critic. The demarcation was vital. If the contentious passages were accepted as being the work of the author then there was no controversy. It was merely one writer's opinion. If the criticisms could be sourced to Wally then there was a sensation because this was Wally Lewis speaking: Australian captain, rugby league figurehead, national ambassador, international sportsman. Since the latter was the better media story we fought a losing battle.

Within a week of the newspaper extracts appearing the sack Lewis campaign began. An unnamed NSW representative player said that if he was selected to play for Australia in the Test against New Zealand that year he would play but he would prefer to have someone else than Wally lead the team. "I've spoken to three other NSW players and we all agree we would not have confidence in him on the field in a Test match," the anonymous player was quoted as saying.

Frank Stanton, the Kangaroo coach with whom Wally had clashed during the 1982 Invincibles tour of Great Britain, entered the fray. Wally should be stripped of the Australian captaincy for not respecting the position, he said. Stanton added, "There is always two sides to every story but only one has been told in this book." Stanton neglected to mention that I rang him for a reply to Wally's version of events and that the book carried Stanton's answer.

The Sydney protest gathered strength. Balmain captain Wayne Pearce and Parramatta captain Peter Wynn objected to the book's descriptions of conflicts on the 1985 tour of New Zealand. Wynn was reported to be considering legal action. He was quoted as saying: "I have already sent a letter of complaint to Australian Rugby League chairman Ken Arthurson. I said I felt insulted by what was written. I said I would like to see the Australian Rugby League take strong action against him (Lewis)."

NSW captain Wayne Pearce said the book threatened to undo hard work establishing a truce between players from Queensland and NSW after the divisive 1985 New Zealand tour. Pearce was quoted, "He (Wally) is inaccurate in what he says about me and a lot of the other situations he talks about. He quotes people who said things in confidence and has brought these statements forward in the book and that is highly unethical."

The crunch came two days after the book's launch when ARL chief Ken Arthurson was quoted as saying he was angry with Wally and that he would be raising the matter at the next meeting of the ARL. Sydney *Daily Telegraph* rugby league writer, Ray Chesterton, reported Arthurson as saying:

"There is no excuse for the public criticisms Lewis has levelled at some of his team-mates and Australia's former Test coach Terry Fearnley. Lewis is entitled to his opinions but he is also entitled to keep them to himself. It's possible people might have an opinion on some of the things Lewis has done but they're not rushing into print with them." Arthurson said he was stunned at the backround and gossip Lewis had included in the book and was particularly disappointed that Pearce was a target. "I owe it to Pearce and other people mentioned in the book to take the matter to the ARL."

The basic tenor of his comments was repeated in a report by senior league writer Alan Clarkson in the *Sun-Herald*. Clarkson's report however added an important comment. Arthurson told Clarkson that he thought it too extreme that Lewis be stripped of his captaincy.

Under this deluge of criticism Wally rang the ARL on 12 May, four days after the book's launch. Arthurson was overseas so Wally spoke to ARL secretary Bob Abbott who admitted he had not yet read the book. Wally told him, "I've sent you a copy. What I'll do now is go through the index of the book, get the names of the blokes I'm supposed to have been critical of and give you the pages where their names appear. You read them and tell me if I have made any criticism there which you think is unwarranted, unfair, or not in the best interests of the game." Abbott explained to Wally that when rung by sports reporters he had replied that IF there was criticism in the book he would be concerned, but that the "if" had been left out of their published stories.

When Arthurson returned from overseas Wally rang him. Wally told me, "I was a bit distressed when I spoke to Ken. I was filthy at the way it was all coming out. It was just getting me down, people going on and on about it, day after day." Arthurson denied many of the things attributed to him. "If I had anything to say I would have said it to you first," he told Wally. "There were a couple of points in the book I've been told about and when I heard I was naturally disappointed." So he too had not yet actually read the book. Arthurson later remarked that Wally sounded emotionally upset during the call. The ARL chief had long been a supporter of Wally's captaincy despite immense pressure in Sydney over the years to have him replaced by Ray Price, Steve Mortimer or Wayne Pearce. In a subsequent press statement Arthurson reminded the public that Wally had been a wonderful sporting ambassador for rugby league and for Australia.

Wally, not for the first time nor the last, was on the receiving end of a full-scale, multi-media beat up, with rugby league officials who had not even read the book making hypothetical remarks which became sensational newspaper headlines. The media had not made Wally and nor would they break him. Nevertheless he set about repairing any damage to relationships with the players he cared about. The first was Wayne Pearce.

Wally had known Pearce since the 1982 Kangaroo tour. Pearce — non-smoker, non-drinker, fitness fanatic, health food follower — was the antithesis of Wally — drinker and smoker, ordinary trainer and fast-food friendly. Despite their differences they maintained a good relationship even when Pearce was drafted by the Sydney push to topple Wally from the Australian captaincy. But problems arose on the Australian tour of New Zealand in 1985. Wally felt that Australian coach Terry Fearnley favoured vice-captain Pearce, even down to seeking Pearce's opinion on Test selections.

Brisbane *Courier-Mail* sports editor, Barry Dick, who reported that bitter 19-day tour, wrote that *King Wally*'s treatment of Fearnley was not tough enough. He wrote:

> It was patently obvious from day one of the tour that Fearnley was going to struggle to build a working relationship with Lewis. His reaction was to turn to Wayne Pearce when he should have been trying to sort out his apparent problem with his captain.

Wally rang Pearce in Sydney and told him, "Listen, I'm supposed to have bagged you in the book but I didn't. It wasn't my criticism of you it was other people's. Just because it's in my biography doesn't mean I'm responsible for everything in it." The next day, 14 May, a week after the book's launch, the Sydney *Sun* carried a backpage headline, "MATES! Wally and Junior Make Up". The story said Wally had rung Pearce to clear himself of any personal criticism of Pearce and that Pearce had accepted Wally's explanation. Subsequently, playing with and against Pearce, Wally detected no animosity and was happy to have buried any misunderstanding.

Wally in vain tried to phone Mick O'Connor who was reportedly upset at a section in *King Wally* in which Terry Fearnley criticised O'Connor. Wally did not get through to his former schoolboys rugby union tour-mate until the furore had died down. O'Connor assured Wally he had no gripe with him. Wally then rang Paul Vautin. Had Fatty read the book? "Yeah, I enjoyed it. There's a lot of funny stories in there," said Vautin. "Just remember there's only a couple of differences between Brisbane and Sydney football. It's how much they get paid and that they believe what they read about themselves in the paper." Vautin couldn't let the opportunity pass. "All the same mate, you've given me up. You've made me out to be a nice critic bagging blokes all the time." Wally laughed, "But you do Fatty. That's exactly what you're like."

Sorting out his private friendships however did not calm the public uproar. Wally's home phone rang incessantly. "I got sick and tired of saying the same thing," said Wally. "I'd pick up the phone and say, 'This is a recording. Pick up the book. Get the index. Check the person's name. Read the relevant pages. If I've criticised the person ring me back and I'll admit that I'm wrong, but I'm quite sure you won't be ringing me back. Now go away, get to it. Start reading. This is a recording.' And I'd put the phone down."

Old Kangaroos even jumped in for a free thump. Johnny Raper said Wally had broken the unwritten code of rugby league tourists. He said, "I could have made a fortune, but there is a code of ethics." Ian Walsh backed him. "Any player who plays beside Wally from now on will be very wary of him. They'll always be wondering what Lewis will say about them."

Noel Kelly thought Wally had put the dollar before his mates. Keith Barnes stayed his hand. Some portions of the book would have been better left unsaid, he said. "But I could never agree that Lewis should be stripped of the captaincy...There is only one place to lose the captaincy and that is on the field."

I sought to redress the balance of criticism with a reply in the *Courier-Mail* newspaper in Brisbane. I wrote that very few books had been written on rugby league and now I understood why. Far from being the greatest game of all it was proving itself the most thin-skinned game of all. I argued that allegations Wally had slandered his tour-mates were baseless. To anybody who read the book it was obvious that Wally could not be the source of much of the material used. I had refrained from putting words into Wally's mouth for the book, why should everybody else now try? Wally was no more responsible for the writing of the book than he had rights to censor it. If he had sought to tone down the manuscript there would have been no book. Unfortunately, by defending Wally in Brisbane, I was preaching to the converted. Wherever Wally travelled in Queensland he was received sympathetically by fans. At Southport, on the Gold Coast, a booksigning session almost became a rally as hundreds of shoppers blocked a supermarket mall to cheer Wally's advertised arrival.

For several weeks I was caught in the cosmic tail of Wally's publicity galaxy and discovered the enormous, perpetual pressure he was under. They were tense days. Sometimes I joined Wally to promote the book in suburban supermarkets and wondered whether he would turn up. Or worse, whether he would turn on me. The relationship between subject and biographer is a sensitive one. After all it was Wally's name, his integrity, his captaincy, his career, which were under seige, not mine. If he needed a scapegoat he had one ready made. But, as you would expect, Wally stood firm. One day, at the height of the fuss, I crossed a parking lot, head down, deep in thought, heading for a bookstore promotion. Wally surprised me, coming from the other direction and burst into laughter. "Mate you should see your face, you look like a man who's lost a winning casket ticket." I was relieved to find Wally's own humour intact.

But the pressure in the Lewis household became intolerable. Jacqui Lewis was pregnant with their second child. "It was getting to us real bad," she said. "We'd had enough. God it was upsetting. Wally just sat by the telephone and made STD calls. He had to talk to someone to let it all out. And then as soon as he put the phone down it would ring. At one stage I thought, 'Why didn't this come at the end of his career?' " One day Jacqui decided to ring the people attacking Wally to tell them off. But when she sought around for a public face to the criticism she could find none. As Wally's mother, June, assured her, "It's all just newspaper talk. Don't worry about it. It's a storm in a teacup." ARL chief Ken Arthurson rang Jacqui with the same message. Arthurson was concerned about the impact of the furore on Wally's family.

That the debate, however sound its foundations, was media-fuelled became evident just three days after the book's launch. On 11 May, the Sydney *Sun* published a state-of-origin story headlined, "LEWIS ROW! Scene Set For Fiery Clash With Kenny." The very afternoon the story appeared Brett Kenny was standing beside Wally in Grace Bros, Parramatta, signing copies of *King Wally* for lunchtime shoppers. Kenny and Bob Lindner had promised to help promote the book at Parramatta. When the row erupted Wally told Brett, "Listen mate, if you don't want to help that's fine, I understand." Brett brushed the offer aside. When Lindner, Kenny and Wally met at the store Wally read out the supposedly offending sections. "Brett just had a giggle at what was written about him," said Wally. They stood together for over an hour, chatting in between autographs. Recalling the Parramatta visit Wally said gratefully, "He'd give you a hand seven days of the week, Brett."

The media tide turned on May 13, five days after the book blasted off. Steve Crawley, who had adapted the original *Sun* extracts, wrote an article entitled, "KING BULL!" taking Sydney rugby league to task for its overreaction. More importantly he wrote:

> King Wally is a biography, not an autobiography. Lewis didn't write it. Adrian McGregor, who did, cleverly worked his words around the subject. When someone is bucketed, nine times out of 10 it is another international doing the bucketing.

As might be expected the Brisbane media struck back on Wally's behalf and his former mentor, QRL chairman Ron McAuliffe, sourced the Sydney reaction to the state-of-origins. He said, "They couldn't push this sort of argument when Queensland was winning on the playing fields. We silenced them from 1980 to 1985 because we were leading. With a few NSW wins the old treatment is emerging again and the best way to overcome it is to smack their backsides again on the playing fields."

Former St George half, now coach, Ross Strudwick cut close to the bone when he wrote in the Brisbane *Sun* that Sydney journalists had always treated Queensland footballers as second-class citizens. He wrote, "I can't see how Wally could have praised them when they've spent a lot of their time bagging him." Columnist Lawrie Kavanagh also pinpointed a few troublemakers among the majority of responsible Sydney sportswriters. He wrote in the *Courier-Mail*, "There are a few ratbags who should have used up their credibility a long, long time ago. They live and breathe sensation and speculation."

Southern vitriol had one last fling. Ray Price pressured the ARL by publicly predicting that the executive would not have the "heart or guts" to censure Wally over the book. The executive met on 22 May, two weeks after the book launch, and Ray Chesterton, in the Sydney *Daily Telegraph* the next day, reported the ARL's findings. He wrote that as a result of the meeting Wally Lewis would publicly apologise for any distress or loss of dignity suffered by rugby league coaches and players mentioned in *King Wally*. He wrote:

> The Australian Rugby League, possibly because of legal repercussions, yesterday rejected the chance to fine Lewis, preferring instead to dress him down for a book many consider has brought aspects of the game into disrepute. Lewis, Australia's Test captain, humbly apologised yesterday after being severely chastised by a full meeting of the ARL in Sydney. He now intends writing full letters of apology to the ARL and to the Sydney and Brisbane media for further public expansion of his distress at any hurt the book has caused.

Wally was incredulous when I showed him that report. He'd

written no letters of apology, either to the ARL or newspapers. His only offer to the ARL had been as follows: if he had offended anybody he was sorry, it was not his intention. He had not criticised anyone and if someone could find such criticism he would write them a letter of apology. "Not only that, I said I'd step down from the captaincy as well, I'd step down the next day," said Wally. "I left that offer open and no one ever hunted it up." Or reported it. Wally's offer was never made public.

King Wally blazed a trail for others to follow — Ray Price's *Perpetual Motion* in August 1987 and Steve Mortimer's *Top Dog* in 1988. Price's book was written with the assistance of *Rugby League Week* senior reporter Neil Cadigan. Price had a slap at Wally for being too sensitive and more or less told him to grow up. But he balanced that with the memory of Wally chairing him off the field after his last Test. Price wrote:

> It was a bit of a shock...but it did show one thing about him; when it came to football he had respect for me and as a team-mate he was a good man.

Steve Mortimer, assisted by respected *Rugby League Week* editor, Norman Tasker, evened a few old scores in his book, reserving a special space for Wally. He wrote:

> He was an absolute grub to room with. His wardrobe was a constant pile of clothes on the floor and I gave up counting how many times he collapsed on the bed and slept in his clothes after a big night out. Getting dressed in the morning was a ritual for Wally that was fascinating to behold. He would dive into the pile of clothes on the floor, pull out those he wanted and get them on nice and early so his body heat would smooth out some of the wrinkles. He also had feet that smelled like he had gangrene. I kept chucking his shoes out the window, hoping the cold air might improve their aroma.

Wally was warned that Mortimer, nicknamed Turvey, had got stuck into him. Said Wally, "I thought, 'Gees, Turvey must have said I couldn't play or that I was the worst five-eighth he'd ever partnered.' " When Wally read it he began chuckling. A friend asked Wally what was so funny? Hadn't Mortimer described him as a grub and the untidiest man on God's earth? Wally kept laughing. He was half inclined to ring Mortimer and say, "You rat Turvey, you've given it to me in your book." And then tell him the truth — that he loved it. The sort of reaction Wally wished his biography had been given.

In the aftermath of the book Wally's close team-mates shed no tears for him. A newspaper published a long profile on Gene Miles and concluded that the big unit, as Miles is known, was probably worth a book — King Geno maybe? Geno cracked up. "No way," he said. "I've seen the other bloke cop too much trouble to fall for that."

The four weeks from 4 May to the first state-of-origin on 2 June 1987, when the furore finally subsided, were the worst of Wally's public career. But if he thought that the Origin would salve his woes, if he thought he could shed his cares on the football stage that he loved best, he was in for a stunning disappointment.

3 FORTY-EIGHT SAD SECONDS

The state-of-origin series has always appealed more to Queenslanders than to Sydney fans. The first match, at Lang Park in 1980, was a sellout and little has changed since. A sports store in the centre of Brisbane has a television displayed in the window which runs non-stop video replays of state-of-origin matches, always to a good audience. The reason is that to "smack NSW backsides on the playing fields", as Ron McAuliffe had recommended, is never easy. Although Queensland won the first five series, NSW were avenged in 1985 and then won 3–0 in 1986, the first clean sweep by either side. Approaching the 1987 series NSW felt rugby league's crown was back in its rightful place.

For Queensland it was desperate stakes. The three losses in 1986 had been by six, four and two points, a diminishing scale but nonetheless devastating for new coach Wayne Bennett and one which put his job in jeopardy. Apart from the losses, Bennett had moved to Canberra to coach the Raiders and the QRL ruled that a NSW-based coach could not coach Queensland. In late January 1987, while the cricket and surf seasons were still in full swing, the lobbying began. QRL officials first approached Wally, fresh from his Kangaroo tour triumph but he declined the responsibilities of captain-coach. "I didn't really know enough about coaching at that stage," said Wally. "I didn't believe I'd get as much out of the players as Bennett. When Benny speaks he puts fear into a bloke. I could imagine me in the state side saying something to Gene and him saying

'Get stuffed!'" Wally compared his coaching with Arthur Beetson's whose appproach was more fun and less intense. "The state side had just got serious under Bennett," said Wally, "and everybody could see the benefit."

The second approach was to Wally again — this time by Bennett. "If you want the job I'll stand aside and give you all the help I can," said Bennett. Wally was mildly surprised and then deeply impressed. He knew how much Bennett wanted to atone for the previous year's losses. It was a remarkable, selfless offer. Wally replied, "If it's all the sa.ne to you mate, I was quite happy with you last year. I'd like to further my education with you." Bennett could not have hoped for better. Without Wally's backing Bennett was unlikely to retain the job let alone topple NSW.

After hearing Wally's decision the QRL relaxed its residential ruling on Bennett. Wally then publicly endorsed Wayne. "Queensland can win the series this year provided we pick the best players and the best coach," he said. "As far as I'm concerned Bennett is the best available." Having spoken his mind Wally wished he hadn't because, soon after, Bobby McCarthy nominated as well. McCarthy had played 18 Tests, 250 first grade games for South Sydney and Canterbury-Bankstown and coached Brisbane Souths to the 1981 premiership. He was a highly respected contender. McCarthy knew Wally well from Brisbane's dramatic National Panasonic Cup win in 1984. McCarthy was coach, Wally captain. Wally liked McCarthy's coaching style. "I had a good time under Bob," said Wally. "He's an attacking coach. He really believes that to win you've got to create points, not just wait for errors." Wally was embarrassed that his previous endorsement of Bennett would weigh against Macca.

The day after McCarthy's nomination, Wally met him at a social function and apologised. "I hope you don't think that I don't want you Bob," said Wally. "To be perfectly honest, and it's a difficult thing to admit, but I forgot all about you. I just thought you were a NSW bloke and that was it." Wally then publicly withdrew from the coaching debate, declaring it a decision for the QRL and no one else. McCarthy was grateful but knew the damage was done. In fact the position was decided by McCarthy's background. Bennett was a Queenslander, McCarthy from Sydney. On 20 February the QRL retained Bennett.

Bennett was haunted by his 1986 Origin failures. His Canberra employers, notably Jim Woodger, hoped to deter him from accepting the Origin post because it would divert his attention from the Raiders. Bennett told them, "I've got to do it. There's no other way I can set the record straight." He shuffled his previous season's notes, rang QRL general manager Ross Livermore and plotted his campaign — training regimes, where and when. He lunched with Wally and listed the likely team. "Belcher will be fullback," Bennett began. "Shearer on one wing, toss up the other, Miles and Meninga in the centres, you five-eighth, there's two or three halfbacks, Langer, Dawes or Spina..." And so on. Mal Meninga's collision with a goalpost, fracturing his arm, caused a further flurry of phone calls. It was easy for a man of Bennett's intense temperament to become obsessive. Said Wally, "There was no way Wayne was going to lose that year."

Wally's own build-up began with Brisbane's National Panasonic team. Their coach was Barry Muir, the former fiery Test halfback who coined the term "cockroaches" for NSW. Muir took the squad to Boggo Road gaol for a game of touch football against the prisoners. "Everybody was full of jokes and carrying on outside," said Wally. "But when they slammed the gates behind us everybody clammed up with fright." The match was delayed a few minutes, the prison crowd became restive and one inmate called out, "Would you blokes get this game started, I stole good money to come in here and watch you play!" Blond-haired and tanned young Allan Langer of the swift step and lightning acceleration enjoyed the adulation of the watching crowd until reprobates of a certain persuasion began wolf whistling.

Muir's admirable four months of preparation ended with a whimper. Brisbane lost 14–2 to a spare parts Penrith captained by Craig Izzard. It had been the same the previous year against Manly, bundled out first round. "I felt sorry for Garbo (Muir)," said Wally. "He tried hard to get us going but we just put in a low game." Langer, selected for his sharp, unpredictable attack, had a quiet game in his first match with Wally.

The next stage was a state-of-origin trial: the Queensland Maroons — a residents' team coached by Bennett — versus the Sydney Maroons — expatriate Queenslanders coached by McCarthy. Wally was chosen to captain the locals and Paul Vautin the expatriates. Vautin withdrew with injury, much to his and Wally's disappointment. As opposing captains they had organised a Three Stooges handshake, where each shapes to shake hands but instead bends forward and shakes each other's foot. It's how they greet each other anyway so they had no need to rehearse their act. "We were going to do that right in front of the grandstand," laughed Wally. Vautin's captaincy was awarded to Bob Lindner so Wally substituted his own little joke. When the two captains ran onto Lang Park to toss the coin, Wally muttered mock-seriously to Lindner, "You low cockroach cat!" and turned aside before his smile gave him away. Lindner's eyes widened with surprise. It was only a couple of weeks since Bob had helped Wally launch *King Wally* in Sydney.

Trials rarely engender atmosphere. Reluctant to risk injury with tough defence, players turn them into quasi-touch football. After 20 minutes at breakneck speed, Lindner panted alongside Wally, "How fast is this game!" Wally, puffing, replied, "It's got to slow soon!"

The expatriates won the trial 20–10 but the real contest was played out afterwards in the selection room. Several state-of-origin positions were a toss-up, none more so than halfback. Paul Vautin, in his Sydney newspaper column, had mischievously advocated that Wally play Origin halfback. The Queensland media picked it up as a genuine possibility. Wally did play halfback in an interstate match in 1979, the year before the Origins began. He had rung Vautin and demanded, "Fatty what are you bunging on!" Vautin was delighted. Yeah, you can play halfback, he laughed. Wally was disgusted: "Pigs I can!" Well who else was there? asked Vautin. "I don't care as long as it's not me," said Wally.

After the trial Wally and Bennett were summoned, individu-

ally, to give their views to the Origin selectors, a tradition begun by Ron McAuliffe. Difficult choices were explained and
comments sought. Wally and Bennett had no vote but if they
had a strong view about a player, the selectors listened. They
could probably even change a selection though rarely was there
such a divergence of opinion. Wally was courteous and never
abused his privilege. The procedure was part of the Queensland
effort to instil unanimity in the Origin team. Yet Wally's experience and seniority were clearly recognised by the QRL. He had
been consulted about the coach and, now, about the team, a
rare thing in any sport at this level.

The Queensland team for the first Origin in 1987 comprised
nine expatriates, a record. It included only six of the losing side
from the third Origin in 1986, by far the greatest Queensland
reshuffle in Origin history, recognition that form alone was now
the main criterion. Although three changes — the omissions of
Les Kiss, Mal Meninga and Mark Murray — were due to injury,
the team ushered in fresh faces for the perilous call to go over
the top against NSW. One was diminutive halfback Allan
Langer, another centre Peter Jackson and a third prop forward,
Martin Bella, all of whom were to become the steel in the Maroon's 1987 reconstruction.

In 1985–86 Queensland undoubtedly had become complacent. In those two years Brisbane's Origin players had, as
preparation for the toughest football in the world, played only
a few four-quarter, early season matches with their clubs. NSW
players had been hardened by various representative trials as
well as Sydney's formidable premiership games. For its 1987
preparation, Queensland sent a domestic team to New Zealand.
At Carlaw Park they met a strong New Zealand XIII including
Test Kiwis Adrian Shelford and Gary Freeman. Cocky half
Freeman roughed up a nervous Allan Langer in the first scrum.
Langer, indignant, lost any hesitancy and displayed skills long
promised by his Ipswich coach, Tom Raudonikis, as Queensland scraped in 18–14. The second match was a 72–6 romp
against Bay of Plenty. For the five Origin players it was still
better than any training run.

Wayne Bennett had coached Souths to defeat Wally's Wynnum team in the 1985 Brisbane grand final, once a source of some coolness between two strong personalities in the halls of the QRL where they were both employed. Since then, in the grinding mills of Origin defeat, they had come to respect each other. Wally said of Bennett's coaching, "It's not practice makes perfect, it's practice until you are perfect." In 1986 when Bennett first took over Queensland Wally was no immediate devotee of some of his coaching drills. After the first session Wally took Bennett aside and, as politely as possible, told him, "That's the kind of stuff I was doing as a schoolkid."

Bennett listened, non-committal. If he was to be accepted by the Queensland squad he had to convince Wally. Before next training he called Wally in and ran an old video, the 1985 Brisbane grand final, a sore loss for Wally. Bennett explained what Wally knew already, that his pass to the left was stronger than to the right. His pass to the left was that wonderful spiralling torpedo which could travel half the width of the field. It was first seen in all its glory in the second Test of the 1982 Kangaroo tour of Great Britain. Wally, from centre field, put Mal Meninga over in the corner with an arcing pass of some 25 metres. That pass was powered by Wally's right arm.

Wally's pass to the right, controlled by his left arm, was not as strong, did not torpedo and tended to float. In fact Wally occasionally turned his entire body to throw a right-handed pass to the right if he sought distance. That took precious seconds. Bennett explained how in the 1985 grand final he had used this knowledge to stretch South's defence wide on the left field and ease up on the right. Wally, a numbers expert himself when examining defences, knew the truth of Bennett's observations. Bennett then rolled a video of one of Wally's recent matches. He hit the pause button at an ill-directed, right-side pass. "Doesn't look like you're doing any better now than you were then," Bennett said with a wry grin.

Wally reassessed those simple skill drills. He told me, "You watch Canberra play. There'll be a break downfield, someone throws a pass and his support will scoop it up off his toes. From the next play they score a try. If the bloke hadn't picked up the loose pass — if he drops it — they aren't in position to score the try." Having converted Wally, Bennett showed the entire Origin squad videos of the 1986 losses. He told them, "In each game there were probably only three instances where we went wrong and it cost us a try every time. There isn't a hell of a lot to change, the mistakes are fairly easy to correct. If you don't change, the result won't. It's that simple."

Wally noticed changes in Bennett as well. "Despite our 1986 losses he was more confident," said Wally. "At first he wanted a particular style of football and he was going to get it. But he was used to working with club sides for a whole year with plenty of time to influence them. Here we were together for five-day camps, three times a year. At first Benny was unrelenting but then he understood the limitations of the team's time together."

All Bennett's preparations could not prevent the awe with which the Queensland side examined the NSW team. "Have a look at this backline for speed," said Wally. "Jack, he's as fast as anybody though he doesn't get credit for it, O'Connor's gone before you know, McGaw can run, Johnston's very quick, Ettinghausen's lightning, Kenny can run and Sterlo..." Wally paused and smiled, "well I guess Sterlo's about as quick as I am." NSW coach Ron Willey tagged it the fastest backline he had ever been associated with. Only Queensland's Dale Shearer could match it for speed.

Yet the one player Wally was glad to see the last of was centre Chris Mortimer, the NSW anvil from 1985–86. "I knew from my time on the Australian tour how good he was," said Wally. "He's just so competitive. If he was playing against his brother he'd bash him all night long and at the end put his arm around him and say, 'Thanks for the game let's go have a drink.'" NSW had also shifted O'Connor to the wing. That made Wally happy. He'd always considered Mick a better centre than winger.

A glimmer of hope for Queensland lay in the injuries to those twin Shermans, Peter Tunks and Steve Roach. In 1986 the giant pair strode through the rucks, slowly grinding the Queensland pack down. At training Paul Vautin, drawing on his vast knowledge of Sydney footballers, assessed the NSW team for his Origin mates. "Player number one: very talented, good mover, strong fend and sidestep off his right foot, must be respected. Player number two: fair dinkum sheila who can't play. Thinks he's Robert Redford, bash him!"

The match was a sellout, due in no small part to the controversy generated by *King Wally*, launched a few weeks earlier. Former Australian coach Harry Bath said he feared aggrieved players would take it out on Wally on the field. Wally was sceptical. "I can't see why anyone would want to get square," he said. "Wayne Pearce is the only bloke involved and I don't think I have ever seen him throw a punch." Bob Lindner and Paul Vautin vowed Wally would not be the victim of any retribution. "We'll be right behind him if anything should happen," said Lindner. "I know Paul feels the same way."

Nevertheless ARL chief Ken Arthurson addressed the NSW team at their first training session at Leichhardt Oval to defuse any aggression created by the biography. Accompanied by NSW general manager John Quayle, Arthurson walked to the centre of the field. Players huddled around him while photographers and television lens zoomed in. "You can play it as hard as you like," Arthurson told the team. "But play it the way the game is supposed to be played. There is not to be any attempt at revenge for the book. It's not a factor." Arthurson told the media separately, "The book has created plenty of problems and ruffled a few feathers including my own. But that's over now, it's been settled." He wanted the players' code of ethics observed and the series played in the right spirit. He would be giving the Queensland team the same message.

In the Queensland camp the players occasionally passed supportive remarks to Wally. "You handling it OK?" they'd ask. "We've read bits, can't see what they're blowing up about." Wayne Bennett kept a close eye on his trump and eventually raised the subject. Said Wally, "Well it's starting to get me down. Anything thrown by those blokes down there won't upset me, but I'm just totally pissed off now. It's not the criticism which upsets me, it's the frequency and ignorance of it."

Bennett donned his psychologist's coat. "You can't let it get you down," he entreated. "You've got to put it aside. You know in your own mind when you're right so just shelve it. Get it out of the way and concentrate on what you've got to do in your football." Obvious words, but when spoken by Bennett in his stentorian manner they penetrated Wally's gloom and righted his equilibrium which had been listing badly from weeks of media denunciation. NSW coach Ron Willey generously added a final reassuring note. He made a point of approaching Wally and told him, "Mate, they carry on about nothing don't they? I read the book and I thought it was good. I got a good laugh out of it."

On the evening of 2 June 1987, I wended my way through the excited crowd milling inside Lang Park. Program sellers and first scorer barkers blocked the grandstand approaches, queues lined at stalls selling T-shirts and match memorabilia and even a stack of *King Wally*s. Hundreds were turned away when the ground was sold out at 5 p.m. There was a dusky exhilaration in the air, a glint in every eye, an anticipation, like a street crowd on New Year's eve. At the Hale Street end of the ground fans climbed trees to get a view. Beside the grandstand stairs I bumped into Wayne Bennett who looked remarkably composed with only 50 minutes to kick-off. "Here's the man responsible for the sellout crowd tonight," he said, grinning, before the crowd pushed us apart. Then came Tony Durkin, Queensland editor of *Rugby League Week*. "No need to ask how they're selling eh?" he shouted and rushed past.

I presented my invitation to the flunky manning the door of the QRL board of directors' inner sanctum and was shown into the expansive presence of the inimitable Ron McAuliffe, chairman of the Lang Park Trust. The boardroom began filling with a coterie of the powerful and influential of Queensland. I shook hands with the Governor, Sir Walter Campbell; Federal Sports Minister John Brown; Police Commissioner Sir Terence Lewis; Supreme Court Justice Angelo Vasta; Lang Park trustee Sir Edward Lyons; Lands Commission chairman Wally Baker; Director of Prosecutions Des Sturgess and author-journalist Hugh Lunn. Each setting at the dining table — silver service and crystal upon white linen — was garnished with a copy of *King*

Wally, inscribed to each guest and signed by Wally. Premier Sir Joh Bjelke-Petersen, on his ill-fated road to Canberra, was absent but Deputy-Premier Bill Gunn arrived to accept an autographed copy on Sir Joh's behalf.

The gathering, and the participants, were unforgettable. Des Sturgess was the author of the 1986 Sturgess Report into Child Sexual Offences, a precursor to the dramatic Fitzgerald Inquiry into corruption in Queensland; Sir Walter Campbell signed the Cabinet documents establishing the inquiry; Bill Gunn hired Tony Fitzgerald QC, to run the inquiry; Sir Terry Lewis became the centre of the inquiry; Sir Edward Lyons was a star witness; Wally Baker was mentioned in passing during evidence from Sir Joh; Angelo Vasta became the subject of a separate inquiry initiated by evidence; Hugh Lunn reported the inquiry for the *Australian*.

Midway through cocktails McAuliffe welcomed into our midst the president of the Australian Rugby League Ken Arthurson. McAuliffe solemnly introduced Arthurson around our august circle until he reached me. "No, no," exclaimed Ron. "You won't want to shake this man's hand," and drew Arthurson away. The other worthies looked amused, and Arthurson confused, until McAuliffe broke the joke and introduced the awful author. Arthurson, a man of some poise, joined in the laughter. A few minutes later, talking with him, I discovered he had read most of the book and thoroughly enjoyed it. But he felt there were things that should not have been said. After all, Wally and Wayne Pearce had to play in the Australian team together. McAuliffe overheard and interceded.

"The book is a work of art, a work of great literary merit which rugby league ought to feel proud to have been published," said Senator Ron. "Other sports, cricket, rugby union and motor racing have books, why not us?" He thrust his generous paunch at Arthurson. "Rugby league is a tough body contact sport. Would you want a namby-pamby book written about it?" Arthurson was ready to agree, but Ron wasn't satisfied. He nailed Arthurson about saying Wally would have the Australian captaincy stripped from him. "No, I didn't say that," said Arthurson adamantly. "I only said the book would be discussed by the ARL. And you know, Ron, that Wally would never have got the captaincy without my support." McAuliffe was in a grand mood. "Now Kenny, we're going to have a wonderful evening here tonight, but you tell me..." I withdrew from that debate, left the boardroom and claimed my seat upstairs for the main contest to come.

The shame of great rugby league matches is that they are so evanescent, so all-engrossing for one evening and then dispatched into a fading memory. The state-of-origins of 1987 deserve to be regularly re-run like famous old movies, introduced with biographies of the stars, an analysis of the plots, an explanation of dramatic moments and then a loving roll of the tapes.

The first 10 minutes of this classic showed what was at stake. Players tensed and winced in tackles. Television spares viewers. If you stand near the sideline you can hear breath expelled from lungs in rushing grunts, hear flesh slap on flesh, the hollow knocks of bone on bone — gruesome sounds. An untrained player would snap a limb in those first 10 minutes.

Cameos emerged. From a scrum Peter Sterling fed Brett Kenny. Kenny ran three steps forward, Wally advanced straight. Kenny propped, Wally propped. Kenny veered out, Wally veered out. Kenny accelerated across field for 10 metres, Wally matched him. They were like similar poles of two magnets, able to oppose but not approach. Ah, but Wally's foot slipped on the turf for a micro-second. Kenny saw, broke formation and peeled into the gap. His body leaning at an acute angle, he eased around Wally like a skier around a slalom pole. Half-way past, Wally recovered balance and with his fingertips snared those fleeing knees. Just a few seconds in an 80-minute match, action at eye-blink speed yet it was pure theatre, with two leading men, confrontation, duel and denouement.

The script for the first half was that Queensland had three opportunities to score tries and scored one, NSW had two and scored twice. They led 10–6 at the break.

For the first 20 minutes of the second half both sides slugged it out, slowly wearying, defenders rising from tackles a little slower, attackers running a little further. Eventually attacking

energy overwhelmed defensive determination and the scoring
began in earnest, NSW always minimally ahead, to 16–12.

During one restart of play I glimpsed a gladiatorial tableau.
As O'Connor of the Etruscan nose toed the earth to place the
ball, Pearce of the haunted eyes bent double beside him, hands
on knees, headband askew. Both stared ahead. They could have
been peasant farmers in the field at day's end, tired, engrossed,
together and strong. A living landscape of toil.

With 12 minutes left, referee Mick Stone sounded the relief
for Queensland with a penalty. Wally found touch on the NSW
quarterline and pelted up for the tap. "Our blokes were just
about rooted," he told me. "I don't know — I just looked back
and the blokes were tired and I thought I'd just hit it up and get
them to think 'Hey that's our job, we should be doing that' and
get them stirred up a bit."

Once there Wally saw that where NSW normally had three
men covering a 10-metre-wide blindside, they had only two —
Steve Folkes and Andrew Ettinghausen. Garry Jack had moved
to cover a chip or bomb in centre field. Wally accepted
Conescu's tap pass and surged straight into Folkes. Ettinghausen
could not resist the temptation to leave his wing and assist.
Wally freed his arms sufficiently to feed Tony Currie who
speared through where Ettinghausen should have been and
scored. Five minutes left, score: 16–16.

A draw seemed a just result to Queensland, less so to NSW.
Lang Park was seething, chants rose up "Queensland! Queensland!" With every dangerous break the crowds in the stands
rose like choreographed human waves. The tension made you
short of breath. If football is a surrogate for battle then it
seemed Queensland's frontline troops had turned the enemy
from the gates.

Queensland had worked their backsides off getting back into
the match. "For Christ's sake don't lose the ball," Wally
screamed. Only the strongest should now handle. Gene Miles?
Yes! But Miles had the ball ripped from his arms first tackle.
Wally put both hands to his head in anguish. "They're working
for the centre," Wally shouted. "Field goal!" Sure enough, but
Sterling's kick wobbled and missed. The bright bulbs on Lang

Park's digital clock blinked the agony, 2m 41s left.

From the quarterline tap Wally called for four tackles and then downtown, meaning that before the fifth he would roof it down field. Conescu ran it out — one tackle. Bella took it up — two. Then Vautin — three. Conescu to dummy half. Belcher ran through, no ball. Gillmeister took off too, hands raised to receive. No pass. Collapse of plan. Wally was standing flat footed, his arms by his side well back from the ruck when Conescu flung the ball straight at him. Wally caught the ball, Royce Simmons and Peter Sterling almost simultaneously. He somehow eluded their charge but had no time to kick. He ran the blindside and passed to Tony Currie. Wally did not want to be caught with the ball. He wanted to be free to kick from the ensuing ruck. But Currie did not go to ground with the ball. Instead he chip-kicked ahead, straight to Brett Kenny on half-way. Possession lost. Hearts in the Frank Burke grandstand collectively missed a beat. 1m 45s to go.

NSW ran four rucks and suddenly McGaw broke through and flew down the blindside flank. Defenders converged and harrassed him and in the confusion the ball rolled loose over the Queensland line. Peter Jackson and McGaw wrestled like miners after a disputed nugget until McGaw broke free and dived to stake his claim in the corner. Lang Park held its breath. Referee Stone looked at both linesmen. The nearest nodded. Stone put that fateful whistle to his lips and stretched his arm towards the criminal spot. O'Connor and Simmons leapt into the air. I glanced at the clock and scribbled 0.48s.

On television an inspired director at Channel 9 cut to a shot of Wayne Bennett. In his maroon blazer and tie, headset and earphones in place, he mouthed, "Oh no!" like an air traffic controller witnessing a runway disaster. In the NSW sideline dugout Ron Willey was embraced by his support team. On the Queensland bench all eyes, except Greg Dowling's, were turned towards the guilty corner. An ice-pack strapped to an injured shoulder Dowling was staring straight ahead, eyes glistening, shaking his head.

On field Cleal, Simmons, Johnston, Kenny and McGaw were cavorting in one group. Ettinghausen, Jack and Pearce in another. Then they split apart like exploding nuclei and reformed in new clusters. Jack whooped, Cleal punched the air. The crowd sound was like nothing I've heard before. A persistent, subdued hubbub, a sense of searching, an agitated uncomprehension. Had they been a volatile soccer crowd the mounted police might have been ordered into position inside the perimeter. Near my seat Sydney coaches Bob Fulton, Ted Glossop, Laurie Freier and John Peard were staring down with surprised expressions, gradually evolving into smiles of relief.

As O'Connor prepared for the conversion the men in maroon toed the line — soldiers of ill fortune, heads down, shoulders slumped, disbelieving, exhausted, beaten. Wally passed along the line briefly shaking hands with every player. Referee Stone spoke to Wally. "If McGaw hadn't got his hand on it in goal I was going to award a penalty try," he said. Why? Wally asked. "Jackson held their player back," said Stone. Wally was too dispirited to care. The final siren sounded. O'Connor's kick missed and it was over. 20–16. O'Connor shook Wally's hand, Pearce gave him a consoling pat on the shoulder. Wally walked slowly off, mouthguard in hand, a sad, ironic twist to his lips.

In the Channel 9 commentary box Alan Thomas was wearing his loyalties on his downturned lips. He said:

I hope you people at home have regained your composure, I'm not sure I have. You often wonder, don't you, why the score couldn't have finished at 16–16, but I guess that's sport eh?

To which co-commentator Mick Veivers, hard-nosed ex-Test prop, replied:

That's why the Blues are hard to hold you know, they play it and they play it, right to the end.

The Queensland dressingroom was a battle dressing station. Bare bodies lay on benches and tables, uninjured physically but mortally wounded in spirit. Bennett did not seek to dispel the agony. He spoke briefly and to the point. "I'm happy with the way you came back," he said. "The way you fought was magnificent. Your ball control was great except for the last two minutes." Bennett's cool words hid a huge heartache which he did not dare display for fear he would irrevocably damage the team's confidence in themselves and him. He walked back to the team's motel in the city. But the 20-minute walk took him an hour because he walked via south Brisbane, pounding the pavement to ease the pain within. "It was an enormous distress to me," he said. "I was very low. I didn't want anyone to be with me. I had to do some cold, hard thinking and sort myself out emotionally."

He crossed the Brisbane River with his long strides, into the territory where he had made his name as a coach with South Brisbane. In that hour Bennett repaired his own wounded will. He rebuilt it, walking block after block, with layer after layer of positive thoughts. "Damn it! I'm not going to let them beat us again," he lectured himself. "I'm not going to let them get on top of us. I'm going to be even more determined. I'm going to display all the qualities a coach needs. I'm going to get it together and fight back." Bennett knew his personal resolve had to be ironclad because once he reached the motel he would be placed under the public microscope in his speech to the team's post-match function. He had to be able to say, "Look, we had a little accident tonight, but nothing too serious." And every player had to believe it.

Wally paid Bennett the ultimate tribute in his captain's speech. "I've always considered Graham Lowe to be the best coach in the world but Wayne Bennett has changed my mind," he said. Wally was one of the few who had seen Bennett's full effort, the meetings, the telephone conversations, the organisation, the training.

Bennett told journalists that the nature of his fourth consecutive loss coaching Queensland — none by more than six points — was the hardest to accept. "We've proved we are their equal but we lose," he said. "I believe we have deserved much better. It really hurts being the beaten half of mighty football games. We are good enough to win. The players know that. If we give it all again in Sydney surely something has to come our way." Jacqui Lewis drove Wally home and, to break the deathly silence, ventured quietly, "We should have won." Wally was in no mood for post mortems. "Look, I don't want to talk about it any more," he said abruptly. At home Jacqui tried another conversation tack. "I recorded the game," she said. Wally's mood was dark. "Well you can wipe the bloody thing, you can get rid of it!" Everywhere Wally went the next day well-meaning words plagued him. "Tough way to lose," said acquaintances. Wally didn't want to hear it. He had pinned a lot on winning, not the least of which was to kill all the rubbish about the book.

Bennett rang him Wednesday evening, 24 hours after the final siren. "How're you feeling," he asked. Wally: "Shithouse". Bennett: "You know there is no way in the world they will beat us again this year." Wally: "Yeah I know, you're not kiddin'."

Wally's conversations with his team-mates had turned up a new determination. Far from being dispirited they were disgusted. Fatty Vautin told him, "Fancy getting beaten that way. You'd rather lose 20–6 than like that, eh? Mate, next time we've just got to belt them." Wally agreed, but the loss sat heavily in Wally's memory, the worst defeat, emotionally, of his career.

4 HAIL, THE EMPEROR

After 18 Origin matches since 1980 the two warring states were 9–9. Queensland had lost the last five in a row. Wally could not pull his Origin career out of the dive it began in 1985. Though Queensland's four losses under Wayne Bennett were by narrow margins, fears arose that NSW were about to dominate the state-of-origins as they had the old interstate contests.

The first training session for the second state-of-origin showed that the senior Queensland hands understood what was at stake. "There hasn't been a training session like it," said Wally. "Phenomenal. Just that session. The determination in the air, you could hear it in their voices." At a group talk Paul Vautin spoke about proving that Queensland was not a spent force. Gene Miles said they must win to maintain state morale. Greg Dowling reckoned he had forgotten what it felt like to win an Origin match. Coach Bennett had just one wish: under no circumstances was his team to quit. He knew his players well. Though they all came from different backgrounds, they were all special guys, he said. Not a lair amongst them. He addressed the team: "I don't care what happens out there, I want you to hang in. Maybe we'll get something good out of it."

He did not tell the players what he told team manager, Dick Turner, after they had booked in to their Rushcutters Bay motel in Sydney three days before the match. Nothing had been printed or said, but Bennett felt the knives being sharpened. As he and Turner strolled that evening around Rushcutters Bay, near where they start the Sydney to Hobart yacht classic,

Bennett said tonelessly, "Dick, if we lose on Tuesday night I won't be embarrassing anyone by asking to remain as Origin coach. I've been given two years. I've done my best with the cards dealt to me but if we haven't done it, that's it." Said the taciturn Turner, "I can't argue with that." The story broke that Monday after Bennett was interviewed by a Brisbane newspaper, but it was not picked up in Sydney. The players were spared the extra pressure that their coach was departing if they couldn't win.

The Sydney Cricket Ground that Tuesday was awash. Rain was still falling as the teams splashed through ankle-deep water to line up for the National Anthem. Wally bit on his mouthguard as a record crowd of 42,048 drowned the anthem with their own hymn of hate, "WALL-LY SUCKS, WALL-LY SUCKS!" He was used to the abuse, but he could scarcely credit that the crowd would desecrate the nation's song. He blocked out the chant. In a similar quagmire in 1984 Greg Dowling had caught a rebound from the crossbar for a miraculous try. Wally heard Dowling warn a doubting Gene Miles before they ran on, "You watch. I'm going to score again out there tonight."

The first tackle focussed media attention on a man known as "The Grasshopper", spindly-legged, hook-nosed referee Barry Gomersall from the north Queensland coastal city of Mackay. Wally decided to clear the ball from his quarter after the first ruck. The Queensland chasers took off to harrass Garry Jack. Gomersall penalised them for being offside — in front of the kicker — a controversial ruling.

Rugby league had only just begun to grapple with the problems of chasers standing offside, anticipating kicks downfield to hem in opposing fullbacks before they had time to move. It was the first penalty ever given for the practice in Origin football. A simple two points for Michael O'Connor. On such a night it could easily have been a winning margin. Wally asked Gomersall as he walked by, "Are you going to penalise all night for being in front of the kicker or just this once?" Gomersall ignored him. Later when Gomersall penalised Queensland from a scrum, Wally asked pointedly, "Is it going to be the same for both sides?" This time he earned a reply. "Isn't it always?" said Gomersall.

For the first 20 minutes NSW played exhibition football in atrocious conditions. They scored the most casual of tries when the ball squirted from Dale Shearer's arms close to Queensland's line. Waiting for the conversion, Wally stood behind the line with an empty feeling in his gut, face muddied, rainwater dribbling off his chin. He said nothing to Shearer. But coach Bennett did at half-time. "Rowdy, that was the softest try you'll ever let in," he said. He could afford the luxury of a snipe because by then Shearer had atoned, driving over to score from dummy half with strength that belied his slim frame. At the break Queensland trailed 4–6 yet Bennett saw small, hopeful signs. Wally was marshalling, Vautin charging. Bennett's week-long theme had been, "If you don't give in, anything can happen." Now he looked out and thought, "These blokes don't want to be beaten," and then, "By gees, they're not going to be beaten!"

Never has a team been more excited at half-time. Wally shouted when Bennett entered, "We've got them!" Vautin jumped up and said, "Yeah, we've got 'em coach." The cry was taken up around the room. "We've got 'em, let's get out there and get them again." Bennett called for calm. "You've still got five minutes to go." Wally was jumping around. "Doesn't matter. Let's go and get them." It was an astonishing scene. The maroons were on a high, bouncing back from their depressing defeat in Brisbane.

In the second half they laboriously, exhaustedly clawed their way back. Though their hands slid off muddied jerseys and greasy ball, though they tripped, slipped and erred, they inexorably pressured NSW. They would not be denied. It was uncanny to see such masters as Sterling and Kenny unable to stem the tide of play. As he predicted, Dowling scored and then Miles put Colin Scott over with one of those risky one-handed passes for which — when they fail — Miles is much castigated. Wally is critical of Gene too. He wished Gene would throw more. Queensland led 12–6 but they were not just winning. In the drenched and quenched presence of Sydney's most ardent rugby league supporters, Queensland were reclaiming the balance of Origin superiority which had deserted them for two long seasons.

Ten seconds from the siren the Queensland players were already clapping their hands. "Gees it was a good feeling winning that game," recalled Wally. "It took so much pressure off us, off Wayne, off everyone." Bennett's face and shirt became progressively smudged as he was embraced by his jubilant players. For once he could not maintain his determinedly impassive expression. His lips split into a large, lopsided grin which lasted into the small hours as the team wound down in various Sydney nightspots, celebrating until the doors finally closed on them at sun-up.

Then they discovered why they had won. Three Queensland tries to NSW's one — and that a gift — seemed convincing enough to Wally. But the following day's Sydney newspapers suggested Queensland had a 14th player — the Grasshopper. "Ref Row" said the *Sun*, "We're Stuck With Gomersall" said the *Mirror*. Their complaints stemmed from the penalty count of 10–5 to Queensland. At one stage Queensland received five successive penalties while NSW went 50 minutes without one. Bennett was furious. "When we win it's because of the referee, when NSW wins it's because they have such a super team," he said. "When Gomersall refereed in Sydney last year and NSW won he was supposed to have done a great job. Anyone who is fairminded can't say Gomersall cost NSW the game."

Gomersall was unmoved. "I could not give a continental what they say," he said. "Sensationalism is the name of the game in the media these days, I understand that." Gomersall quoted a South Australian survey which showed that losing sides complained about the umpires 75 per cent of the time but winning sides only 5 per cent. He said, "It boils down to this, if you can't find any other reason for your loss, blame the referee." As he moved around the SCG members bar he received unanimous praise. Asked by one intrepid reporter how he thought he performed, Gomersall replied, "I thought I had a blinder!" Wally loved that. Gomersall was not a showy referee, just idiosyncratic, as demonstrated by his practice of letting brawls on field sort themselves out. The southern media couldn't fathom him and he treated criticism with contempt. Yet he seemed to possess an immunity to any official reprimand. NSW coach Ron Willey

diplomatically admitted his team had conceded too many penalties. Gomersall was, after all, to referee the third and deciding
Origin in Brisbane.

The week of the third match Wally awoke with the flu. Within
days it had spread through the camp. Worst affected were Allan
Langer and "The Axe" Trevor Gillmeister, whose Origin tackling
had further justified his nickname. But nerves were the major
team affliction. Martin Bella was out, injured, for Queensland;
Peter Tunks had returned for NSW whose pack now outweighed
Queensland's by an average four kilos per player. NSW had
broken the Parramatta connection, Sterling-Kenny, of five Origin matches. Kenny was moved to inside centre to make way
for the form Sydney five-eighth, Manly's Cliff Lyons. O'Connor
was moved from wing to outside centre to produce what Wally
described as "Surely the most lethal attacking combination ever
selected" - Kenny and O'Connor. Opposing O'Connor was Gene
Miles who needed pain-killing injections in a swollen ankle. The
day before the match Wayne Bennett sensed — smelt is how he
puts it — a lack of intensity within the team. At a team meeting
first Wally and then Paul Vautin rose and spoke emotionally
about the imperatives of winning. Bennett left them to it. He
always believed the will to win could not be imposed from without by the coach. It could only come from within the players.

On a more practical note Queensland would need to heed the
advice of Australian rugby union captain Andrew Slack. In an
open letter to the team, published in the *Courier-Mail* on the
morning of the match, he wrote:

> For all the analyses that might have raged over why Australia lost
> the rugby World Cup, I can tell you the reason was that we missed
> tackles. Brighten up my week boys, please. If you have to tackle until
> 10.30 tonight, do it.

That evening the team boarded the bus for the inspirational
drive from their motel in Roma Street to Lang Park. Wally chose
his traditional left-side seat. In 1986, the year that Queensland
lost badly, Wally had boarded the coach and sensed a flatness
among his team-mates. "Drive by the Caxton," he commanded.
The coach driver did then as he has since. After leaving the

Travelodge, he did a u-turn, drove back along Roma Street, right into Petrie Terrace, past the old police barracks and left into Caxton Street. The Caxton Hotel, a block from Lang Park, has a large car park. On Origin nights cars are barred as thousands of drinkers spill into the area from packed bars. Queensland manager, Dick "Tossa" Turner, calls the Caxton from the motel: "We'll be past in 10 minutes." The hotel relays the message over its public address system. Patrons throng to the footpath as the coach swings into Caxton Street and gives the signal, three blasts of its claxon. The crowd surges forward, cheering, raising cans in salutes and toasts to the maroons. As the bus inches past, the crowd's closeness penetrates, lifting the players as no coach's inspirational harangue could. "The crowd goes off their melons," said Wally. "Even though I know it's coming I know what it does for me. It's second only to running on the field. The noise is so loud then it's like someone poking you in your ears."

The week before the third Origin I wrote a story for the Brisbane *Courier-Mail* suggesting that when Wally led Queensland on to Lang Park I'd like the band to strike up a song, the crowd to sing and the words to be flashed up on the scoreboard so everyone could join in. At previous matches the brass band, as they marched from the field, played the chorus of a well known television advertisement. I wanted the crowd to sing the first verse which went:

Here's to Wally Lewis, for lacing on a boot,
Sometimes he plays it rugged, sometimes he plays it cute,
He slices through the backline like a Stradbroke Island shark,
There's glue on every finger, he's the Emperor of Lang Park.

There was no need for the crowd to sing the chorus, in praise of beer. To those who would criticise the idea I wrote that Queensland owed Wally a special welcome back to Lang Park to erase the extraordinary castigation he received at the SCG in the previous match. At Cardiff Arms Park the rich voices of Welsh rugby union crowds launch into, "Bread of Heaven, feed me 'til I want no more", and English soccer crowds swing into "You'll Never Walk Alone". Lang Park fans could sing a hymn to their Emperor.

Sing that song they did and much more. A figure dressed as the Emperor of Lang Park, in jersey number 6 (Wally's number) paraded around in royal crown and maroon and gold flowing robes while leotard-clad dancing girls genuflected before him. The Emperor chased a pantomime cockroach and sprayed it with a giant can of pesticide and the cockroach rolled on its back.

The mock Emperor — alias QRL consultant Chris Elder — maintained his presence during the match as well. With his ground microphone he had the crowd urging the home pack to "heave" during scrums and led a chant of "Queensland" whenever the maroons pressed the NSW line. It became too much for NSW general manager, John Quayle. He left his seat in the main stand, hurried down to the office of QRL managing director Ross Livermore, and demanded Elder be cut off. Quayle felt Elder's use of the microphone was unfair. Livermore reined Elder in but by then his job was done.

Queensland led 4–0 after 10 minutes, through a piece of premeditated razzle dazzle near the NSW line. It was codenamed "hooch", an apt description for the illicit way the Queenslanders smuggled the ball through seven pairs of hands in as many seconds. If the ball's path was a coloured light on a computer screen it would have drawn a scribble as it reversed, skirted and criss-crossed, mesmerising the NSW defence. Wally was the master, Gary Belcher the penultimate handler. As Belcher was felled a metre short of the line he heeded a call and dished the ball blind to his right for Bob Lindner to juggle and plunge over. "It was an old Wynnum move," said Wally. "You can see three of the blokes who handled were Wynnum — Dowling, Lindner and me." That is how modern rugby league teams break straight line defences, why the theory of man-on-man defence has no perfect application, why rugby league does not stagnate into scoreless draws. Precisely planned attack can open the gates of victory.

Wayne Pearce roams the field like a medieval warrior, fearless, hitting evil where he finds it and surviving gang tackles. With a headband of black electrical tape over white bandage, both wrists and several fingers similarly strapped and chewing on his mouthguard, he looks the stuff of comic book heroes. With NSW trailing he led by example. Wally essayed a low trajectory clearing kick. One step for rhythm, two steps for momentum and kick. In that time Pearce ran 10 metres, charged down the airborne ball and collected the rebound. Wally frantically chased and brought Pearce down but they both rose in time to see the concluding stages of a runaway 40-metre NSW try. Wally trotted slowly back, head inclined down. "I had a big watermelon in my throat," he said. "You know it's your fault, and the blokes look at you, and you know they're filthy at you and... Oh, it's a mongrel of a feeling."

Being thus thwarted was not new to Wally. In 1985 Steve Mortimer and Ben Elias, with their speed off the mark, effectively stymied Wally's kicking game and won the Origin series. Rugby league kickers could learn from Australian rugby union great, Roger Gould. As Test fullback he was called upon to clear twenty times per match under severe harrassment from opposition breakaways — tougher pressure than Wally faced from NSW's forwards. Gould practised and became expert at the standing punt. No two steps, no stutter preparation, not even body weight going forward if there was no time — just receive and swing the leg through.

Queensland regained the lead with a try from a grubber kick by Greg Dowling. In the melee I could not tell who scored. "Dale Shearer," said Jacqui Lewis sitting nearby. "How do you know?" I asked. "I saw Wally give him a hug," she grinned. Grubber kicking is not a finesse usually associated with front-row fowards. "GD fancies himself as a kicker," said Wally. "Every training session he mucks around kicking." Admittedly Dowling got his instructions from Shearer who was pointing behind the NSW defence and shouting "Put one down!" Queensland led 8–6.

NSW equalled minutes later when Cliff Lyons intercepted and ran to the Queensland quarterline. Wally dived headlong at his ankles, Lyons arched his back, nearly escaped, staggered and fell. Wally jumped up and lay all over Lyons, a professional foul. The consequent penalty was close to the sideline, difficult for most, not for Michael O'Connor. Before that kick O'Connor, with 69 points from eight games, was second only to Mal Meninga (109 from 16) in state-of-origin pointscoring. Mick made that 71 points and the score 8–8. Tension mounted. In the stands coach Bennett looked upwards and thought, "Not tonight. Don't let it be tonight."

Fate now alighted on the man responsible for much of Bennett's state-of-origin misery — Michael O'Connor. A minute before half-time Lyons made as though to kick through. O'Connor motored up from behind. At the last moment Lyons changed to a little lofted chip kick and to do that he slowed abruptly. O'Connor tried to halt too. A cartoonist would have sketched him like the Roadrunner with legs locked and clouds of dust billowing behind as he skidded. O'Connor finished a half-metre offside, saw the kick, took the chance, whipped through and caught the kick on the full. Even before O'Connor caught the ball Wally, who had nabbed Lyons, was pointing and calling offside. As O'Connor heard referee Gomersall's whistle, Wally was already looking over his shoulder to gauge the distance to the goal posts. The ruling was indisputable, and no NSW player said otherwise.

The penalty was as easy, or as difficult as O'Connor's. But Colin Scott had missed his last five kicks, three in the second Origin and two tonight. Wally, reluctantly, decided to take the kick himself. Dale Shearer, wandering by, inquired, "Do you want me to kick it?" Wally looked at Shearer, the quiet man known as "Rowdy", a poker-faced, nerveless competitor. Wally remembered the Ella brothers from his schoolboy days, natural athletes, adept at picking up skills in any sport. Shearer was their soul brother. "You better not miss the bastard," quoth Wally. "Oh, I'll get it," said Dale. And he did. As Shearer ran by, Wally shook his hand and Dale broke into a rare smile.

So Queensland led 10–8 at half-time. Vautin told the tense dressing shed, "If they don't score, we don't lose." And they didn't and that was the final score. Yet the second half remains as one of the epic 40 minutes of modern rugby league. It prompted ARL chief Ken Arthurson, in his address to the crowd afterwards, to say they had witnessed the greatest exhibition of rugby league football for many years. "In fact, personally, I have never seen better in my life," he said.

For the first 10 minutes neither side held sway and then NSW sustained 20 minutes of running offence beyond Queensland's imagination. Queensland's nemesis, Michael O'Connor, broke clear from the half-way line. Steve Rogers may have been the Rolls Royce of centres but O'Connor is the Ferrari with his unmatched changes of speed and legendary cornering. He cruised to the Queensland quarterline — a try, the match and the series now within his sights. The only person anywhere near him was referee Gomersall. But if tries win matches, tackles save them. Wally, in deep defence, was galloping across field like the cavalry. Coming almost at right angles to O'Connor, he should have been an easy mark to beat. O'Connor ran 14 strides and on the 15th planted his left foot and leaned infield for his trademark, a glorious inside step.

"I've known Mick for years, since a schoolboy," said Wally. "I knew his big step was off his left foot. He has a habit of making a mug of you with it. I knew the step was coming next so I had to put the brakes on, stop going across and drive up towards him. The important part was that instead of letting him come to me I had to go to him. You haven't really got a lot of time to think, you've just got to get there and hope."

It was not a tackle, it was a collision. As O'Connor stepped left at near full pace Wally hurtled into him at equal velocity. Had they been automobiles they would have been write-offs. Wally is immensely strong, the best part of 95 kilos; O'Connor 83 kilos of sprung muscle. They hit like two battering rams, flew into the air, legs flailing, and fell slam-bang to the unyielding turf. About 35,000 people held their breath, fearing some mortal injury. As the collapsed pair slowly rose, as the rest of play caught up with them, a roar of wondrous applause spread into a crescendo along the stands.

Experienced rugby league writer, the Sydney *Sun*'s Geoff Prenter, devoted an entire story the next day to that tackle. Under the headline, "Tackle King" Prenter wrote:

Wally Lewis last night leapt over a metre into the air to make the greatest tackle ever seen in state-of-origin football. The tackle was so devastating that it took the capacity crowd of 35,000 at Lang Park some moments to respond. It was a tackle that saved Queensland from defeat...The King saw O'Connor step off his left foot. As O'Connor was about to accelerate Lewis jumped into the air and threw his entire body at him. You could feel the impact in the stands...It was as though Lewis had driven a sword into O'Connor's belly...For once it is a tackle rather than a pass that will be talked about as long as state-of-origin is played.

After the match O'Connor ruefully praised Wally. "He's a smart bastard," he said. "I thought I had him when I stepped inside but he anticipated my move to the letter and just swamped me. Had his timing been out a fraction I would have scored under the posts." O'Connor's captain, Wayne Pearce, agreed the tackle was awesome. "I've got to hand it to him, that was one of the really great tackles," he said.

But NSW were not defeated with that tackle alone. Within two rucks fullback Gary Belcher produced a further try-saving tackle which Wally himself rates as better than his own. NSW winger Brian Johnston crossed the Queensland quarterline with Lyons in support, Belcher the only impediment. The equation was compelling, NSW must score. Belcher covered Johnston, Johnston passed to Lyons a fraction early. Lyons ran 5 metres clear of Belcher with the line open. Belcher turned and chased. Lyons is no slouch — perhaps he felt in no danger — but Belcher, from a standing start, his legs whirring like wagon wheels, caught Lyons 10 metres from the line. When I rolled Wally a video of the play he was still full of admiration for Belcher. "Gees he showed some speed to cover two blokes," he said. "Belcher saved us the game there." Coach Willey ordered a replacement and Lyons became a forlorn figure trudging from the field.

After those two busts Belcher suddenly, furiously, yelled "Queenslander!" Wally picked it up and shouted "Queenslander!" The call bumped and ricocheted among the men in maroon. Coach Bennett had told the team to pick a code word to fire them when they were doing it tough. The team talked about how it felt to play for Queensland and simultaneously overheard on a radio the Bank of Queensland advertising jingle, "You can count on a Queenslander." That was it.

"It was a chain reaction," said Wally. "Every tackle someone would yell it out, another bloke would take it up and make a tackle and he'd scream it out and four or five others would relay it along. The blues must have thought we were a bit strange, but it picked us up, you could feel the heart come back into the team." When Bennett told Wally afterwards, "I don't know how you held out," Wally replied with the one word, "Queenslander".

For the final seven minutes Queensland laid seige to the NSW line. With five kicks into the NSW in-goal, Queensland held the ball for 21 consecutive tackles. It was total dominance. One of those kicks was by Paul Vautin, a clever, not totally intentional, floating chip. The irrepressible Vautin turned to Wally, at the critical moment of the most tension-filled match of the year, and said with a grin, "Ohhh mate, skills!"

Wally was concentrating on keeping NSW in check — marshalling moves and counting tackles, watching the clock. "I was thinking what was the best way to waste time," said Wally. "Was it take the five rucks and put the ball in behind the line like we had been doing? Or should I make it four rucks and then kick when they're not expecting it? Or should we have four rucks and then field goal, which would waste another 20 seconds? " The ability to think ahead delineates great captains. To adjust to every new combination of events and yet never allow the planning to detract from his own performance. Bennett regards Wally's play in those seven minutes as possibly the most disciplined performance by a footballer under pressure he has ever seen.

With 29 seconds left Queensland played the ball almost flush with the NSW line. For several minutes Lang Park had been a standing, stamping, chanting mob. It was hard for dummy half to hear Wally's calls. "Six rucks!" yelled Wally. It meant dummy half was to run at the line. No passes. Gillmeister ran, rose, played the ball and Lindner passed it back to Wally. A blue blur leapt forward from the NSW line and plucked the ball from the air — Michael O'Connor! Lang Park was pandemonium. A woman beside me in the stand was in tears. Other fans who could not bear to watch collapsed back in their seats.

Wally screamed "Offside!" and then belted back in defence. One thought raced ahead of him — "Jesus Christ, don't tell me we're going to lose it from here." NSW careered up to the half-way, O'Connor, McGaw, Kenny and Sterling dealing the ball between them like cardsharps. "We were all over the shop," said Wally. "There were blokes running from side to side. Everybody says cool heads prevail but I've got to say this, there was absolute bloody panic." But this time Queensland were not to be denied in the dying seconds. Full-time sounded, skyrockets lit the night, Wally lifted Langer skyhigh, Bennett smiled for the second time that series, and Mick Veivers for Channel 9 emotionally summarised the feelings of millions of viewers: "That is the best game I have seen for many a long day. What a ripper game!"

Wally called the team together and said, "Let's go and meet the crowd." He led them to the four corners of the stadium. In front of Fourex Hill a fan threw a can of beer to Wally. "I remember it was half-full, it wasn't real cold, but it was one of the nicest beers I've tasted," recalled Wally. He took a grateful sip and hurled the can back. The scoreboard was lit with just two words, "King Wally".

Some players take defeats better than others. Brett Kenny chatted with Gene Miles, his room-mate from past Kangaroo tours. "Have a go at these two having a yap," said Wally, shaking his head, but glad that football friendships were not sundered by victory or defeat. While the official speeches began Pearce stood alone, swallowing his disappointment. Allan Langer was man-of-the-match. He summoned his courage, tears welling in his eyes and told the world, "I'd like to thank my brother Kevin. I did this all for him tonight." His brother was in Boggo Road jail.

Wally accepted the Winfield Origin Shield, commiserated with NSW and, his right eye closing from the collision with O'Connor, embarked on his captain's duty. He announced, "I'm up here accepting this shield and getting these photographs taken but I'd like everyone to cast their eyes down on 14 of the bravest footballers ever to set foot on Lang Park." He praised the choice of Allan Langer as man-of-the-match. "He's only 10 stone...9 stone 13 pounds of that is heart." And he left the best until last. "I'd like to thank one bloke who completely and utterly plotted our victory." Wayne Bennett, smiling nobly, gazed up at his captain. Wally continued, "He's a guy I used to have a few blues with playing club football. It wasn't until I came under him in the state side that I recognised what a magnificent coach he is. I've already gone public and said he's the best coach in the world and Wayne, you've proved it tonight. Thanks mate."

The next day Wayne Pearce and half a dozen of the NSW team were at the Breakfast Creek Hotel with the Queenslanders who were still intoxicated by victory as much as by alcohol. The beaten NSW players were not gluttons for punishment. They were there because they had been selected in the Australian Test side to play New Zealand in just six days' time.

5 KIWIS, YANKS AND OLD BOYS

The 1987 Test against New Zealand at Lang Park stands condemned as the worst piece of scheduling ever devised by the Australian Rugby League. Since their inception in 1980 the state-of-origins had come to be recognised as the pinnacle of world rugby league. Two undefeated Kangaroo tours of Great Britain, in 1982 and 1986, had shown where international strength lay. But in Wally's representative career New Zealand had won two out of 10 Tests since 1982. In two Tests Australia was fortunate to skate in with last-minute solo tries, by wingers Eric Grothe (in 1983) and John Ribot (1985). Had the Kiwis won those matches Australia would have led New Zealand by only six Tests to four. Nearly every major British and Australian club harboured a New Zealander gaining valuable experience. Clearly the New Zealanders were formidable opponents.

The ARL could not have known that 1987 would produce the most fiercely contested Origin series ever, but the interstate matches had long since gone beyond being a mere forum for selection of the Australian team. The state-of-origins, though recent compared with inter-city New Zealand rugby union or Lancashire-Yorkshire cricket, had become one of the finest provincial sporting contests anywhere. NSW proudly defends its traditional status as senior state, Queensland challenges with an underdog, chip-on-the-shoulder resentment. The formula is just right.

Less than a week after that torrid final Origin encounter in 1987, 13 of the players — seven from NSW and six

Queenslanders — backed up in the bottle green and wattle gold jerseys of Australia against New Zealand. The psychological and physical bruising had scarcely healed. Wally himself still had the remnants of a black eye, received in his momentous tackle on Michael O'Connor. Wally was forewarned of the Kiwis' class when he captained a Queensland Residents XIII against the tourists at Lang Park, a match sandwiched in between the second and third Origins. The Residents, coached by Wayne Bennett, included Wally, Langer, Dowling, and seven other players contracted to the Brisbane Broncos for the following year. Playing the match mid-Origins was itself asking a lot of Queensland's senior players. The New Zealanders won 22–16 and that score flattered the locals. New Zealand surged with new blood: centre Kevin Iro — a Meninga clone even down to kicking goals — halfback Gary Freeman and lock Mark Horo. The Test was no sure thing, despite media barking to the contrary.

Wally was unequivocal about the timing. "It was a hell of a hard game that last Origin and then we had two or three days of celebrating and letdown," he said. "You don't go looking for excuses, but the Test was too close." Wally also pointed out that Queensland had just won back the Origin shield, lost in 1985. "Inevitably there was a little bit of feeling there," he said. "It wasn't carried into the Test but playing the Kiwis a week after a game of that magnitude is a strange idea."

Three days before the Test, former coach Bob Bax wrote in his Brisbane *Sunday Mail* column:

> The rugby league Test between Australia and New Zealand has been pushed into the backround by the State of Origin decider. Believe me, I hardly know a sports fan who isn't still talking about that game.

Other warning lights were glowing. In the Residents-New Zealand match, Test prop Greg Dowling retired shaken after a big hit on Christchurch amateur Ross Taylor. Taylor subsequently displaced rugged Canberra Raiders prop Brent Todd from the Kiwi Test team. The New Zealanders had a surfeit of hit-men.

Australian coach Don Furner sensed the anti-climax in his team and was at his wit's end to lift them. He confided his fears to Wally and Peter Sterling. They understood but were themselves afflicted. The team looked so flat Furner abandoned one training and tried to refresh them with a game of indoor cricket. Wally looked at his team-mates and was uncertain how they felt. "It's very hard to pick the difference sometimes between an air of confidence in a side and an air of complacency," he said. "Some blokes build up for a game with an arrogance towards the opposition. You can't tell until you hit the paddock." Furner had no doubts. He regretted later, "I could only get them half-way up the mountain."

Wally noted other disturbing signs. He wrote later in his Brisbane *Sunday Mail* column:

> There were a few late nights among the players who were catching up with some close mates made on the Kangaroo tour. A couple of nights before the Test and on the night before the match there was conviviality. Some people can do it and get away with it...it's a matter of picking the right time. It certainly wasn't the right time against the unknown New Zealanders.

Apart from their mental and social attitudes many of the Australians were suffering injuries from the Origin series. Brett Kenny hoped an injured knee would free up once it was warm, Gene Miles's ankle was still suspect, others carried injuries to which they did not admit. "To be honest some blokes just shouldn't have been on the field," Wally wrote. "One in particular had trouble getting into a jog on the morning of the match."

Opposed was a rookie team, super-fit, ultra-keen, with a new coach Tony Gordon anxious to prove his appointment over his sacked predecessor Graham Lowe. A glance at some names, with hindsight, showed how they could never be underestimated: Hugh McGahan, captain of Sydney Easts; Sam Stewart, captain of the Newcastle Knights; and Sydney premiership stars Darrell Williams (Manly), Dean Bell (Easts), Clayton Friend (Norths) and Gary Freeman (Balmain).

Separating the teams was New Zealand referee, Neville Kesha, who Wally remembered from Queensland's tour earlier that year. "He absolutely caned us with penalties in one match," said Wally. "Then after the game he came up and said, 'Sorry about some of those penalties, but you always had the game in control and you must remember, I've got to live here.'" In the Test, Kesha upset Australia with his lax application of the five-metre ruck rule. "We couldn't believe it," said Wally. "The game in Australia over the past 10 years has enjoyed freedom because of the strict adherence to five metres. That's why it's so open, fast and exciting. Here we found dummy half would pass to first receiver and he'd have a Kiwi charging him down."

New Zealand, playing with their sleeves rolled up, playing David to Australia's Goliath, were hyped and deserved their 13–6 lead at half-time. Coach Furner could not help uttering what the team already knew, "They're a lot better than everyone expected." Wally listened listlessly. Mid-way through the first half he had hit his head on fullback Darrell Williams's knee in a tackle. Wally's chin hit his chest, he heard a sharp crack, shooting pain in his neck and pins and needles in his limbs. He lay motionless. "That's when you sweat," said Wally. "The noise frightens you even though it may just be some vertebrae shifting, like when a chiropractor cracks your spine. I thought 'Can I feel my fingers and toes?'"

Australian trainer Larry Britton urged Wally to come off but after treatment he resumed, albeit lacking enthusiasm for any more big hits. Late in the second half he rose from a tackle, started running and felt his right knee start clicking. At full pace it hurt. His neck hurt, his knee hurt. He decided to go off but at that moment Brett Kenny, limping from his knee injury, was replaced. Australia had already used their two permitted replacements — Wally had to stay on. He spent much of it on the wing unable to influence the course of New Zealand's convincing 13–6 win.

In the dressingroom Wally's neck and knee cooled, stiffened and ached. ARL medico Dr Kevin Hobbs put Wally's neck in a brace and strapped his knee. He looked a mess, exacerbated by his shiny black "O'Connor" eye, bumped again by the Kiwis. The first glimpse Jacqui Lewis, who had not been allowed in the medical room, had of her husband came an hour after the match as he was wheeled by on a stretcher to be taken by ambulance to Wesley Hospital. Wally's father Jim drove Jacqui in pursuit.

Tests and x-rays showed Wally had concussion, strained ligaments in his neck and torn cartilage tissue in his knee — the price of a rugby league player's representative season. He awoke the next morning groggy from sedation and for the next three days his only visitors were family and Gene Miles. "He looks the worse for wear," Gene told media in the foyer of the hospital. "The rest won't hurt him." The hospital issued daily bulletins on his progress.

Wally lay flat on his back recuperating. Nurses wound the back of his bed up to a 45-degree angle for meals. He did not want Jacqui to bring their son Mitchell to visit. Wally was not a sight to see. Strapped to his bed he stared at the ceiling and contemplated what football cost him. Though it was setting him up financially he hated the loss of good health, the helplessness of hospital. He was irritable and dispirited.

Footballers rarely speak of the time-consuming nature of their sport and the stress it places on their marriages. Wally had been away from home for the final Origin team camp, followed immediately by the Test camp and now hospital. Visiting him, Jacqui listed her problems at home, including her loneliness. Wally's temper was edgy. He painfully got out of bed. "I couldn't turn my neck — it was in a brace — my knee was in a big, long cast to my toes," said Wally. "I said to her, 'Oh well, there's absolutely nothing wrong with me. I'm lying here because I haven't had a holiday for some time and just felt like having a few days off.' " A surprised nurse asked where he was going. Wally said sarcastically, "I'm going home to look after my wife who's lonely." So Wally, stiff-necked and on crutches, watched by ward staff, hobbled down the room and out of hospital. Wally laughed at the recollection, "I can see the funny side of it now, but gees I was dark then. Probably the only time I've ever been absolutely filthy on my missus."

A week later, out of his cast and brace, Wally consulted Dr Fergus Wilson about his right knee cartilage which hurt when he ran above half pace. Dr Wilson, who reconstructed former Australian Wallaby five-eighth Paul McLean's knees, said Wally could have an operation then or later, but surgery was inevitable. Wally chose later. He was keen to play in one more representative match that season, the fourth state-of-origin in Los Angeles, America.

Testimony to Australia's historical isolation is that its two major winter sports, rugby league and Australian rules, are among the world's minority football codes. Aussie rules is unique to Australia and league is only marginally better off. Rugby league is played by 34 first and second division clubs in the north of England, 24 amateur, college and university sides, and 200 grassroots village, pub, colliery, factory, company and old boys teams. Despite this apparent depth, English rugby league's dominion extends over just two counties, Lancashire and Yorkshire, an area that would be encompassed by the 80 kms from Sydney to Gosford. French rugby league comprises 28 teams in two divisions in the south of France, but its ranks have been depleted by rival rugby union clubs. Recent French tours of Australia have been cancelled through lack of finance. New Zealand rugby league, though rapidly increasing in popularity, remains the poor cousin of rugby union.

The ARL, like Columbus seeking the New World, organised a fourth Origin clash in America to promote rugby league there. American universities play rugby union but rugby league is unknown. An American rugby league team toured Australia in the 1950s featuring giant American football players who threw the ball in torpedoing, overhead grid-iron passes. It was rumoured the team had to be boosted with players from a South Sydney sub-district club and the Yanks were slaughtered by NSW at the SCG.

An Australian team, returning from the inaugural World Cup in Britain in 1954, played two exhibitions against New Zealand in America. The first match was called off after 10 minutes because of a fog. Australian second-rower, Kel O'Shea, recalled, "At one stage the Kiwis yelled out the ball had been kicked because they heard the sound of it landing." The second match went ahead at the Los Angeles Coliseum and drew a crowd of 4,000. O'Shea said the Americans enjoyed the non-stop action of rugby league, its lack of protective clothing and tolerance of injuries. For the next 33 years rugby league did not approach the shores of America. The game could never take on in America without enormous financial investment but as ARL chief Ken Arthurson said, "You don't always win when you try something. To me there is no disgrace in losing. The main thing is to have a go."

The LA match was scheduled for 7 August 1987, two weeks after Wally left hospital. At the medical check-up for the tour Queensland coach Wayne Bennett asked with a knowing smile, "You all right to play?" Wally smiled back, "I'm fine." Wally told me, "There was no way I was going to miss the trip. Wayne half knew my knee wasn't worth two bob, but he didn't put me under too much pressure. Maybe he thought it would be okay by the time we got there." Wally was safe. QRL chief Ross Livermore intended to invite Wally along in a public relations role had he been unfit. Not everyone shared Wally's enthusiasm for the tour. Brett Kenny was injured, Wayne Pearce's first child was due, Garry Jack had other personal reasons for withdrawing.

Though dubbed the Tooheys interstate challenge, Wayne Bennett took the commonsense approach. He told the excited Queenslanders, "We've won the Origin series. This is a reward trip. When we get over there we'll train hard and do all the normal things. And we'll play it for what it is, a game to promote rugby league in America." The Queenslanders took their seats at the back of the aircraft, the NSW players were seated towards the middle. The first sign that NSW regarded the game rather more seriously was their ban on players drinking alcohol. Said Wally, "We were having a great time down the back when Noel Cleal came down on his way to the toilet and whispered, 'This is crazy', and snuck in a smoke and a beer. We couldn't believe it."

The Queenslanders caught a connecting flight from San Francisco to Los Angeles with their Aussie preconceptions alive — Disneyland, Hollywood, the Beach Boys and Californian girls. The LA airport bus drove for so long — over an hour to reach their hotel — that they pulled in half-way for hotdogs. It was past midnight when they finally arrived and Wally asked for the hotel's bar. "Sorry sir, Californian law, too late for alcohol." Wally smiled. Was there a secret bar? "No, sir, nothing like that now." What about room service? "Sorry." Wally was indignant. California, and you couldn't get a beer anywhere? The players hailed down some cabbies. Wally acted as spokesman, "Look you blokes, you know all the desperate dens. We just want to get a beer, nothing else, no action, just beer." The cabbies apologised. The players retired unquenched and disillusioned with legendary LA.

The next evening they started promptly to beat any early closing and finished at a local bar where the stage show for the night was a body-building contest. The contestants warmed up in full view of the bar, flexing and posing in their tiny briefs and rubbing oil on their glistening, outsized torsos. The Queenslanders secretly nominated diminutive Allan Langer and proceeded to prime him with sufficient drinks to ensure he took part. "Allan had become a lot more confident with the blokes," said Wally. "A lot more cheeky. He's the sort of bloke if you half push him, away he goes. He got on stage, took his shirt off, put the oil on and did all the poses." Langer, nicknamed Alf (Alien Life Form) can affect a somewhat silly, yet wicked grin, and he had the bar in stitches as he went through his routine flexing muscles half the size of the other contestants'. Australians have enjoyed novelty status in the United States for years. The American nightclubbers were delighted with the high-jinks of their guests and cheered when the judges awarded Langer third place.

Next day they trained in a heatwave at the University of Southern California, finished early and drove down to Huntington Beach where 15,000 people lounged on the sand watching an international surfing contest. The beach was so crowded the team drove further on for a swim. It was the US west coast's spring, scarcely football weather. They took a drive to Universal Studios and saw the island stage set for the television series, *Gilligan's Island*. The tour included a boat ride on the water where the horror movie, *Jaws*, was filmed. "I was sitting next to Gene Miles and this big, bloody shark comes up and jumps out of the water right beside the boat," said Wally.

"Gene nearly wet himself, almost threw his camera overboard. But the funniest thing was he'd been there before on holidays and knew it was coming and it still frightened the pants off him."

Another day they visited Disneyland which was jammed with American tourists. Wally spent the day hunting souvenirs for his son Mitchell. Several of the team, notably Colin Scott, lined up in long queues for what was reputed to be the scariest fun park ride in the world. "They stood for an hour, which is the normal wait for a ride over there," said Wally. "They got four from the top of the queue and the ride broke down."

A week before the match, to be played at Veteran's Stadium, Long Beach, Brisbane *Courier-Mail* reporter, Miles McIvor, rang the sports editor of the local newspaper the *Press-Telegram*. "Rugby league? You mean rugby?" said the editor. "Hell man, what's the difference? There are heaps of rugby clubs in southern California and I imagine a lot of them will go along out of curiosity." The *Los Angeles Times* did not run a line and another newspaper described rugby union and league as both having 15 players.

Wally and Peter Sterling had their work cut out trying to explain rugby league at media conferences, even with the assistance of short videos. The Americans were interested and friendly but afterwards the team would search five pages of sports news to find a tiny item about their match. The ARL's American promoters hit upon a novel match poster — a graphic spear tackle, long outlawed by the ARL. As a bait for spectators it was excellent though it might just as well have been promoting all-in wrestling. As Wally observed, "It was a silly way to encourage people to play the game, a bloke getting jammed into the ground headfirst."

The match took on a different note at an official launch the day before the match. Peter Sterling said NSW was desperate to level the Origin series 2–2 and win back some lost pride. The Queenslanders ignored this as promotional hype. Coach Ron Willey backed his spokesman, accusing Queensland of holding NSW players down in tackles in the third Origin. Wally thought better sense would prevail on field. Bennett had his toughest three days coaching ever. "The boys were ready to play, but not at footie," he said. "I tried to be as serious as possible, but they weren't switched on."

Former coach and now television commentator Jack Gibson approached both teams and told them to use the headbin for all injuries to ensure there were always 13 players on each side. Even in Australia crowds do not generally understand that the headbin may be used only for players recovering from head blows, not injuries to the rest of the body. "The Yanks, with the number of replacements allowed in their games, won't understand if there's less than two full teams on the field at all times," said Gibson.

At the 8 p.m. scheduled kickoff about 2,000 people sat in the stadium with long queues at the gates. "Apparently in America everybody gets there 10 minutes before the game," said Wally. "So they kept us waiting." Wally worked through his warm-up stretches again and prepared to lead the team out once more. Hang on, another 10 minutes, came the call. After a third warm-up they ran out and were pleasantly surprised. The field was well lit, well grassed and clearly marked. But they could not start yet. "We were told to go out on the field, run around, kick a few balls, do some ball skills and come back in again," said Wally." That's what they do over there. So then we came back off for another 20 minutes."

Wally estimated the match was delayed an hour by which time a crowd, variously estimated at between 7,000 and 12,000, had given the 15,000 capacity stadium a true match atmosphere. The stadium was used for the final rock concert scenes in the film *The Rose* starring Bette Midler. Instead of bouncing Bette, a giant blow-up kangaroo bumped around the field and marching girls and cheer squads provided essential colour and movement. The crowd patiently drank beer from plastic cups and munched peanuts and popcorn. Peter Sterling ran out, burst through a big plastic sign, got tangled up in torn strands and cursed. The crowd laughed. It seemed we might have a rugby league sideshow instead of a showpiece.

But from the third tackle, which erupted into a brawl, the match became more than an exhibition. Wally rushed in and shouted, "Turn it up! What's going on here? This is supposed to be a promotion." To which several NSW players snarled, "Pig's arse it is, you cats!" Said Jack Gibson, commenting for Channel 9, "They're getting a little bit excited out there, probably jet lag." At half-time Mike Gibson invited feedback from fans in the stands and the articulate Yanks did not disappoint — "Non-stop, fast, rough, they knock the hell out of each other, wear no protection, no helmets, they're real men, it's great," came the comments.

As Origin losers, NSW had the greater motivation. With their lightning backline they were always going to win a try-scoring shoot-out and led 24–2 with only 15 minutes left. Jack Gibson's mind had drifted elsewhere. He told Darrell Eastlake, "I can't tell you too much about the game but I can tell you we're about half an hour away from Disneyland." NSW ran out winners 30–18 after Dale Shearer scored a try for Queensland on the final siren. Wally shook his head with wonder when he heard Sterling berating his team for the Blues' last second defensive lapse. In fairness to Sterling it was precisely because NSW took the match seriously that the experiment worked. The crowd sensed as much as saw this was genuine rugby league, not a plastic substitute.

Wally called out at the end, "Sterlo, grab the blokes and let's thank the crowd for turning up." That seemed the way to go as guests in America. They all walked to the stands, waved and clapped. Wally held Sterling's arm in the air as the victor until Sterling sheepishly pulled it down. Wally gave Darrell Eastlake the pro forma comment, the better team won. Eastlake pressed him: "There was a bit of feeling in a lot of those tackles?" Wally nodded. "Yeah, there was. It was confusing for us because we came over here to play an exhibition and it was a little more fair dinkum than we thought." It was 11 p.m. but still humid when the players emerged, showered but perspiring, to be greeted by scores of fans. By the time they escaped it was past Californian closing time again so they adjourned to an all-night diner for pizzas and burgers.

Ken Arthurson justifiably accepted the plaudits. The whole exercise — to airlift the state-of-origin theatre comprising 30 players, two coaches, two trainers, a doctor, referee, linesmen and a dozen other officials half-way around the world — had cost the ARL $400,000. "I smiled today for the first time in a week," Arthurson said. "I admit I was worried no one would turn up." The ARL could have drawn a larger crowd had they returned the following year and played the second state-of-origin match there, when the series result was still undecided. But as one American fan said, "If you guys play like that in Australia all the time there may not be enough players left alive to come back next year."

Vengeance theirs, most of the NSW team flew home the following day but for Queensland the tour had just begun. They booked into a hotel in Las Vegas for three days and discovered their hotel was a casino. Shades of the Dragonara, the Kangaroos' headquarters in Leeds, except this was far more ritzy and glamorous. The first evening Wally lost, Miles lost, but Allan Langer, full as the proverbial state school hatrack, could not help winning. He was laughing so much and winning so easily, no matter where he placed his chips, that he drew attention from the casino heavies. Their expressions asked, "How's this bloke winning?" They had their answer the next morning when Langer, cold sober, lost the lot back again.

Their hotel was across the road from Caesar's Palace where the Beach Boys were the stage show, $30 a ticket plus two free beers. "They're legends, we can't miss them," Wally announced. About 15 of the tour party went, led by rugby league's oldest rock and roller, Wayne Bennett. Said Wally, "They were on stage for well over two hours. There'd be 2,000 in the audience and though we were towards the back we could see." They could also see the Dallas Cowgirls, cheer squad to the Dallas Cowboys NFL team. Wally assured me, "They were American beauties, not a bad sort among them." The music was infectious and the team was amazed to see coach Bennett, of the stern visage and unbending bearing, tapping his feet and bopping about. "What are you doing?" Wally called out in mock disgust, "Behave you goose!"

Dean Martin was performing in another hotel but the lads had become blase and were choosy about which famous entertainer they'd see. Sometimes the guys would be gambling in one casino and decide to change to another across the road. "We'd walk out and it would be broad daylight," said Wally. "That's when we noticed that you never see a clock. The whole town is open 24 hours a day. There's no closing time. Even the Beach Boys were doing three shows a day, or night. There was one digital clock, away on top of a building. You'd ask some bloke the time and he'd drawl 'Aw, it's mebbe 10 in the mornin' ' and you'd think, 'Hell I better go get some sleep!' "

From Vegas the team flew to the Grand Canyon which didn't impress some players who'd seen Carnarvon Gorge, but Wally enjoyed it all. "It was a great trip," he said. "We did things most football teams wouldn't get a chance to do, been half-way around the world, seen America's biggest sights and had a game of football while we were there."

Back home, Wally rested his knee and resigned himself to missing seven straight premiership matches with Wynnum, the team he coached. He selected himself for Wynnum's semi-final loss which confirmed medical advice — his knee required surgery. It had been a strange year. Though Wynnum had a comparatively poor season Wally led the Rothman's Gold Medal until injured. He captained Australia in the Test loss to New Zealand yet was named Queensland's Sports Star of the Year, a distinction which had eluded him even in his halcyon year of 1984.

He had one more match that season. The 1977 Australian schoolboys rugby union tourists had a reunion in Sydney, the first in ten years. Wally flew down one Friday night with fellow Queenslander Richard Leslie and linked up with former tourmates George Gavalas and Warwick Melrose. They batted on until 2 a.m., woke the next morning and decided to have lunch at Doyle's seafood restaurant in Watsons Bay. Proprietor Peter Doyle looked after them royally. "We got there about 11 a.m.," said Wally. "Threw three schooners down, had lunch, washed that down with half a dozen schooners and suddenly remembered we had to play a match at 3 p.m." They drove to the University of NSW oval at Randwick for their friendly against a Randwick club XV. "It was all very hush-hush, just a fun game," said Michael O'Connor, whose Manly club would not have been amused had he been injured. They arrived to find their hush-hush match had been advertised on radio. A crowd of 1,500 had turned out to observe whether time had dulled the old boys' skills.

Wally stood on the sidelines, can in hand, hoping, after such a long lunch, not to have to play. When the call came he ran on and, the first time he was tackled, rose and deliberately played the ball rugby league style much to the amusement of the rah-rah crowd. Wally played inside centre, beside Mark Ella, and was suddenly in the thick of it. A Randwick winger scooped up a dropped ball and set off towards Wally, who knew that if he missed the tackle he would get a shellacking from the rugby types on the sideline. He managed to bundle the winger into touch and thought, "Thank bloody goodness for that." A noticeably stouter Mark Ella, grinning hugely, said, "If all those bastards weren't on the sideline watching, you wouldn't have even tried there."

At the reunion dinner in the Randwick clubhouse Wally marvelled at the different directions various players' lives, and looks, had taken. Some he did not even recognise. To reintroduce themselves each player had to stand and tell the dinner what he had been doing for the last 10 years. With 30 players talking for at least five minutes, depending upon their state of inebriation, the hours wore wearily on.

Wally was brief. "I couldn't play rugby union because I couldn't get a trendy haircut," he said, patting his receding hairline. "I couldn't get a job so I switched to the game that paid. We've got a little boy Mitchell, and another on the way and me and the missus intend doing a fair bit of practice in the future." And sat down. But Wally did not need to introduce himself. He was by far the most famous among them, exceeding O'Connor, the Ellas, everyone. "He only had to stand up and that was it," said his old tour-mate George Gavalas. "We all knew it from the tabloids." Gavalas felt the inner Wally had not changed but the public man had. At Doyle's restaurant, where Wally had signed autographs, Gavalas sensed Wally would have been happy to unwind more. "He doesn't bow to anyone," said Gavalas.

"When he wants to speak his mind he does. But now he's also got this position to uphold."

Wally enjoyed seeing Mark Ella with whom he had always kept in contact. Ella was climbing the corporate executive ladder, becoming a respected identity in Australian Aboriginal sport. Although the reunion recalled past good times for Wally, he was looking to the future, about to embark on probably the last great challenge of his football career.

6 SYDNEY OR BUST

When Wally led his undefeated Kangaroos of 1986 back to Australia just before Christmas, he briefly contemplated retirement. It would have been a grand note on which to depart. He had captained a team which had equalled the feats of the 1982 Invincibles. He was carrying yet another partial dislocation of his shoulder — an injury becoming increasingly common with him. His taxation problems had subsided, reducing the need for lucrative match payments, and he was scanning the media and political worlds for a new career. It seemed there were no new heights he could scale in football.

He had hoped the Queensland Rugby League would enter a team in the Sydney premiership for 1987 but when the QRL dithered and finally withdrew, Wally and Gene Miles negotiated to play in Sydney with Manly. It would have been the finale to Wally's sporting life. But the QRL's consultant Ron McAuliffe and managing director Ross Livermore outgeneralled Manly and signed Wally and Geno to stay in Queensland for 1987.

The personal cost of the QRL's contractual dexterity dawned on Wally as he lazed around the swimming pool of his inner suburban colonial home that Christmas of 1986. He was about to slide from the heights of leading the Kangaroos to the low of a massively depleted Brisbane domestic season. In the coming season Brisbane lost 59 first-grade players to Sydney, the equivalent of four teams — nearly half the nine-club Brisbane competition.

In 1986, his first year as captain-coach, Wally had guided

Wynnum to the premiership. "I only ever intended to coach one year and then go to Manly," he said. Another season with Wynnum would be his tenth consecutive year in Brisbane first grade. He had won three grand finals — with Valleys in 1979, as captain of Wynnum in 1984 and as captain-coach in 1986. There was nothing left to achieve. Wally faced the same psychological let-down he encountered after winning just about every conceivable rugby league honour in 1984. The corollary was that 1985 became one of his worst seasons ever in senior football. Wally thrived on challenge and this 1987 club season loomed like a desert.

To inject some interest he had accepted an offer from Graham Lowe, coach of Wigan, to play 11 matches in the 1986–87 English season. Wally had always respected New Zealander Lowe, the best coach he had played under until he met Wayne Bennett. The main attraction was the match fee, nearly $5,000 a game — $55,000 for half a season's football in the less competitive English first division on England's softer playing fields. Jacqui Lewis had enjoyed a few weeks with Wally at Wakefield Trinity in 1983–84 and she was looking forward to an extended visit.

St Helen's coach, former Great Britain halfback Alex Murphy, mischievously publicised Wally's match fees and a row ensued at Wigan with players threatening not to play with Lewis. Lowe assured Wally he could solve the Wigan team's discontent. The British scuttlebutt was that the trouble within Wigan was fomented by English star Ellery Hanley objecting to Wally's match fees. Hanley was said to be jealously guarding his stellar role at Wigan and was not about to welcome a challenger of Wally's stature.

Wally's experience with Wakefield Trinity, when his new team-mates had refused to shake his hand when introduced, persuaded him against returning to a cauldron of resentment. Or as he put it, "Once the blueing began I wasn't interested in playing with a bunch of sooks." He used his shoulder injury as an excuse to rescind his agreement with Lowe and Wigan.

That still left Wally stuck with Wynnum who, from 1986, had lost Bob Lindner to Parramatta, Ian French to North Sydney and Greg Dowling to Brisbane Norths. He knuckled down and led Wynnum to their fourth consecutive pre-season State league victory. In fact it was Wally's fifth consecutive win, having won in 1983 with Valleys.

Coaching in 1986 at Wynnum, dealing with players of the calibre of Miles, Lindner, Dowling and Scott, had at times been awkward for Wally. One moment he was their overlord as Wynnum coach, the next he was one among equals as their state-of-origin and Test team-mate. Gene Miles was a particular friend. On the Brisbane Panasonic team's short tour of New Zealand in 1987 the pair were drinking together one evening when Wally performed his usual mouth contortions to suck beer froth from his walrus moustache. Gene commented on the habit and Wally decided to shave it off. Miles didn't believe him. I will, said Wally. Geno bet $100 he wouldn't. Done! said Wally. "I don't care about the cabbage, I'm just tired of it," he said. An hour later Miles ran into Wally and burst into laughter. Wally had shaved one side of the moustache off. When the rest went Miles disputed the bet on the technicality of the half-moustache interlude and paid Wally only $20.

They had an easy friendship and Miles's laid back outlook on life enabled him to cope with being the lesser half of rugby league's most famous double act. He objected to a cartoonist depicting him as a dog on the end of a leash, running after Wally during their 1986 negotiations to play with Manly, but had his day when he won the 1987 Rothmans Gold Medal in Brisbane, one of the few rugby league honours to elude Wally. Wayne Bennett thought Wally expected too much of Geno but Wally knew he needed him.

The week of the 1987 State league final Miles was nursing a painful torn rib cartilage. He had already missed three matches and Wally-the-friend knew Miles should probably not endanger himself for the approaching state-of-origins. But Wally-the-coach desperately wanted to win the final and the $44,000 winner's cheque for the struggling Wynnum club. At training he asked Miles how his ribs were. Gene wasn't sure he could play. "You'll be right," said Wally. Before the match Miles passed a few balls and told Wally, "It's still not right." Wally flung aside his friendship cap and jammed on that of the coach. "What are you, a cat?" he demanded. "You're the biggest girl I've come across! You're as big as a house, you've got all that weight. You're nothing but a big sheila." Miles was silently indignant. He had pain-killing injections, strapped the ribs and annihilated Redcliffe, smashing through tacklers at his awesome best.

Wally had distanced himself from his Wynnum players at club level in 1986 and was rewarded with Wynnum's premiership. In 1987 he became more relaxed. One day fullback Colin Scott arrived 15 minutes late for 6 p.m. training. Wally's rule was that if players could provide a genuine excuse they were not punished.

"I was watching *Perfect Match*," explained Scott.

"Instead of coming to training?" asked Wally, incredulous.

"Yeah. Three really good sorts. The bloke matched with one so I thought I'd just watch and see if he matched with all three. Then it got time to leave and I just thought I'd see which one he chose because they were all good sorts."

Said Wally, "Well that makes it five to six."

"I saw the one he picked and you know how they say they'll be back in a minute to tell you where they're going? I was interested to know whether they'd go away for a romantic thing or just be given a night out to dinner."

That would take you to 6 p.m., said Wally.

"Then I was coming down the road up there and I hit a dog," said Scott.

Wally started to giggle, not at the dog, at Scott's ingenuity.

"I didn't hit him hard, but I knocked him over. I picked him up and he had a phone number on his collar."

Go on, said Wally.

"I didn't have the right coins on me so I went to a shop and bought a drink and then used the change to phone the owner. He didn't have a car so I said I'd bring the dog around. When I got there his missus thought I was upset so she insisted I have a cup of tea. I couldn't refuse..."

What made Wally laugh was that with Scott it was probably all true. He interrupted. "Scotty I've never heard anything like it. You're clear. Piss off."

Wynnum eventually made the Winfield Cup semi-finals but were knocked out by Redcliffe. Their coach, Darryl Van de Velde, claimed credit for devising a plan to blot out Wally. The more likely reason for Wally's quiet performance was that he had not played a club game for seven weeks. His right knee, injured in the Test against New Zealand in July, had not been improved by the fourth state-of-origin in Los Angeles. After that defeat Wally retired from coaching. As he slumped in the loser's dressingroom he admitted he had run out of ideas. "I'd much rather play than coach anyway," he said.

He had received yet another English approach, from his old Wakefield Trinity club — $250,000 for three years. It was not a sensational offer and Wally declined. Besides, there were plans stirring on the Brisbane football scene that were about to whet his appetite for rugby league all over again.

The decision of the Queensland Rugby League to consider once more entering a Brisbane team in the Sydney premiership was made with all the hesitancy and uncertainty of a state's football administrators overturning 80 years of tradition. The QRL's withdrawal from their 1986 bid was such a tortuous affair that ARL president, Ken Arthurson, was determined to avoid a replay of that *Blue Hills* saga. But even Arthurson's great conciliation skills could not prevent a re-enactment.

It was always expected that, having failed to make up its mind for the 1987 season, the QRL would have plenty of time to prepare for a 1988 entry. It was imperative that rugby league embrace the trend to a national competition. The Brisbane Bullets basketball team had been up and running for several years. A premiership victory meant Bullets fans filled whatever sized stadium the Bullets could book, even the 12,000 capacity Boondall centre. When the Brisbane Bears joined the Sydney Swans in the VFL Australian rules competition in 1987, rugby league finally budged. They had already given the Bears a season's headstart.

In mid-January 1987, the NSW Rugby League appointed Ken Arthurson to chair a sub-committee including QRL chairman Bill Hunter, managing director Ross Livermore and Brisbane clubs delegate Tom Drysdale to guide the Brisbane entry into

Sydney. The committee set February 27 as the closing date for applicants, the winner to be announced on April 30. The committee laid down guidelines for finance, sponsorship, player strength, advertising, promotion and marketing. It was well organised and seemed to justify Arthurson's confident comment that Brisbane was 100–1 on to link with Sydney.

The 1986 trailblazers, a consortium led by Redcliffe coach Darryl Van de Velde, re-entered the race. They were followed by a group which became known as the Norwood-McKay consortium. Alister Norwood was the Jeans West clothing magnate who had unsuccessfuly bid for the Bears VFL licence; Jim McKay was a Melbourne marketing strategist who had been consultant to both the Australian and Queensland Rugby Leagues. Another to declare an interest was a consortium chaired by Brisbane businessman Barry Maranta — an associate of Greg Chappell — and backed by Brisbane stockbroker Paul Morgan. A fourth Gold Coast-based group had as its principals ex-Test footballers John Sattler and Bob Hagan.

Coincidentally Wally had called on Morgan to investigate floating a "people's bid" under the name of Corporate Queensland. The concept was to issue shares and raise money from football fans to fund the bid. Wally was promised a position on the board which, apart from providing a business future, would have enabled him to look after the interests of players. Wally's role with Corporate Queensland lasted two weeks. Gene Miles mumbled to him one day that he might be late for training that evening. Wally casually reminded him to be on time. Miles persisted but was vague about his reasons, something to do with work. "You never have anything at work that can keep you from training," said Wally, puzzled. "You be here." They parted uneasily and when Miles did not appear at training at Wynnum's Kougari Oval, Wally became progressively angrier. When he read the paper the next morning he was livid. There was Miles, large as a photograph, shaking hands with Alister Norwood. The reason Gene had not trained was that he had attended a news conference at which the Norwood-McKay consortium signed him to promote their bid.

The next day's newspapers in Brisbane reported that Wally

had fined Gene Miles $500 for not attending training the previous evening. The size of the penalty was unheard of in Brisbane football, worth several winning match payments. It was popularly supposed that the size of the fine imposed by Wally had more to do with Miles opposing Wally's consortium than with missing training.

"That hurt me more than anything the whole year," said Wally. Miles rang the morning his photo appeared and drove around to an icy Lewis household. He explained he had been committed to secrecy and could not tell Wally the reason he could not train. Wally listened and felt suddenly estranged from his friend. "We'd always enjoyed a very open relationship," he said. "I felt funny he thought he couldn't tell me." That's when Wally hit Gene with the fine. "$500?" queried Gene, half smiling. Wally nodded, "You think I'm joking, well I'm not." With time Wally realised that Gene was genuine in his explanation and that he could not have broken his word to Norwood-McKay. The fine stood but after Gene left, Wally pondered the problems of being associated with the competing consortiums.

He expounded his fears to Jacqui. "This is lovely! We're going to have the greatest bunfight of all time," he said. "Next week another consortium will grab Greg Dowling and then another Bryan Niebling. Each bloke will be used as a marketing tool to swing the vote their way. It will become a contest to see which group has the top blokes up front. I'm getting out." The bidding had the potential to split apart the close knit family of footballers who had lifted Queensland football to parity with NSW. The very spirit which had proved Brisbane footballers were worthy of Sydney league was in danger of being destroyed. Wally rang his consortium and withdrew.

Yet a unilateral declaration of non-involvement was not the answer either. Wally publicly played down the Miles fine. "There's no feud between Gene and me," he said. "We both realise that whoever wins the bid, we'll both be there." Alister Norwood, hearing Wally was now free, invited him to join his board. Wally was impressed by the 34-year-old Perth multi-millionaire but declined.

The favoured consortiums were honed down to two major

contenders: Norwood-McKay and Maranta-Morgan. Comrade Ron McAuliffe intervened to upset Wally's neutrality. He invited Wally to meet him in Fortitude Valley. "Wear a suit," commanded McAuliffe. Wally parked behind news media vans outside a building with Jeans West plastered over it. He knew what to expect and accepted his fate. "Alister Norwood was a cluey businessman," he said. "He'd come east and taken on all the big jeans manufacturers. He was young and football is a young players' sport." Ron McAuliffe grandly announced, "Wally's joined our team." Norwood-McKay, with McAuliffe, Lewis and Miles on board, became hot favourites.

The Maranta-Morgan consortium was not dismayed. "We were initially advised we were wasting our time," said Maranta. "We didn't know how authoritative those reports were, but they just made us more determined." Maranta classed his consortium principals as commercial animals, not political animals. If their submission was right it would win. Said Paul Morgan, "When we were told categorically ours was the best bid but we weren't going to get it anyway, the boys started getting aggressive." The other two members of the consortium were hotelier and restaurateur Gary Balkin and marketing executive Steve Williams.

Williams is credited with the initiative. He rang Maranta, his father-in-law, and on 20 February 1987, the four directors met in Maranta's company boardroom at the town reach end of Charlotte Street, Brisbane. Morgan was well versed in the bid. He had lunched with QRL chairman Bill Hunter two months earlier advising Hunter how to set up the corporate structure to take Brisbane into Sydney. Morgan had already entertained thoughts of backing the consortium entering a team from the Gold Coast. Morgan classed the old pros in that bid, John Sattler and Bob Hagan, as "the funniest mob of buggers I've ever met in my life".

Maranta recalls that the enthusiasm at their first meeting was infectious. "Let's laugh a bit, let's enjoy ourselves," was the rallying call. "We all had heavy business commitments but we were all for it," said Maranta. They discussed ideas like developing an idiosyncratic Brisbane team playing the close-passing, contract football style devised by the Toowoomba Clydesdales in the 1950s. They would incorporate American football techniques with specialist skills in coaching. They wanted families, wives and girlfriends back at Lang Park, and they wanted to clean up league's unsavoury aspects.

Maranta's accountants, who were involved in a submission for a Brisbane entry into the VFL, prepared a cash flow for a Brisbane rugby league entrant. "It showed a loss in the first 12 months," said Maranta. "We would be pumping our own cash in, $120,000 in the first year, just to set the company up." The Bears Australian rules consortium had spent a massive $10 million — $4 million to buy a VFL licence and then buying an entire team. The QRL estimated it would cost the successful rugby league consortium only $1.5 million. Maranta's accountants put the cost at $2.2 million, with an income of $1.8 million for a net loss of $400,000. Buying players would cost $1 million.

But the accounting almost became a hypothetical exercise as the wisdom of the whole Sydney bid was once more questioned. An article of faith for the Brisbane clubs was that the winning consortium commit itself to the future financial restoration of the Brisbane grade competition. The Brisbane clubs had a perfectly rational argument against allowing a Sydney premiership team to be based in Brisbane. The local competition would be decimated by the emergence of a Sydney team. The rival would skim the cream of Queensland players as well as sponsorship, attendances, club membership and media publicity. The local competition would enter a decline from which it might never recover.

The opposing argument was that Sydney player raids had already reduced the local competition to a rump with diminishing standards, pitiful crowds and bankrupt clubs. Two of the oldest — Wynnum and Brothers — were trying to sell their football grounds to pay huge debts. As Ken Arthurson put it, "They aren't going that crash hot as they stand." So the Brisbane Rugby League was contemplating the Sydney move with a gun at its head. Yet if the Sydney alternative looked too bleak the BRL, with all the memories and traditions of a long established tribe, might choose slow death at home than risk a fast-track ride to reconstruction and possible annihilation. "We won't be giving away the farm," said BRL chairman Tom Drysdale defiantly.

On March 19 1987, the BRL met in farcical circumstances. They called for all consortiums to make increased provisions for the local clubs in their entries. But because the confidentiality of the consortiums' bids had to be protected, the BRL had only sketchy knowledge of their actual detail. After a three-hour meeting they voted 8–0 to block the QRL's move into the Sydney premiership.

Number crunching now began for the QRL vote. The QRL board of 10 consisted of five directors from the country, three from the BRL and chairman Bill Hunter and managing director Ross Livermore. The BRL therefore had only to gain the support of two country delegates to tie the vote 5–5 and derail the Sydney-or-Bust express. If the vote was tied, QRL chairman Bill Hunter could exercise a casting vote and, from his comments, he was definitely pro-Sydney. "This is stage one towards a national competition," he said. ARL chief, Ken Arthurson, fearing a weakening of the line, remarked, "There seems to be an ever-growing thought in Queensland that the NSWRL wants Brisbane in their competition. Nothing could be further from the truth. If Queensland votes 'no' it will be a long time, if ever. before Brisbane is given the opportunity again to join us."

On March 23 1987, the day the QRL board met, Hunter came under immense pressure from the Brisbane clubs, even to the point of veiled threats to disendorse him as QRL chairman if he used his vote to override them. Hunter told me that if two equal and opposing views were vehemently held by directors he had rarely used his casting vote to break the deadlock. He had decided before the meeting to vote for Sydney but not to use his casting vote to ensure that happened. Had ARL chairman Ken Arthurson and Australian captain Wally Lewis known that, they would have had apoplexy. The directors' voting intentions had become so generally known that without Hunter's unwavering support the Sydney bid was dead.

When Hunter called for a vote the count was 5–4 against Sydney. The five votes against belonged to three directors from the BRL and two from the country; the four votes in favour were from three country directors and managing director Ross Livermore. Hunter was about to lift his hand in favour of Sydney when he suddenly realised that if he abstained, the vote would remain 5–4 and he could not be accused by either side of having to use his casting vote. He actually lifted his hand to vote but withdrew having now decided not to vote at all. "I made a bad mistake and I've lived with the criticism ever since," Hunter told me. For not having the courage of his convictions Hunter had to field the flack about the QRL's decision and defend his own abstention as well.

Thus did history repeat itself. The stayput QRL board was consistent only in that they demonstrated the same timidity and lack of pioneering spirit they had displayed in their original rejection eight months earlier. Perhaps a braver, or more ruthless, chairman than Hunter would have defied the Brisbane clubs and returned a 6–5 Sydney vote. Former chairman, Ron McAuliffe, would have had no compunction but that is also how McAuliffe made enemies.

Wally, Geno and other players were under a huge marquee in the centre of Lang Park assisting a league promotion when news of the vote from the upstairs boardroom reached them. They were dumbstruck. Hunter emerged and murmured to Wally that it would be best for rugby league in the long run. Wally was so angry he simply brushed past. He heard Hunter, interviewed for television, admit that he had abstained from voting. Gene Miles wrote in his sports column, "I've never seen Wally so angry as he was yesterday." Despite subsequent events, Wally and Hunter have scarcely exchanged a word since.

Wally said he would obtain legal advice to seek a release from his QRL contract. He had signed in 1986 to stay in Queensland only on the verbal assurance that the QRL would put a team into Sydney in 1988. His home phone ran hot with calls from Sydney players who had expressed interest in joining a Brisbane team in the Sydney table. They included such luminaries as Paul Vautin, Brett Kenny, Dale Shearer and Steve Roach. The NSWRL declared its confidence shaken by the QRL's dramatic eleventh hour turnaround. A year of planning an expanded

Sydney premiership was in turmoil. With the Newcastle and Gold Coast clubs now accepted, Sydney had to prepare for a 15-team premiership instead of 16. Privately Arthurson was furious with Hunter and the Brisbane clubs. Media polls showed the Brisbane public wanted a team in Sydney. Rugby league was being held up to ridicule.

Bill Hunter declared the Sydney venture dead and buried but neither Norwood-McKay nor Maranta-Morgan accepted the verdict. Jim McKay flew to Sydney to unveil to Arthurson a foreshadowed deal — the QRL could become a one-third consortium partner with Norwood-McKay or accept a once only payment of $2 million. Maranta and Co. threw in their hand. They could not match that sort of cash from private sources. Then they learned it could be obtained through a public float. "We could raise that no trouble," said Maranta. "Paul Morgan could float a $2 million company over afternoon tea." They were back in it.

Behind the scenes Maranta tugged the ears of the club presidents who comprised the BRL. Using the convivial surroundings of director Balkin's Bonaparte's Hotel, the consortium set about turning the BRL around. Maranta, who had honed his persuasive skills as a schoolteacher, assured the club presidents that no four individuals could run the Brisbane team by themselves. They wanted strong club support and a strong Brisbane competition. In real terms he matched Norwood's $2 million up front but argued that dropping a large bag of money in the laps of the clubs would not solve their long-term problems.

They needed to boost the public image of rugby league and bring crowds back to the game. So, as an alternative to the $2 million, Maranta offered the clubs a stake in the future — 30 per cent of his consortium's profits, no liability for losses and no need to outlay capital to invest in the project. He promised also to match each club's seasonal sponsorship on a dollar-for-dollar basis up to a maximum of $10,000. Paul Morgan, no mean dealer himself, applauded Maranta's negotiating skill. "He was brilliant," said Morgan. "He's a fabulous operator. Only trouble is he's usually got a thousand things on at once and you can't concentrate on more than two."

The BRL suddenly rescinded its opposition to a team for Sydney and within days, on April 5, the QRL unanimously voted to go ahead. It all happened so quickly that Ken Arthurson, who only days earlier had been issuing ultimatums and setting deadlines, found himself presented with a *fait accompli*. Though the NSWRL was bound to accept whichever consortium the QRL nominated, in the face of such erratic behaviour by the banana league, Arthurson could only muster some dignity. "The appointment of a licence to a Brisbane team will be made finally by the NSWRL," he said. "The Brisbane division is not going to make that decision." He had his 16th team, but from which consortium?

In the two weeks it took the QRL to perform its reverse somersault Maranta-Morgan snatched favouritism from Norwood-McKay. A key element in the changing fortunes was the involvement of Ron McAuliffe with Norwood-McKay. To an outsider — like Alister Norwood — McAuliffe seemed the man to have onside. As chairman of the Lang Park Trust, confidant of Ken Arthurson, and with so many contacts, McAuliffe could have joined whichever consortium board he wished. Maranta, alone, perceived that power lay with the active Brisbane clubs, not with retired chairmen. He did not need showpiece names. McAuliffe later told me that when he spoke with Maranta regarding a fee to sit on the consortium's board, Maranta had not rushed him with an offer. From then on, McAuliffe's opposition to Maranta stiffened.

Yet McAuliffe himself recognised, and was frustrated by, his powerlessness. He publicly blamed himself for the QRL's original decision to stay out of Sydney. He said, "Since my retirement as QRL chairman in 1985 I have been a paid consultant to the QRL. In that time the chairman of the Brisbane division Tom Drysdale and the QRL chairman Bill Hunter have not spoken to me." The BRL saw a conflict of interest in McAuliffe's position as Lang Park Trust chairman and probable executive chairman of a Norwood-McKay football team. When he'd been QRL supremo, McAuliffe had run Queensland rugby league with such an iron hand that, when he retired, club executives were glad to have done with him. They were not anxious to throw open the gates for Senator Ron to ride back in, more powerful than ever, with the Norwood-McKay circus.

Another element assisting Maranta's consortium was their Brisbane base, compared with Norwood's Perth base. Brisbane's parochial clubs were steeped in suspicion of anything beyond the state borders. At a BRL meeting on April 10 the executive instructed its votes on the QRL to go to Maranta. The day before the QRL vote, Ron McAuliffe rang Wally. "We're in a bit of trouble," he said. "These bastards are against me and so they're against Norwood-McKay. Backing Alister (Norwood) was the worst move I could have made." McAuliffe's politicking was lost on Wally. "Despite joining Norwood-McKay with Ron I wasn't sure what was in the consortium proposals," he told me. "I was happy to go along with whoever got it as long as they recognised the players had to be looked after."

On April 14 the QRL met once more. Three country members, John McDonald, Jim Gallagher and John Garrahy, wanted the QRL to put a team in itself. That vote was lost 7–3 though Bill Hunter told me that if, a year later, the board had the vote over again, it would have backed the country proposal. After initial euphoria about Norwood's $2 million the board discussed Maranta's offer of 30 per cent of the team profits, with the licence to be renewed after three years. In the final vote the three BRL directors backed Maranta and the three go-it-alone country delegates switched to Maranta as well. Hunter followed suit to make the vote 7–3 to enter a Maranta-Morgan team in the Sydney premiership. Instead of being a cause for celebration the drawn-out procedures had exhausted the participants. The Maranta group rang Wally and told him there were no hard feelings. They knew he had backed the losing group but they would call him as soon as they were organised.

Thus did the code of rugby league football in Brisbane reluctantly and fearfully commit the pride of its players to the unknown perils of the 1988 Sydney premiership.

7 BIRTH OF THE BRONCOS

The first player signed for Brisbane's new team was Wally Lewis. A week after the Maranta consortium's victory Wally and Gene Miles made their way to the boardroom of Paul Morgan's stockbroking company in the city's new Riverside centre. The peaceful and picturesque view of the broad Brisbane River contrasted with the confrontation which ensued on the 29th floor. In the boardroom sat the four consortium directors. The two who did all the talking were Paul "Porky" Morgan playing bad cop to suave Barry Maranta's good cop.

At 2 p.m. Morgan welcomed the two players and told Wally to wait outside for 10 minutes while they dealt with Geno. "We'll have you out of here by 2.30 p.m.," Morgan assured Wally. An hour later Morgan burst out of the boardroom fuming. "How do you get that bastard to listen to common sense," he roared. Wally tried a little joke. "Well Porky I've tried for two years at Wynnum without finding the formula for success." Morgan decided he didn't need a laugh, whirled and stormed back into the boardroom. He told Miles, "Geno, buddy, if you don't listen to me I'm gonna throw you straight through that glass window." Women clerks paused momentarily at their green video display screens. The world of stocks and shares waited while they calculated, perhaps, that Geno would land on the Riverside forecourt somewhere between Michael's and Friday's restaurants. It would be an interesting contest, a heavyweight bout with both men over 100 kilos. "I got aggressive all right," said Morgan. "The sheilas were all worried it was a blue."

Paul Morgan can swear, drink and stay up as late as any football firebrand and he prides himself as a powerful persuader. He was going to sign Wally and Geno come hell or high water but he knew he hadn't won them yet — hearts or minds — and he wanted his motives understood. "I didn't blame them, because we were raving on about life after this and life after that," Morgan told me. "But I knew all the old troupers, those who were set up for life, and others who weren't. Arthur Beetson, an immortal. Footy should have done more for him." So here was Morgan with a chance to get it right. He launched into Miles again: "The difference between us and Sydney, Geno, is that when you're burnt out in Sydney you'll end up hanging off the back of a garbage truck." Morgan was striding about. "Sure, we don't want you after you're burnt out, but let's make sure the net money you've earned after tax is still there. We've got lawyers and accountants ready to give a hand. Then we'll open doors and you can go for your life." Morgan punched a thick fist into a tough palm. "Geno, if you don't commit yourself to this you'll never commit yourself to anything."

Wally cooled his heels for another half hour. Miles finally emerged, rolled his eyes at Wally, and muttered, "Gees, didn't it hit the fan in there!" Miles had accepted the consortium's terms but wanted time before he signed. The consortium wanted Miles's signature before he walked out. Miles was obstinate. Wally, having been delayed nearly two hours, walked into the boardroom to face four frustrated, fed-up directors. "This is lovely," he thought, glancing about. "Gene's got them all steamed up for me."

Wally should have thanked Miles. Morgan had exhausted his rhetoric, if not his energy. "What about these other offers?" he demanded, sitting on the edge of a desk. Wally took a deep breath and played the hand he wished he held. "There's only one you've got to be concerned with. You know who that's from." Morgan nodded, yeah, he knew. Barry Maranta knew Manly had offered Wally close to $150,000 the year before. He did not know Manly had not contacted Wally since. Wally had one last, genuine approach left with Manly who were still miffed at having been used as the underbidder when the QRL retained Wally in 1986. Wally could not push the probability of another Manly offer too far. He told the directors, "The offer from the other place is a bit better than yours, but when I think how much it will cost to move to Sydney it brings them back a bit." Morgan was exasperated. "So what are you telling us?"

Good cop Maranta was calculating. The consortium had announced it would pay players an extraordinary $1,500 per match win. In the Sydney competition few teams pay more than $500 a win. As was standard, players would receive only $50 if they lost. Wally's highest win bonus had been $1,500 for state-of-origin games but there were only three of those a year. Fifteen wins from 22 competition matches in the Sydney competition — a semi-final performance — would be worth $22,500 in win bonuses, $15,000 more than Sydney clubs paid. Maranta knew that Wally had always valued not having the hassle and cost of moving to Sydney. Maranta added the extra win-bonus and stay-in-Brisbane factors together and subtracted their value from Manly's 1986 offer. And waited.

Morgan pointed his pen at Wally to hurry him up. Wally pursed his lips. "I'm not going to play ducks and drakes, I've never dealt that way with McAuliffe," Wally said. "But I set myself a figure and it's five grand on top of your original offer." He ploughed on before Morgan could butt in. "I haven't got carried away and said I want an extra $15,000 and hope for $10,000. Five is my realistic figure." Maranta smiled. Wally's figure was almost on the button. "I think that's fair," said Maranta. "You haven't tried to bite us. That's OK." He altered the contract. Morgan, standing, still unsure whether they had secured rugby league's most prized player, demanded, "Well what are you going to do? You going to keep buggerising around?" Nettled, Wally shot back. "Well if you give me a bloody pen Porky I'll sign!" He snatched Morgan's pen and scribbled on the contract, the flourish to start the W, the long tail on the y, the lower case l starting the surname and the circle to dot the i.

Why Wally subjects himself to the stress of these contract confrontations is a mystery. Barry Maranta had negotiated Michael O'Connor's transfer from St George to Manly. It would

be entirely proper, and advantageous, for an advocate to nego-
tiate on Wally's behalf and for Wally merely to attend a final
ceremonial signing. But not Wally. He sits and sweats, runs his
own game, beards financial giants like Kerry Packer and Paul
Morgan in their dens, suffers a bit and lives with the results. It's
partly ego, partly independence and partly the habit of his
working-class background. Wally is as good as the next bloke,
better if modesty permitted him to say, so what had he to fear
from this lot? In any case Wally negotiates as he tackles, with
a big, front-on hit that by rights would stun most adversaries.
He scorned the piddling adage that' whosoever represents himself has a fool for a client.

No one else in that boardroom — not Morgan or Maranta,
Balkin or Williams — and few outside could guess Wally's intense satisfaction as he signed the last club contract of his career.
It had taken him 30 minutes to embark upon the last leg of his
life's long league journey. North Sydney had offered him $7,500
a year to go south in 1979. Nine years on, for a six figure
amount, he had finally signed a NSWRL contract — without
having to leave his beloved Brisbane. He signed for three years
but believed his career would last only two. "It's Official and
It's Final!" said a newspaper headline. The Sydney premiership
beckoned to Wally like a medieval jousting tournament to the
kingdom's top knight.

The four directors who confronted Wally were no football
naifs. In just eight weeks, from their first meeting, the former
rugby league footballers — second-rower Paul Morgan, fullback Barry Maranta, winger Gary Balkin and five-eighth Steve
Williams — hijacked the Brisbane bid like old masters pulling
a heist, except in this case it would eventually cost the gang $4
million. Behind their approaches to playing staff was the promise that the directors would help with post-football careers. Part
of Paul Morgan's rant to Gene Miles was a description of the
aftermath to Morgan's own five years in rugby league — about
the hole it left in his life and how hard it had been to cope. Barry
Maranta's input into the consortium's submission to the QRL
was introducing footballers to life after football, teaching them
public speaking, budgeting, investment and career analysis.

Wally, still uncertain about a vocation, felt reassured.

Before switching to league Paul Morgan had represented Queensland in rugby union and might have in rugby league too had he chosen to ignore a damaged ankle which sidelined him during a city-country trial. Having thus underachieved he has since sought to prevent others similarly erring. Morgan left Brisbane State High — the city's equivalent of Sydney High — eight years before Wally enrolled. Now, as principal of leading Australian stockbrokers Jarden Morgan, he reasoned that good sportsmen, like himself, were as likely good businessmen. Morgan's company and its subsidiaries, at one time or another, were sown with former Australian rugby union stars Stuart Gregory, Andrew Slack and David Codey, Australian rugby union coach Bob Templeton and former Test cricketer Bob Cowper. Apart from being a sports fanatic Morgan is popularly famous for having floated the company which raised the finance for Paul Hogan's fabulously successful *Crocodile Dundee*. Yet all that pales beside his commercial achievements. Jarden Morgan is one of the world's largest dealers in currency and precious metals. An estimated 7 million visitors a year passing through Hong Kong airport have no choice but to buy their foreign currency from money booths owned by a Jarden Morgan subsidiary. Paul Morgan could certainly afford Wally.

Barry Maranta, consortium chairman, played first-grade rugby league, was once selected for Brisbane and later coached rugby league at Queensland University. His career spanned schoolteaching, writing textbooks and CAE lecturing before he branched into real estate, life insurance and sports management. He is now chief executive of Northern Securities Management Ltd, Queensland's largest private fund management company, of which Greg Chappell is a director. Maranta managed Chappell and then transformed him from Australian cricket captain to a captain of Queensland commerce. Maranta's son Michael, who later bowled for Queensland, was a contemporary of Wally's in GPS sport: Maranta at St Joseph's College, Gregory Terrace; Wally at Brisbane State High.

Bon vivant Gary Balkin has enjoyed too much *bon vin* to be recognisable as the slim, fleet-footed winger who was the leading Brisbane rugby league try-scorer in 1964. He is known internationally for his two paddlewheel riverboat restaurants, the *Kookaburra Queens*, the city's most visible tourist attractions. Balkin represented Brisbane in rugby league but his off-field support is just as impressive. He donated the trophy for the interstate primary schools rugby league competition which was won in 1971 by Queensland after a clever try by baby-faced lock W. Lewis. A life member of Souths (Brisbane), Balkin brought Bobby McCarthy and Wayne Bennett to coach the club and each won premierships, McCarthy in 1981 and Bennett in 1985.

Steve Williams, 36, the youngest director, moved to Queensland from Sydney in 1973 and therefore has not acquired the half-a-lifetime residency necessary for diehard Queenslanders to accept him as a local. A strong, wiry five-eighth, he played for North Sydney and after moving interstate represented Brisbane and Queensland. His last year in A grade Brisbane rugby league, 1978, was Wally's first. His business career has been in advertising and he is credited with establishing the hugely successful marketing division of the QRL. Williams was a good friend of Redcliffe coach Darryl Van de Velde who sought in vain to enter a Brisbane team in the 1987 Sydney premiership.

Though out of playing action for at least a decade, these were four immensely experienced rugby league businessmen. To make their venture work, rugby league had to be dragged into the 21st century. They were seeking nothing less than the middle-classing of the game, a sport steeped in nearly a century of working-class tradition. To transcend old boundaries league would need to attract Australian rules, basketball and rugby union followers from greater Brisbane's 1.4 million population. Rugby league crowds in Queensland had diminished because sports contests were no longer sufficient to lure home-body audiences away from the safety of a video film in their loungeroom or the leisure of an airconditioned cinema.

The challenge was to convert rugby league to the family-oriented image of the Bullets and transform Lang Park, one of the city's oldest arenas, to the comfort of Boondall, its newest. Rugby league had cleaned up its act on field, but off field? I sat in Lang Park's outer Badlands for the first state-of-origin in 1986 and saw women in long queues outside inadequate toilet facilities. Young men publicly urinated, too drunk to care. Obscenities filled the air, hooligans hurled half-full cans of beer. The price of a fool on the hill is the absence of a footballing family. Consortium director Steve Williams attended a Superbowl in the United States and noted the American crowd did not drink and was non-violent. Barry Maranta conceded that the directors had not encouraged their wives to attend rugby league matches because of the risk of unpleasant experiences. Yet women constituted a potential 50 per cent following for the new Brisbane team. Maranta spoke of "dry" (non-alcohol) and "wet" drinking zones and vastly upgraded public facilities. "Everything is predicated upon a comfort zone," he said. "Once the first ladies attend in safety and comfort the word will spread quickly."

The image of their team was uppermost in the consortium's mind as they invited applications for coach. Seven responded, including Brisbane premiership winning coaches Johnny Lang and Ross Strudwick. From Canberra Wayne Bennett recommended Wally Lewis but, as with the state-of-origin, Wally again shied from the burden of captain-coach. With Bennett apparently tied to Canberra for four years, Wally said, "I thought someone like Bobby McCarthy would be considered the pea."

The four directors flew to Sydney and met Jack Gibson and Arthur Beetson. Maranta wanted a winning coach but equally important, one who would fit the consortium's vision of respectable rugby league. The coach had to fulfil this ethical image — the Bullet's Brian Kerle reincarnated in rugby league. Gibson and Beetson were unanimous. There was only one man — Wayne Bennett. Steve Williams rang Bennett and told him, "We've found the best coach in Australia...Will you come home?" Bennett said he was too committed in Canberra. Williams persisted, "But would you like to?" Bennett could not deny that. Paul Morgan, who had snatched top staff from the most powerful finance companies in Queensland, flew to Canberra. He sold Bennett the integrity of the directors, the potential of their new club and the promise of a long-term future for Bennett and his family in Brisbane. Morgan achieved what very few have ever managed — he convinced Bennett to change direction. Morgan then stiff-armed the Raiders' administrators: "Benny's coming home. Forget about any alternatives, we haven't any."

The Raiders acquiesced, provided Morgan and Maranta did not try to steal their other ex-Queenslanders. Maranta noted the irony of Canberra's demand: "I don't imagine Canberra were too concerned about the impact on (Brisbane) Souths when they took Mal Meninga, Gary Belcher and Peter Jackson." Before joining the Raiders, Bennett was employed by the QRL as director of coaching with an office adjoining others where Wally was schools liaison officer and John Ribot development officer. The consortium had Bennett and Lewis and now they poached Ribot to become their general manager.

John Ribot had an illustrious playing career: in Brisbane with Wests, Valleys and Redcliffe; and in Sydney with Newtown, Wests and Manly. He played lock for Queensland and second-row for NSW before Wests coach Roy Masters rang the position change, to winger, which made Ribot a 1982 Kangaroo. Ribot retired in 1985 after a magnificent last season, scoring match-winning tries for Queensland and Australia. He was a contemporary of Queensland's senior stars and quickly signed up the nucleus of the state-of-origin side. Hooker Greg Conescu was a priority, and then fullback Colin Scott. Prop forwards Bryan Niebling and Greg Dowling were snatched from the contracting jaws of Sydney clubs. After a drawn-out transfer fee battle, Allan Langer was secured from Ipswich and the Brisbane team had seven state-of-originers.

From Brisbane's local competition came winger "Smokin'" Joe Kilroy, voted the world's best fullback after Queensland's 1983 UK tour, and Grant Rix, Wally's heir apparent until a succession of knee injuries. Ribot toured the state and arrived back with such unknowns as fearless fullback Shane Duffy from Mt Isa, winger-speedster Michael Hancock from Toowoomba and the nuggety Gee brothers, Keith and Andrew from Beaudesert. In Sydney Ribot signed the old and the new from St George —

star forward of 1985, Billy Noke and lightning young centre Chris Johns. From Sydney Easts came goal-kicking rookie, lock forward Terry Matterson.

By mid-July the consortium's team name had been narrowed down to the Broncos, Bulls, Bombers, Kookaburras or Cowboys. At directors' meetings — lunch aboard Balkin's *Kookaburra Queen* — Balkin plumped for his feathered jackass but it lacked the straightforward alliterative appeal of the Brisbane Bears and Bullets. The board all wished for an Aussie flavour such as the Boomers, but the Australian basketballers had snaffled that. Brisbane Brumbies was nicely colloquial but could be shortened to the Brissie Brums, a devastating headline after a loss. Thus the Broncos were born. The Broncos jersey was also displayed, at first glance an uninspiring combination of colours and designs. "Not a lot of the blokes liked the jersey but if you were asked it was hard to come up with a better one," said Wally. "It took a couple of months before we took pride in actually pulling the jersey on."

The sponsor's name across the jersey front, Power, was a curiosity. Apart from being a wonderful rallying cry, as in Power-to-the-Broncos, it was the surname of Brisbane hotelier Bernard Power, promoting a beer he had not yet even brewed. Rather impudently he was seeking to extract a percentage of the Queensland beer market from international giants, Bond Brewing and Carlton United Breweries. Bernie Power was a former First XV captain of St Joseph's College, Nudgee, where his successors included Australian rugby union captains Mark Loane and Paul McLean. He remained a rugby union buff but did not exercise his undeniable right, as sponsor and former prop forward, to instruct the Broncos how to pack a scrum. He paid $3 million for a three-year contract and the Broncos repaid him by quickly becoming the biggest name in sport on the Australian east coast. To challenge the two brewing giants Power had the sympathies of a loyal Queensland public which had noted with displeasure Alan Bond's removal of the Castlemaine Perkins Brisbane address from the XXXX can, replacing it with Bond Brewing Perth. Paul Morgan helped float Power Brewing but, when it came to refinancing, Bernard Power found traditional lending institutions fearful of taking on Bond and CUB. Power let the people judge. He placed a prospectus in a Sunday newspaper and was overwhelmed with investors — four times as many buyers as there were shares offered. Queensland backed Wally, the Broncos and Power Brewing. All three drew strength from Queensland's renowned xenophobia.

The first Broncos muster took place in November 1987, at Kooralbyn, a sport-health-holiday resort in the subtropical Gold Coast hinterland. On the first evening Wally and the experienced players settled for a moderate drink while the younger blokes hit the resort's disco and bars. Wally told Gene Miles, "I think these blokes are going to be sick and sorry in the morning because if I know Bennett we're not up here for a holiday."

Wally had learnt his lesson as a young hero in his first year in Brisbane A grade. His team, Valleys, were playing a lowly placed opponent and Wally, just turned 18, went to a pub with a friend for lunch before the match. One beer couldn't hurt, tasted good. Another? Thanks. He drank half a dozen cans, enjoyed a few laughs and headed off for the game. For the first 10 minutes he alternated between heartburn and hot stomach refluxes. He cursed himself aloud, "You dickhead! Fancy doing that!" Valleys prop forward, Peter O'Callaghan, a friend of Wally's, called a move from which Wally often scored close to the line. But Valleys were in their own half. "Cal! What are we doing?" shouted Wally. "We're too far out." O'Callaghan called back, "It's on, it's on!" Wally got the ball, ran 60 metres and scored but, when he staggered back, roundly abused O'Callaghan. "You bastard Cal! Don't you ever pull that on me that far out again." O'Callaghan gave a knowing smile. "Doing it a bit tough this afternoon are we big fellah?" Wally looked back in surprise. "I can smell it," said O'Callaghan. Afterwards O'Callaghan asked Wally where he had drunk the night before. Wally sheepishly confessed his lunchtime misdemeanour.

Sure enough at Kooralbyn coach Bennett roused the Broncos at 7 a.m., sent them on a long loosening-up run and prepared a full day's skills and drills training. It was a hot, muggy day. Bennett pointed to a 400-metre oval he had flagged and told the squad he wanted to see how far they could run in 12 minutes.

Bennett, who works out for half an hour every day, ran with the leaders for the first few laps and then took off. As he lapped slower players, especially those who had been living it up the night before, he turned and looked them full in the eye. Wally and Greg Dowling, running last in an unspoken pact, were the first lapped. Bennett finished three-quarters of a lap ahead of the first player home. Never has a coach conveyed his message more clearly. The squad was humbled.

Training was interspersed with meetings with doctors, psychologists, physiotherapists, dieticians and even a cleric. The psychologist explained how the human brain consisted of negative and positive sides and that when the athlete was enduring pain the negative side encouraged the body to stop. The positive then said, "Yes, you can do it." And the negative came back, "No I can't, I'm hurting." The players digested this sombre dialogue. Any questions? Wally piped up, "How come Mr Negative's always a lot stronger than Mr Positive!"

When Pastor Russell Hinds of the local Baptist Church was introduced, the players greeted him with doubtful looks. Hinds skilfully disarmed them. "If you're ever doing it tough and things aren't working out for you, if you ever need somebody to talk to away from football, I'm the bloke to do it," he said. "I'm not going to call you in and put you straight on the phone to the bloke upstairs, but I might be able to give you some alternate means of approaching your problem." Wally was suitably impressed. "If he hadn't worn his church gear you wouldn't have picked him," he said. Several players chatted to Hinds after the lecture.

Wally's psyche and soul were in good shape thanks, his physiology less so. Dietician Holly Frail, a consultant to the Australian Institute of Sport, told the Broncos that though none was overweight, some were "over-fat" - like Wally who must shed 6 kilos of excess body fat. Wally sent the Kooralbyn scales to 102 kilos, the weight to which he had soared on the 1982 Kangaroo tour. He had not touched a beer for five months but that abstinence did not include food. Slim and shapely Jacqui Lewis is a chocoholic — she can nibble through a family block in an evening in front of the television, comfort food for long solitary evenings. Wally's irregular training and work hours often left him with no alternative to fast food. But the real reason for Wally's weight blow-out was that he could not train adequately. At Kooralbyn his right knee, injured against New Zealand and aggravated in Los Angeles, flared again.

In mid-January 1988, a week before the Broncos embarked upon an arduous weekend at the army's Canungra jungle warfare training base, in the southeast Queensland rainforest, Wally underwent surgery. Gene Miles shook his head: "You'll do anything to get out of training won't you?" Wally booked into Holy Spirit Hospital on 18 January 1988, ravenous from fasting for the anesthetic. Jacqui wisely refused to smuggle him in some late tucker before the operation. He awoke at 2 a.m. in a daze and suddenly wished he had chosen Canungra. Bloody hell, his knee! "I started yelling," he said. "And then I remembered the buzzer so I pushed the shit out of it." When the nurse did not materialise Wally grabbed the buzzer and held on. "You could hear it going bzzzzzz...right through the ward and down the hallway," said Wally. After a minute a nurse rushed up and admonished him sharply, "That's enough!" Wally does not like hospitals and has never been a model patient.

A nurse woke him at 6 a.m. with breakfast. Wally blinked sleepily. Turn it up, he said, and rolled over. The nurse insisted. Wally said indignantly, "Listen, you ask my missus, she'll tell you I don't have a feed, don't even wake up for breakfast until eight o'clock." He pulled the sheets back over his head. The breakfast tray hovered. He must eat breakfast now. "Listen, I'm a fair judge," said Wally, humouring Florence of the Food. "If you have breakfast this early I can go back to sleep, wake at 8.30 and you'll be just about bringing lunch around. I'll eat that." At 9 a.m. Jacqui arrived and Wally struggled to the car on crutches. The Broncos orthopedic surgeon Dr Peter Myers had conducted an arthroscopy and removed a piece of torn cartilage.

After his knee operation Wally's rehabilitation began at 5.30 every morning in a swimming pool near his home. Wally, a former lifesaver, had been a fair swimmer since his days as a youngster hanging around the pool run by Steve Holland's dad.

With his legs strapped to a float, Wally thrashed down his first few laps and stopped, his shoulder muscles aching from disuse.

Still on crutches he accompanied the team to Canungra, camping the weekend in four-man tents. The players donned jungle greens and tackled the army's obstacle course, scaling rope ladders, crawling through mud and over barbed-wire fences. The army kindly lent the Broncos several instructors who shouted at the footballers as though they were new recruits, earning strained stares from the Broncos' less agile big men. Fullback Shane Duffy came close to breaking the army's record for the course and he was soon to show that form on the field. From the sidelines Wally watched, giggled occasionally, but admitted, "I really felt sorry for the blokes. They were flogged for three days. They'd have only six hours sleep and be back at it again."

On day two the team rose at 6 a.m. and took off on a difficult cross-country run. Miles and Dowling arrived back shattered, covered in cobwebs and dirt and drenched from having forded creeks. "How did you go boys?", Wally called cheerfully from his crutches. Geno and GD turned on him: "You big whimp, you cat, you big sissy, you big girl," and every other demeaning insult they could hurl. Heading back to Brisbane that Sunday afternoon Wally and the driver had the bus conversation to themselves. "I'd say three miles down the road every other bloke on the bus was asleep, out like lights," said Wally. "They wouldn't have been watching the Sunday movie that night either."

The public interest in Wally's progress amazed Broncos staff unused to Wally's exalted status in Australian rugby league. The Prince and Princess of Wales were in Australia, Susan Renouf was sparring for possession of her harbourside mansion, but Wally's health commanded the spotlight. Even the phlegmatic Wayne Bennett was moved to write in his *Courier-Mail* column:

> In the three months since my return from Canberra the number of inquiries about "King Wally's" health, fitness, dedication, enthusiasm and hairline have overwhelmed any other topic of conversation.

Wally could not play in the Bicentennial Sevens tournament at Parramatta Stadium on February 6. In 14 manic minutes the

Broncos were bundled out by Canberra 12–4. Two weeks later Wally was still consigned to the grandstand with coach Bennett when the Broncos ran on against Canberra in a full rehearsal at Lang Park. Said Wally, "I remember thinking when Canberra racked up the first two tries, 'Uh oh, we're in trouble already. Maybe we're not up to it yet.' " But in the second quarter the Broncos piled on three tries with free-wheeling attack. "The cohesion in the team amazed me," said Wally. "They played as though they had teamed together all year." The Broncos victory, 22–16, against the previous season's losing grand finalists, was as satisfying as the crowd of nearly 10,000. The Broncos experimented with all the hoopla that had annoyed NSW general manager John Quayle in the previous year's final Origin. On the ground PA system, snorting horses and cracking whips accompanied Bronco attacks and a chatterbox ground announcer kept a running commentary on incidents in play, like "Ooh, that hurt" and "Off!" when Canberra's Sam Backo was cautioned.

Every aspect of the Broncos show was being broken in. At training the team had watched with keen interest the auditioning of the scantily-clad Broncette dancers until one evening there came a shocked cry, "Hey! There's blokes out there!" and so there were — five — to lift the 30 girls during the squad's more acrobatic routines.

Some players felt they were put into equally uncomfortable positions by the Broncos publicity machine. Shy, tongue-tied tyros like Allan Langer had to bone up on public speaking as the Broncos shared the escalating demand for promotional appearances. The Queensland Governor, Sir Walter Campbell, held a reception for the Broncos in the grounds of Government House, with its panoramic views to city and mountains. Some of the younger Broncos, either bushies or unskilled workers, looked distinctly collar-proud as they graciously clutched drinks from waiters in cummerbunds and epaulettes. Wally, an old hand, chatted amiably with Sir Walter. The semi-finals or bust, King Wally told Governor Wally. Nothing less would do.

Channel 10 signed a $750,000 one-year contract for the rights to televise Broncos matches. That particularly pleased Wally.

Channel 10 had flirted with Australian rules in 1986 and, with Alan Bond from Western Australia (an Australian rules state) in charge of Channel 9, Wally had feared rugby league was losing ground in Brisbane.

On 27 February 1988, Wally played the second half of a trial against a New Zealand President's XIII at Lang Park. He had not played a match for six months. He was 28 and returning from the most prolonged injury in his career. How would he fare? Former coach, now Broncos consultant Bob Bax, wrote in his *Sunday Mail* column:

> From the moment Lewis took the field everything changed. He was like a traffic cop directing play and calling the shots for his team to come alive. Yet while he was there I doubt he ran more than 100 metres overall. Regardless of that Lewis put Gene Miles away for two tries...scored one himself...made three of the biggest hits I have seen...and drove the opposition back with well directed line kicks.

Wally even had time, in his idiosyncratic fashion, to exchange a few friendly words with the Kiwis towards the end of the Broncos' 38–6 win. Wally crashed through two New Zealanders to score a try and one player gave him the sort of lip junior opponents reserve for legends. Wally replied, "They're pretty strong words from a bloke who's just missed me." The second Kiwi joined in and Wally turned and said, "Oh yes, I forgot to compliment you. You were in on that tackle as well, weren't you?" And added sarcastically, Richie Benaud style, "Oh yes, marvellous effort that." Brisbane referee Eddie Ward intervened, "That's enough of that, six."

Ten days later Wally produced close to the game of his career as the Broncos, running on high-octane adrenalin, opened their Sydney campaign with the smashing victory over previous year's premiers, Manly, by the incredible margin of 44–10.

8 IF YOU CAN MEET WITH TRIUMPH...

From day one John Ribot was certain the Broncos would succeed. "I played in Sydney, I knew what the Sydney market had to offer," said Ribot, Broncos general manager. "I played with Wally, Gene and the others. They were better players than I was and I had reasonable success in Sydney. I could see they were going to take Sydney by storm." But neither Ribot nor the team's most ardent supporters could have predicted the series of performances by the brash Broncos in the months of March and April 1988.

Wally was personally elated by their first up victory over Manly, the Sydney champions. He felt relieved of a great burden, slaying the canard that he might not measure up to Sydney's exalted standards. Coach Bennett spent the week wrenching the Broncos down from their Manly euphoria. At training nothing was beyond them. Like kids after exams they bubbled and bantered non-stop. Bennett warned them, "That wasn't a true indication of what it's going to be like all year." But as Wally said, it was impossible not to get carried away. "I remember picking up the Sydney papers," he said. "We'd gone from complete underdogs to the team that could win the premiership." The Broncos had been installed at 5–1 second favourites to the 9–4 favourites Manly.

Wally approached the next match, against Penrith, as a more realistic test. The excitement had subsided, the thrill of their debut was over, they would have to win on merit. Penrith were semi-final chances. Their coach was NSW Origin coach Ron

Willey, their captain Test hooker Royce Simmons. They bristled with first-class backs like Greg Alexander, Brad Izzard and Chris Mortimer, backed by a heavyweight pack boasting two of Sydney's hardest hitting forwards, tank-like prop Peter Kelly and 195 cm second-rower Mark Geyer.

Early in the match Wally put a stop to Kelly and Geyer's ambushes. After the two forwards swung in with consecutive high tackles Wally opportunely dashed in, grabbed Geyer by the jersey front and waltzed him a few steps, provoking a general melee. Referee Kevin Roberts stopped play, lectured Geyer and penalised Penrith. Not a punch was thrown but Wally had made his point to Roberts.

The Broncos took up with Penrith where they had left off against Manly, running to an effortless 16–2 lead at half-time. Of three tries none was more damaging than that by Allan Langer. In a solo run from near half-way he beat Penrith full-back David Green with a sidestep so comprehensive that Green may as well have been trying to catch a fox terrier on the beach. Penrith were shaken. They expected such individual brilliance from their own 1986 Kangaroo half Greg Alexander, not their opponent's.

A mediocre Saturday evening crowd of 13,621 at Lang Park settled in for a comfortable win. Bennett cautioned as the team filed out for the second half, "You can't go to sleep against these blokes." Wally sensed complacency sedate the side as surely as if they had been hit with a syringe. "Penrith were supposed to be the gun side of 1988," he said. "Yet here we were way in front." Suddenly the Broncos went off the boil. Tackling became sloppy, handling grew careless. Test trumps Greg Conescu and Greg Dowling went off, injured. Penrith scored twice within two minutes to trail 16–12. "They got 10 feet tall and bullet proof," said Wally. "I laid it down to the blokes, we couldn't let them score again." But Penrith did, to lead 18–16 with nine minutes left. Wally had the team in a huddle under the posts but in truth he was as distressed as anyone. "WHAT are we doing here?" he said violently. "We had this on toast!" Messages were being relayed from Bennett, control the ball, push it wide, kick...chase.

The Broncos then allied the skills they had been taught by Bennett with a hitherto unrealised team spirit. In just three rucks, comprising 19 passes, every member of the team, except Bryan Niebling and Billy Noke, handled the ball as the Broncos swept 75 metres up field to score. The sequence began on the Broncos quarterline. In the first movement Wally handled three times, in the second Matterson twice and the last Langer twice. They ran helter-skelter, hither-thither, deftly palming passes in a style reminiscent of The Entertainers, the early 1980s Canterbury-Bankstown teams. They looked capable of anything. The Broncettes, in their skin-tight gold leotards and white belts, boots and stetsons, pranced with genuine delight on the sideline and skyrockets exploded overhead. The Broncos had won a 20–18 cliffhanger.

Wally walked slowly off, blessing the two competition points. Penrith captain, Royce Simmons, a close friend from the 1986 Kangaroo tour, walked over and shook hands. "Mate, we threw it away," Simmons said with a sigh. "We should have won that." Wally did a weary double take. "Royce, you threw it away? Have a look at us, we led 16–2." In the dressingroom Bennett surveyed his battered team and said loudly, "Welcome to the real world of Sydney football." He was glad of the win but even more delighted by the Broncos' recovery. He told newspaper reporters, "Now they know the true intensity of Sydney football. They can expect that most Sundays. I'll have no trouble motivating them for next week against Wests."

Two matches, two wins. It was party time. The team adjourned to their Red Hill club. Wally usually began with a few drinks in the massive ballroom where a live band dished out dance numbers. Not that he's a dancer. He considers it the most ridiculous recreation ever invented. Few of the players, stiff, sore and winding down after a slogging match, felt like dancing. If Jacqui Lewis asks her husband to dance she knows his standard reply will be, "Love, I did dance with you, remember, on November 10, 1984, the bridal waltz." The Broncos were such a new club that members were unused to brushing shoulders with their heroes. "I probably signed 100 autographs a night at first," said Wally. "It can be a pain, but the members are good and they'll settle down." For more privacy Wally and friends would retire to the club's restaurant bar, a smaller, quieter area with subdued lighting, indoor greenery, cocktail stools and black, cushioned elbow rests. On the restaurant walls hang lifesize coloured photographs of old guardsmen Wally and Gene, and new boys Duffy and Matterson. The young Broncos too were fast becoming celebrities.

The team flew to Sydney the following Saturday, a flight which took less time than the ensuing long, hot drive southwest to Campbelltown where they booked into a motel. The next afternoon a record crowd of 10,000 packed into Orana Park for the Broncos' first away match, against Wests. The famous old club, once home to the 1950s Test halves, Keith Holman and Frank Stanmore, had been relocated in Sydney's outer western suburbs. The club was still rebuilding and Wayne Bennett counted nine Queenslanders in Wests grades, many of whom he had himself coached at Brisbane Souths. One of them, Wests captain Scott Tronc, Brisbane's 1986 Rothman's gold medallist, subsequently signed for the Broncos for 1989.

In the 1950s and 60s, when St George were demoralising the rest of Sydney with their interminable premierships, Wests in vain bought players and so became known as The Millionaires. A quarter of a century on, Wests coach Roy Masters fostered a battlers image at the club, calling them the fibro mob compared with the silvertail set from Manly. Wests' new coach, Laurie Freier, had coached Easts to a losing grand final against Wally's Brisbane team in the 1984 Panasonic Cup. Freier's civilising influence had not yet permeated Wests. When the Broncos walked into their warm-up area they were roundly abused by the fibro mob. Perhaps Wests' new citizenry perceived the Broncos as interstate silvertails. Wally glared about. "What annoys me is that those who are calling out Wally wanks or sucks or whatever, are often eight and nine-year-old kids," he said. "They parrot the adults and don't even know what it means."

The Broncos won 38–4, despite referee Mick Stone's 11–2 penalty count in favour of Wests. The crowd howled down the Broncos' best moves and Wally, in response, made a hand gesture indicating he could not care less. After the final whistle three police and several officials protected Wally as he was surrounded by hundreds of jostling spectators, mostly children seeking his autograph. Police warned off a youth and his girlfriend for throwing plastic bottles of soft drink at Wally. Another long queue of children waited for autographs outside the dressingroom. Manager John Ribot asked Wally if he was OK. "I saw a couple of those bottles in the air," he said. There was a knock on the dressingroom door. The Wests cheer squad, consisting of seven young girls, had seen the jeering and the flying plastic bottles and wanted to apologise to Wally for the crowd's behaviour. Bennett introduced them to Wally and their beaming faces did much to restore his faith in Sydneysiders.

Small boys kept wangling their way in, clutching autograph books. Said one loudly, "Where's that little kid that plays for you?" The dressingroom broke up while Allan Langer pretended he did not hear. Langer became inured to such innocent children's remarks but he tired of the same from adults. Once Wally was in a bar with Langer when a drinker approached and addressed Langer, "Gees, you ARE small aren't you? How tall are you?" Wally held his breath. Langer looked evenly at the interloper and said, slowly and succinctly, "Six . . . foot . . . (*expletive*) . . . three!"

Wally was privately looking forward to playing Norths, coached by Frank Stanton. The Broncos flew to Sydney on Sunday morning and caught cabs to North Sydney Oval. On a clear, warm autumn day the team bought sandwiches and sat in a nearby park. At run-on time Bennett looked closely at an unusually thoughtful Wally. "You sure you're in the right frame of mind?" he asked. Wally glanced up. "You've forgotten who's coaching this other mob Wayne." Bennett's comprehension took a millisecond. "Oh, right. No trouble motivating you today." Norths coach Frank Stanton had been the Australian coach who dropped Wally from the Test side on the 1982 Kangaroo tour of England. Although Wally had long forgiven this, Stanton had also publicly demanded Wally be stripped of his Australian captaincy during the *King Wally* furore. The Sydney premiership promised Wally opportunities to settle a few scores.

Desperate defence saw the Broncos lucky to be level with

Norths 6–6 at half-time. Bennett, for the first time, took Wally aside for specific instructions. "We're not getting into position to attack. We've got to work for field position," he said. "We'll attack the middle of the field and catch them short on one side." Nor were the Broncos spinning the ball sufficiently wide to evade Norths' powerful pack. The Broncos ran in three second-half tries to finish 24–12 winners and to their amazement were applauded from the field. "The crowd was so well behaved," said Wally. "At Wests kids were spitting at us and even after you signed their autograph books they'd walk away and call you a wanker. It was a pleasure to play Norths." Four on the trot. A gleeful cry was being bandied from the shower recesses to the lockers, "That's another $1,500." The unbeaten Broncos were now equal competition leaders with Canterbury, but with a far superior points for-and-against aggregate.

Every week in the Sydney league was like a grand final to the Broncos. It excited many of the younger players just to hear the names let alone face the players. Eric Grothe, Steve Ella, Peter Sterling, Bob Lindner and Peter Wynn were the Kangaroo quintet who arrived with Parramatta for a Sunday showdown at Lang Park. The Broncos may have claimed the scalps of top-notchers Manly and Penrith, but the Eels, the 1986 premiers, were from rugby league's heartland, with legendary skills, guts and heroics. No other Sydney team was held in such awe.

Parramatta coach John Monie primed Wally with an unusual analysis of the Broncos' strengths in his column in the Sydney *Daily Telegraph*. He wrote:

> Wally Lewis has maximum effect for only eight minutes of a match...The only time Lewis is really a threat is when his team is in the opposition's quarter — and even then it's brute strength and not guile which makes him a danger. The simple rule is that every time Lewis sets himself to run near your line he must be hit — and hit very hard...For 90 per cent of the game it is the likes of Gene Miles and Greg Dowling who are the danger players.

Wally shrugged off the criticism. He was more concerned about Parramatta's 64–12 hammering by Manly two weeks earlier. What was the story there? Were Manly flawless on the day? Ray Price and Mick Cronin had retired and Brett Kenny was out for the year. Had Parramatta gone bad?

A record Brisbane crowd of 23,000 jeered the Eels but were quickly silenced as Parramatta jumped to a 12-2 lead within 20 minutes. One of the Eels' tries was by front-rower Peter Wynn whose last appearance at the ground had been with NSW in the third state-of-origin in 1985. Wynn took a hammering then from several Queenslanders intent on showing NSW coach Terry Fearnley he had erred in dropping them from the Test side on the just completed tour of New Zealand. Wynn later strenuously objected to criticisms of him on that tour, reported in *King Wally*.

Wynn had his revenge. Wally was marker as Parramatta played the ball about 15 metres from the Broncos line. Wally saw Wynn steaming up, moved out from marker and dived at Wynn's legs — a regulation tackle. But simultaneously Wynn, a huge strider, stepped away, skirted Wally's outstretched hands, straightened and plunged over between Greg Concescu and Chris Johns. Wally could not forgive himself. "I got up and called myself every name under the sun," he said. "I've never been so filthy with myself for missing a bloke." Bennett did not miss Wally at half-time. "Do you know who you missed?" he said pointedly. For much of the first half the Broncos looked lethargic, their defence loose, their attack blunt. They managed to keep pace with Parramatta through several pieces of opportunism, including a 95-metre solo try by Michael Hancock in a desperate race against the looming cover defensive tackle of Eric Grothe.

In the second half the Broncos' adrenal glands opened and when Allan Langer popped over for a try to give the Broncos an 18-16 lead, both Gene Miles and Wally were on hand to lift him from the ground like a rag puppet. Then the drama began. Wynn was terrorising the Broncos pack. Wally stopped him a metre from the Broncos line. Fearing Wynn would toe the ball forward for a dive-over try, Wally tripped Wynn with hand and foot. A professional foul? "Yeah," said Wally. He did not dispute referee Eddie Ward's ruling of five minutes in the sinbin. The loyal crowd chanted "Bullshit, bullshit!" Ward had excellent control and because his decision was plainly justified, there was no untoward behaviour from the packed stands. Parra's penalty made it 18–18.

The afternoon sky grew darker. From Moreton Bay a squall swept in, sheets of rain swirling beneath the floodlights, bathing the ground in a brilliant white glow. The Broncos edged ahead. Allan Langer darted towards the line but, confronted by Bob Lindner, angled a chip kick behind the defence. It was no great kick, miscueing and stopping on the soft, wet turf. Wally, back from the sinbin, followed through, almost overran the ball, cleverly toed it twice and fell upon it for a triumphant try. So Monie was right and wrong. Right that Wally was dangerous inside the opponent's quarter, wrong that he had no guile. Broncos 24, Eeels 18. "That settles it," said a Sydney visitor. "They're blessed."

Now Parra needed the ball. Wally teased them. In a ruck he held the ball tantalisingly close to the ground, hoping the marker would strike illegally and give away a penalty. Marker's foot twitched but held back. Wally looked up and smiled. Marker was Sterlo, no sucker. Minutes from the end Sterling at last got his chance. About 15 metres out from the Broncos line he twisted a full 360 degrees and arrowed in. He was in the air, he was over, he was in goal. He had only to land to score. Bryan Niebling hit him mid-air and the slippery ball popped from under Sterling's arm. He looked up in agony. The siren sounded. Sterlo explained, "He hit the ball with his fist and knocked it out of my hands. He couldn't do it again in a hundred times."

Coach Bennett was a man with a contradiction. His team showed glaring weaknesses, principally close to the ruck, but were winning. The Broncos were now outright premiership leaders. They were on a five-strong winning streak and like a downhill toboggan, gathering speed but slightly out of control. Coach Bennett was on board but could not change direction. At his Monday media lunches he said, "We're playing badly. With enthusiasm, individual skills and luck we keep coming up with wins. But we're playing terrible football."

For years the Panasonic Cup had been Brisbane's chance to challenge Sydney teams. Brisbane's 1984 Cup win was up there with state-of-origin success. Now, faced with a mid-week rematch against Penrith, the Cup was a diversion Wayne Bennett did not need. He was more concerned about the following weekend's match against fellow freshmen, the Newcastle Knights. Seven Broncos withdrew with injury and to Wally it appeared that they were likely to lose this game. Wally and Greg Dowling were also carrying mild injuries. "Why don't you pull us out too," Wally asked. Bennett replied, "I can't make a mockery of it." Wally said, "Well put two other blokes back in and pull me and GD out." Wally's argument was valid. He had a heavy representative season. Bennett refused. Wally's presence would help shield the Broncos from accusations of not taking the Panasonic Cup match seriously.

Wally was resting in his Parramatta hotel room the afternoon of the Cup game when his phone rang. A newspaper reporter downstairs with a couple of questions. "I'm trying to have a sleep before the game," said Wally. Won't take a few minutes, said the reporter. Wally, like 99 per cent of other players, on match day hated talking about the game to anyone except teammates. The reporter persisted. Just a couple of questions then he would be out of the way. Wally trudged downstairs. The interview began:

Reporter: How do you think you'll go in the game?

Wally: Well, we're very depleted but we'll give it a go.

Reporter: What? Is it still going to be depleted on Sunday?

Wally: What's that got to do with it?

Reporter: When you play the local team you'll want your top side in.

Wally (blinking, thinking he'd been asleep too long): We are playing the local team, we're at Parramatta aren't we?

Reporter: No, no, no, the Newcastle side.

Wally: Where did you say you were from?

Reporter: I didn't. I'm from the *Newcastle Herald*.

Wally: What interest is this game to you blokes?

Reporter: None. I'm writing about Sunday's game.

Wally blew up: Spare me bloody days mate. Fair dinkum, do you mind if I get this one over with first?

Wally rose to terminate the interview but the reporter pleaded that if he didn't get the story his editor had told him not to bother returning to work. Wally said he was sorry, it was not his problem. He told the reporter to punch the editor's lights out if he was sacked. The reporter, in a subsequent story, wrote that Wally had offered to punch the editor's lights out. In the event the editor's lights were preserved because Wally consented to the interview over a snack of spaghetti and chicken. Afterwards he had just returned to his room to reclaim his shut-eye when the reporter reappeared at his door. He had forgotten about six footballs the newspaper wanted Wally to sign to give away as a match promotion. Wally swore a blue streak and waved a pen over the leathers. Thus while the rest of the Broncos Panasonic Cup team slumbered in their rooms Wally helped promote the following week's match.

In teeming rain at Parramatta Stadium the Broncos played as though they wished they weren't there. Trailing 24–0 at half-time, more passes had been dropped than held. Penrith were content and the match dragged to a 24–10 end. As Wally slumped in the dressingroom Bennett said, " Well, that's out of the way, isn't it." Penrith felt avenged for their close loss a month before at Lang Park. Sydney collectively celebrated with one memorable newspaper headline, "Good On Yer, Panthers", revealing the depth of antagonism towards the Broncos. Already there was talk that because of the Broncos winning streak, Brisbane should field two teams, from north and south of the river. The Broncos Panasonic loss merely whetted Sydney's appetite for a Broncos premiership defeat.

Steelworks city and coalfields capital Newcastle has a rugby league tradition as old as the game. The city has retained more of its identity and spirit than its industrial sister in the south, Port Kembla, home of the Illawarra Steelers. Inviting Newcastle into the Sydney premiership was as masterly a stroke as including Brisbane. The Knights easily led the competition in drawing large hometown crowds and their fans genuinely believed the rough-riding Knights would be the first in the competition to tame the Broncos.

The Broncos travelling caravan of 60 footballers and auxiliaries flew to Sydney where three Fokkers ferried them

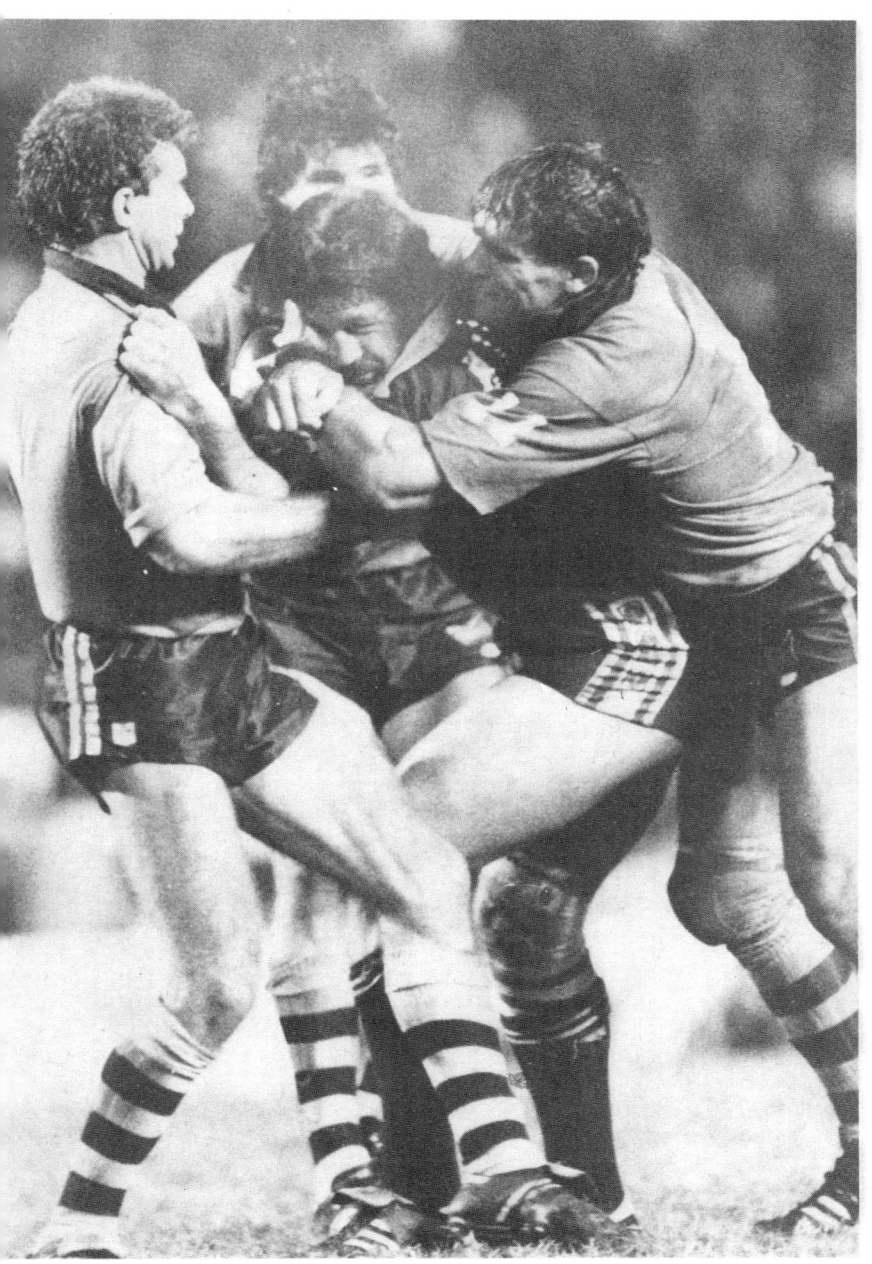

1987. How to stop Gene Miles — NSW's Brian Johnston, Les Davidson and Pat Jarvis in the first Origin.

1987. Wally does a Geno despite NSW's Mark McGaw (tackling) and Brett Kenny in the second Origin.

1987. Second Origin, from left: Brett Kenny, Garry Jack (obscured), Wayne Pearce, Dale Shearer, Allan Langer, and Brian Johnston (right) are hunting — but Wally is the one catching the ball.

1987. Muddy marvels — Wally and Allan Langer after winning the second Origin before a record crowd.

1987. Gene Miles doesn't give Brett Kenny an inch in the third Origin at Lang Park.

1987. Wally, right eye swollen, and Allan Langer, jubilant after winning the third Origin.

1987. Gary Belcher, Peter Jackson, Colin Scott and Wally after winning the third Origin and the series.

1987. Wally holds aloft the Origin shield on which he and Brett Kenny are engraved.

1987. Coach Wally watches Wynnum with
Gene Miles, Peter Tunks and Australian coach
Don Furner the day before the Kiwi Test.

1987. Fierce faced Sam Stewart leads the Kiwis
in a haka before the Test at Lang Park.

1987. Gene Miles in classic pose. Sam Stewart, driving low, and Shane Cooper are the Kiwis.

1987. Australian trainer Larry Britton attends Wally after he injured his neck in the Lang Park Test. Kiwi fullback Darrell Williams and referee Neville Kesha look on.

1987. Real Aussie rugby league! The ugly spear tackle poster advertising the fourth Origin in L.A.

1987. Wally acknowledges the victor in L.A. An embarrassed Peter Sterling pulled his arm down.

Lang Park Trust chief Ron McAuliffe (left) and QRL executive Ross Livermore — challenged by the Broncos.

ARL secretary Bob Abbott (left) and president Ken Arthurson with Ron McAuliffe — a Brisbane team, but which consortium?

1987. QRL president Bill Hunter belatedly toasts the yes-no-yes decision to send a team to Sydney.

1987. Wally formally signs. Broncos manager John Ribot (left) and director Gary Balkin supervise.

Broncos director Paul Morgan — played it tough.

Broncos director Steve Williams — it was his idea.

1987. Broncos directors Barry Maranta (left) and Gary Balkin launch their snorting steed.

THE TEAM TO BEAT IN 88

THE T   T IN 88

1988. Allan Langer's first try for the Broncos, in a trial against Canberra. Gary Belcher is the Raider.

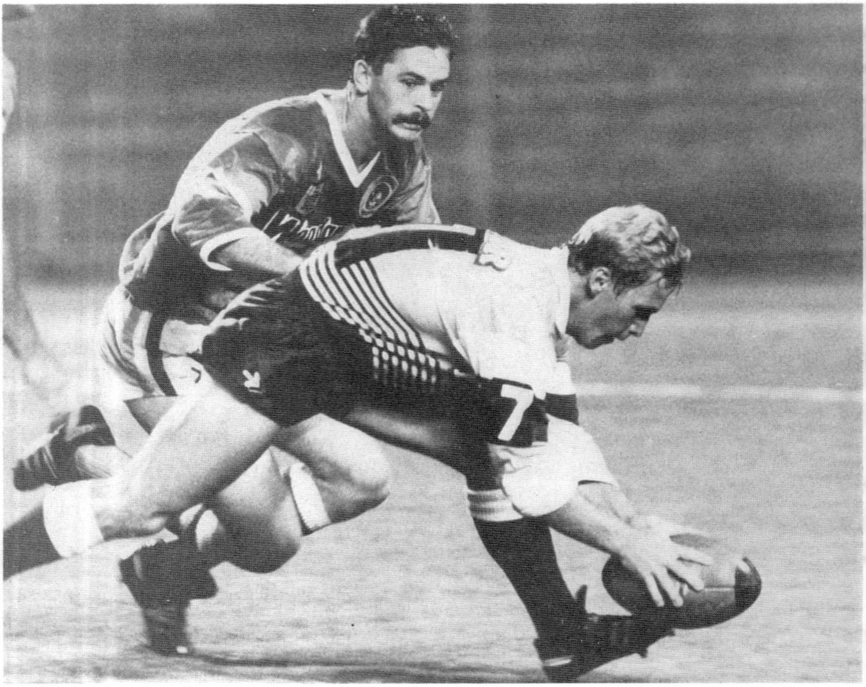

Manly's Cliff Lyons hangs ineffectually onto Wally in the Broncos' amazing 44-10 victory.

Wally triumphant after toeing the ball through to score the winning try against Parramatta.

Welcome to Sydney football! Greg Dowling collides with Balmain's Paul Sironen. Benny Elias is at right.

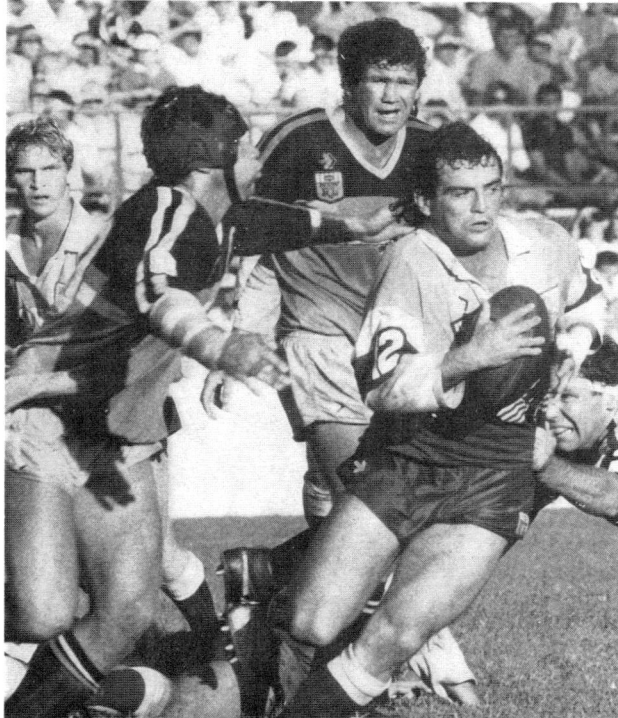

The dream run ends. Wally and lock Terry Matterson after the Broncos' first defeat, by Balmain.

Watched by Gold Coast's Peter Smith, Greg Conescu flees Ron Gibbs during the Broncos' shock loss.

A Giant hit. Gold Coast's Ron Gibbs and the tackle that dislocated Wally's shoulder.

Wally appeals, unsuccessfully, to referee Bill Harrigan against a St George try. The Broncos won 26-22.

Wally distributes in the Broncos' waterlogged win over Illawarra at Wollongong Showground.

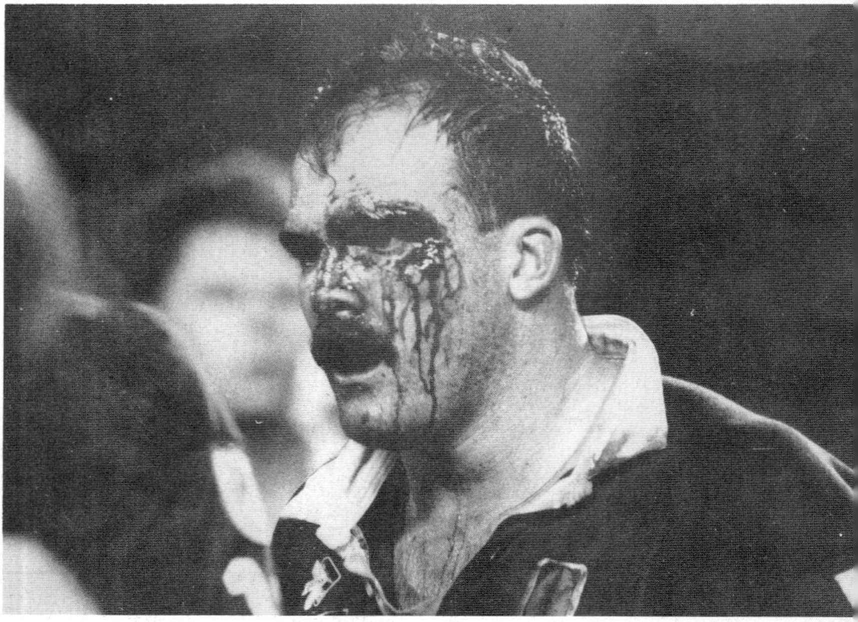

1988. Martin Bella, nicknamed Eddie Munster, bleeds for the maroons in the second Origin.

1988. Sam Backo in agony as a trainer resets a dislocated finger in the same match.

1988. Allan Langer after the second of his two magical tries in the first Origin. Joe Kilroy is elated. NSW fullback Jonathan Docking deflated. Referee is Barry Gomersall, alias the "Grasshopper".

1988. Wally, pestered by Terry "Ba" Lamb, on the burst towards Michael O'Connor in the second Origin. Tony Currie (left) and Trevor Gillmeister are in support.

1988. Superb broken field runner Garry Jack rounds Peter Jackson and Wally during the second Origin.

1988. Second Origin culprit, Steve Roach, gets two handfuls of sinbin from referee Mick Stone.

1988. Start of the beer-can Origin incident. Wally takes out Phil Daley centre stage. Others are (from left) Tony Currie, Allan Langer, Bob Lindner and Steve Roach (both obscured) referee Mick Stone, Paul Langmack, Sam Backo and Steve Folkes.

1988. Why it rained beer cans. On the linesman's word, referee Mick Stone gives Wally five minutes.

1987. Happier days with Wynnum. Wally, despite being penalised, shares a laugh with referee Ian Irwin.

1988. Rarely seen — Wayne Bennett smiling, chaired by Wally and Martin Bella, after the second Origin win.

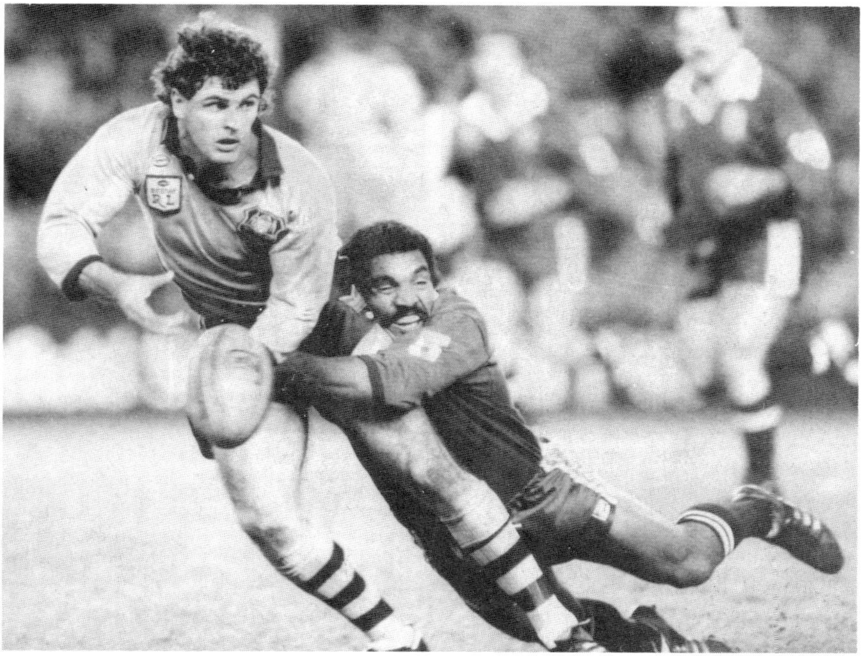

1988. Queensland's winger, Joe Kilroy, halts Michael O'Connor — no mean feat — in the third Origin.

Australian coach Don Furner — respected Wally.

British coach Mal Reilly — won one Test.

1988. The game cock and Black Power — Andy Gregory and skipper Ellery Hanley after downing Newcastle.

1988. The fastest man in rugby league. British winger Martin Offiah stretches his athlete's legs.

The 1988 centenary Test. Wally indulges in a little Bulldog baiting with Andy Gregory. Ellery Hanley intercedes while Britain's Phil Ford and Australia's Tony Currie look on.

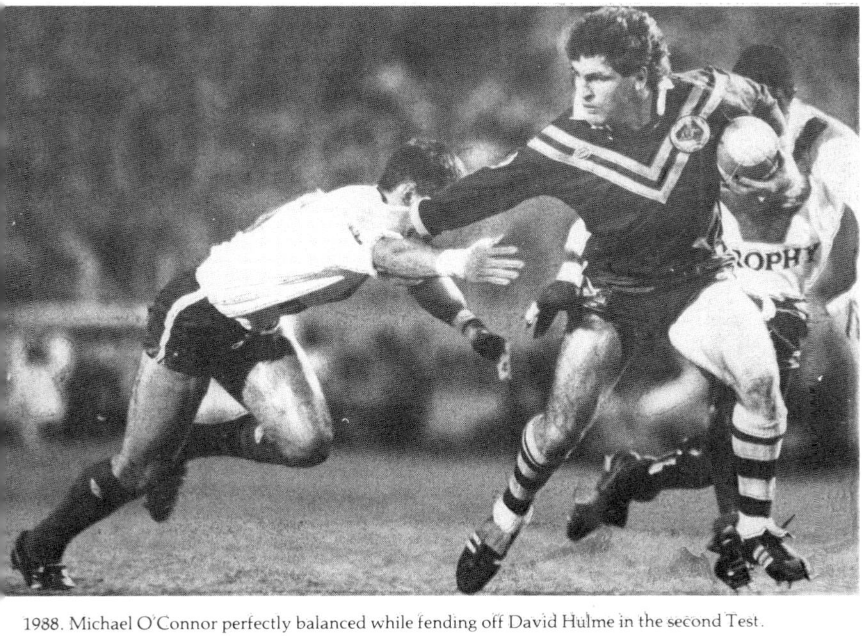

1988. Michael O'Connor perfectly balanced while fending off David Hulme in the second Test.

1988. Kevin Ward dispenses with one Aussie and takes on Wally and Sam Backo in the second Test.

1988. Clash of the quick men. Andrew Ettinghausen eludes Britain's Martin Offiah in the second Test.

1988. Boots and all. Martin Offiah and Phil Loughlin harrass Sam Backo in the third Test.

1988. Ellery Hanley — Led the British Lions, but looked even better as a Balmain Tiger.

End of the Broncos' 1988 road. Wally dejected after the last match loss to Balmain.

Broncos sponsor Bernie Power and Allan Langer sample the new brew.

1988. Wally nurses his painful broken arm soon after retiring from the World Cup final.

Two adoring fans — sons Mitchell (left) and Lincoln greet Dad at Brisbane airport.

Using a huge arm protector Mal Meninga survived this Presidents XIII match against Britain. Soon after, playing for Australia against the Rest of the World, Meninga tragically broke his arm again.

Wally calls this his new relaxation! He later survived a 100 kph crash at the Exhibition Speedway.

Life after football: Wally Lewis, television newsreader.

Jacqui with Lincoln, 10 months and Mitchell, 2 years — looking forward to seeing more of Wally.

Into 1989. Wally emerges from the Canungra jungle at the Broncos' tough pre-season training camp.

north to Newcastle in atrocious weather. The flight exposed some poor flyers in the side. "It was stormy and blowing us around and even though I'm a good flyer I got a bit windy," said Wally. "But Bennett, Langer and Colin Scott were cases. Langer's the worst. He's a disgrace. Even the sound of the wheels retracting scares him." At touchdown Langer, lathered in sweat, finally ceased choking the armrests on his seat and declared, "Never again!" He had a few friends. On Sunday evening, after the match, the white-knuckle brigade, Bennett, Langer and Scott, opted for a two-hour drive to Sydney rather than relive the 30-minute horror hop by aircraft.

Ticket sales for the match were boosted by a controversy begun by a Novocastrian entrepreneur marketing a Wally-Buster T-shirt depicting King Wally eye-to-eye with a football Knight. Wally has become so famous his Christian name is a byword in rugby league. It is easy to forget that his name, and portrait, are his legal property and that anyone seeking to profit from their use should first seek his permission and probably offer him some compensation. A Knights spokesman said their supporters club had designed the T-shirts and proceeds from sales were going to Newcastle's junior rugby league. Wally countered that he was happy to donate his percentage to the Broncos juniors. Basically Wally wished the Knights had exhibited a little courtesy but at John Ribot's request did not proceed with any legal action.

After the match a Knights official approached Wally with a bag. The official said, "There's something in here for you. We hope it will suffice. We apologise if we upset you and hope this will make up for it." Wally felt the bag. Could it be a slice of the T-shirt action? He opened the zip and pulled out three Wally-Buster T-shirts. "There's one for you, one for your wife and one for your son," said the nervous official. Wally smiled. The whole matter was such small beer he did not have the heart to reject them. He said, "Oh thanks mate, I'll make sure I look after them." He has found them useful too, every time he polishes the car. Newcastle may think Wally ungrateful, but they have not suffered a decade of their name being exploited, abused and misused.

Sunday morning, match day, was time for Wally, Gene and Colin Scott to liven up their Newcastle stay. Wally inquired, "Who are we going to get?" Gene and Scotty chorused, "Anybody!" Wally, who is a passing good mimic, dialled general manager John Ribot in the hotel and pretended to be Sydney *Daily Telegraph* rugby league writer, Ray Chesterton. Wally put on the voice, "Mate, I hear there's a bit of controversy about those Wally-Buster T-shirts?" Ribot agreed that Wally was upset. "It's understandable because there's probably a few dollars in it somewhere," he said. Wally was giggling a treat, his hand over the mouthpiece. Ribot continued, "He gets crap put on him everywhere he goes...But you know Wally mate, he gets carried away and he's just getting carried away here as well." Wally's expression changed and he reverted to his own voice. "Is that so Reebs? I'm getting carried away, you low cat, you won't even back me up!" Ribot stuttered into the phone. Who's that, who's speaking? "It's me, you weak bastard." Ribot forced a laugh, "Oh mate, I knew it was you all the time, ha ha." Wally hung up and 60 seconds later there was a knock on his door. "Rack off, you're as weak as piss!" called Wally. Ribot protested his innocence outside while Wally, Gene and Scotty rolled about inside. They pulled the same trick on promotions officer Kev Keliher but Wally hung up without revealing the subterfuge. Miles said, "You should have let him know." Said Wally, "No, it's better this way. We'll get him at the awards night."

That week Fatty Vautin, tossing around ideas for his newspaper column, rang Wally and said, "I'm going to give it to GD (Greg Dowling). How's he been going?" Wally thought Dowling's form was fine but that everybody kept writing he was going like a busted backside. Said Vautin, "Yeah, I've seen a few of his games. He's going OK, but he's not breaking any records. I think I'll give him a kick in the ribs." Vautin wrote in his Sydney *Sunday Telegraph* column:

> Wayne Bennett must be concerned with the form of one of his forwards who has a reputation as one of the hardest and toughest men around. But at the moment his form is said to be about as hard as a Tontine pillow.

Someone dropped a copy of the column outside Dowling's hotel room on Sunday morning. Though GD knew Vautin was writing tongue-in-cheek no player likes to see his form publicly questioned, especially if he senses it contains a grain of truth. Dowling bore enormous responsibilty in those early Broncos days. He was their sole big forward, their best ball runner and their most constructive distributor. Dowling is a noted big match and wet weather performer and Newcastle's International Sports Centre supplied both that afternoon. The stands were awash with umbrellas which shook with ecstasy when the Knights ran on and fanned to both sides of the field to greet a record 30,220 fans.

Gene Miles had an inauspicious first half. Bennett had impressed upon the players they were not to push their passes with the slippery ball. Yet 25 minutes into the game, the first time Gene handled, he threw a dicey, one-handed pass which Chris Johns could not gather. Then, two minutes before half-time, Miles ran the ball 15 metres from the Broncos line and pushed another loose pass, this time to Joe Kilroy. No fault of Kilroy, the ball went astray and presented a gift try to Newcastle. Miles was crestfallen but Wally felt dutybound to speak to him. "Show some bloody brains," he snapped. "You're a better player than that. I just hope you're going to make up for it later." Bennett understands Wally and Gene's special relationship and sometimes thinks Wally goes overboard, asking too much of Gene. In this case Bennett was not so gentle either at half-time. "I'm glad the PA was blasting through our dressing-room," said Miles, "because it drowned out some of what Wayne had to say. I deserved every word of it."

The Broncos rode a Dowling-dominated pack to a 24–10 win, Miles sealing the match with a surging, solo try. So both errant Test men, GD and Geno, came good. Bennett had been curiously critical of Allan Langer's attack after the Parramatta game but refused to reveal why. He repeated his dissatisfaction after the Knights match and he eventually told me why. "Allan is a fine individual player," he said. "When he gets his hands on the ball he's so good he never has to play for the team. But at our level he has to initiate plays as well. That's where Wally's so great. He tells forwards to take the ball there or run here because he can see gaps they can't. Allan's been living on the ball he has in his hands. But he has to think ahead, help others and set them up."

Despite the storm in a T-shirt Wally enjoyed his Newcastle visit. It gave him a charge to see rugby league and its followers so vitally involved. "The competition's best sportstown by a mile," he pronounced. Wayne Bennett organised a police contingent to escort Wally from the field but it was not necessary. The only untoward incident was a farce generated by Ray Hadley, Ray Price's rugby league co-commentator on Sydney radio station 2UE. Monday morning's newspaper published a photograph of Wally apparently blowing up referee Greg McCallum, with a hand on the ref's shoulder, after McCallum awarded Newcastle a try.

Hadley demanded that NSWRL general manager John Quayle investigate the incident with a view to indicting Wally with one of the most serious charges in the game, manhandling a referee. In fact Wally was drawing McCallum's attention to Broncos winger Joe Kilroy who had been injured trying to stop the Knights try. On field McCallum at first had told Wally, "No, it's a fair try." Wally had said, "I know, I know, I'm not arguing, one of our blokes needs a doc quick." McCallum glanced at Kilroy and immediately whistled for medical help. Kilroy went off on a stretcher and McCallum told Wally before play resumed, "Sorry, I thought you were disputing the try." After contacting McCallum and hearing the correct sequence of events Quayle dismissed the media inquisition against Wally. Weeks later Wally bumped into McCallum and the referee volunteered, "I couldn't believe that inquiry. I didn't think you even got close to me."

The following Tuesday night, after training, the Broncos gathered for their weekly Goose of the Week awards. Wally had already awarded one to Fatty Vautin on the phone the previous night. Wally had pleasure in telling Vautin, "I don't think GD is too flash with you." Vautin answered, "Yeah, I know, he had a big game. If we're both in the state-of-origin side I'll just hide for the first 24 hours until he settles down." At training the

Goose nominations flooded in. Geno for his pass to the invisible man, Chris Johns for turning up late at the airport again. Johns had a habit of reporting to Australian Airlines if they flew Ansett and vice versa, and the Broncos even held a plane for him once. The final nomination was promotions man Kev Keliher. Keliher was astounded. What for? For talking to the media. So bloody what? Wally went into his mime, "Gooday Kev, Ray Chesterton here, about those Wally-Buster T-shirts..." *Touche!*

With six wins from six matches, and now undisputed premiership leaders, the Broncos were in fine fettle as they prepared for Balmain. But their bonhomie clothed internal stresses which were about to crack the Broncos wide open. Some senior players were not consistently measuring up, some rookies were good for one match but not another. Moments of magical play were offset by elementary errors. The whole winning sequence had been held together by a fine skein of genuine talent, enormous verve and good fortune. But with every passing week the pressure grew. Newcastle and the Gold Coast were suffering expected losses. The Broncos felt an inevitable, impending fate. They feared not so much a loss, but life after defeat.

9 ...AND DISASTER

After six weeks running free the Broncos were about to be stalked by the Balmain Tigers. "I knew we weren't playing with enough discipline to survive," said coach Wayne Bennett. "We had enormous commitment and enthusiasm, but no discipline. Once another team matched us for the first two and were better disciplined, they were going to kick our backsides."

At first blush Balmain were no threat. In six matches they had scored only 81 points against Brisbane's 174. The Balmain backs did not exactly personify strikepower compared with Lewis, Langer and Miles. Coach Warren Ryan had encountered Wally once before, when Canterbury-Bankstown lost to Brisbane in the quarter-finals of the 1984 Panasonic Cup. Ryan was now unstinting in his praise. "I think he is the smartest footballer I have seen," he said. "The reason he is so unpredictable is that he has so many areas he can be creative in. He has made a few boneheads down here eat their words."

Ryan was studiously ignoring Balmain's obvious strength. Wayne Pearce was ill with viral meningitis but Steve Roach and Paul Sironen represented double the hitting power of Greg Dowling. Bennett had waged his own propaganda campaign to convince any who would listen that Brisbane did not need forwards who would run in like a smash-up derby to assert authority in the first 10 minutes. However Broncos consultant Bob Bax was writing differently. He observed in his *Sunday Mail* column:

While the Broncos forwards are holding their own, they don't ruck the ball up with the same intense hostility as players like Peter Wynn, Phil Daley, Peter Kelly and Mark Geyer. The Broncos defence is strong...But here again the Sydney defence is hell-bent on putting the opposition out of action.

Before a Lang Park crowd approaching 20,000 and a live television audience of a million, the Broncos lost a close struggle 26–18. The defeat may be exemplified in four acts — three errors by young Broncos and one con job by wily Benny Elias. First act: former Sydney Easts junior, lock Terry Matterson, kicked out on the full when restarting play. From that handy possession Balmain scored. Second act: young Stanthorpe winger Michael Hancock saved a ball from going into touch by knocking it back towards his line. In the confusion Broncos fullback Colin Scott thought the ball had gone out, Balmain's Scott Gale knew it hadn't and scored. Teenager Hancock lay face down and slammed his fist into the turf. A few Broncos forwards, flushed from grappling in the furnace with Roach and Sironen, muttered about making Hancock join them for a while. Wally put a hand on Hancock's shoulder. "C'mon mate, you know you've done wrong. Sulking's not going to help anyone." Third act: young Oakey centre Rohan Teevan, three minutes from full-time, dived over for a try but his body height was too high, allowing Test fullback Garry Jack to cannon in underneath and jolt the ball from his arms.

The *coup de grace* was delivered by Benny Elias. Wally knew Elias had all the skills. "It was just a case of when he was going to show the lot," he said. "What sets him apart from other hookers is that he can kick so well. If you asked Turtle and Royce Simmons to kick the ball you'd get some light-hearted entertainment." At 18–18 referee Graham Annesley awarded Balmain a penalty from a scrum. From that gift Balmain rucked to within four metres of the Broncos line. Said Wally, "I heard Benny calling out 'Field goal, field goal!' and I set myself to charge the kick down. Then something clicked. Elias never telegraphed a field goal in his life." Too late. Elias spun out from the ruck with the ball held in one hand, dummied outrageously and speared through a thin Broncos defence to score.

Disappointment shrouded the Broncos dressingroom. There was no relief at their winning streak ending, no lifting of any pressure. Coach Bennett was not angry with the young Broncos. "That's the price you pay when you have kids in the team," he said philosophically. But he was angry when Warren Ryan returned to Sydney waving the formula to beat the Broncos — through the forwards. In defence of his pack, Bennett quoted Jack Gibson. "Jack told me the first thing a player needs is football ability," said Bennett. "You don't want someone who is mad or big. If you do have one and he can play then it's a bonus." Wally knew what to expect. A Sydney scribe had warned him what the theme would be: the Broncos were finished as grand final hopes; Balmain had shown Brisbane had nothing up the middle; teams would steamroll them there all year.

Warren Ryan questioned the legality of Allan Langer's tackling. Ryan wrote in the *Sydney Morning Herald*:

> Allan Langer...at times employs a very doubtful style of tackling. It is reminiscent of the outlawed "Cumberland Throw" and involves throwing the ball-carrier over his leg.

NSWRL referees co-ordinator Denis Braybrook commented that he could see no problems with Langer's mode of tackling. "If a player first grabs hold of an opponent he is permitted to use the leg in the tackle," Braybrook said. "If he uses the leg first it is illegal." Langer had perfected his style — a variation on the Asian martial arts theory of turning your opponent's strength to your advantage — to bring down players heavier than himself. And that was just about everyone. Wally, first opportunity, told Langer, "They had a go at me, they had a go at GD and now he's showing better form, it's somebody else's turn. Yours. It'll go on and on." In the Broncos' early matches, forwards deliberately selected Langer as the small-man, weak-link to run at in the Broncos defence. Wally said, "They tried to smash through him and he just knocked them over. They got shitty because the harder they ran the harder they fell. They soon learned."

Right in the thick of the hurly burly, controversy-ridden,

back-biting, knock-'em-down Sydney rugby league premiership, the Broncos were back to being equal competition leaders.
When the team gathered to train for their away match against
Cronulla, Bennett signalled his growing impatience. "I'm sick of
penalties," he said. "Players are giving in to their feelings and
it has to stop." It was no secret he was referring to two penalties
conceded to Balmain, both on the fifth tackle when Brisbane
was due to regain possession. The culprits were Test men Miles
and Dowling. "Gene got roughed up in a tackle and retaliated,"
said Bennett. "GD wanted to show Roach he still had some
gorilla in him."

Penalties may have hindered the Broncos against Balmain,
but how to diagnose the Broncos' malaise against Cronulla?
Some exotic virus must have infected the team's bloodstream.
They played like a spent team, their reserves of nervous energy
exhausted. They could scarcely manage the semblance of first-
class rugby league.

Wally's head thumped the ground as he missed a tackle on
fleeing Cronulla halfback Barry Russell. Wally shook his head
and looked at the scoreboard, 18-0. Then he looked at the clock
and saw 7 minutes. "We're down 18-0 with only seven minutes
to go in this half," he thought. Then his head cleared. No. They
had only been playing 7 minutes! Surely not. The bad dream
flooded back. The first try had come after just two minutes. "It's
hard to say to your team, 'This is where we're going wrong',
when you've only been on two minutes," said Wally.

Cronulla were running the angles on Brisbane. They moved the
ball slowly across field and as soon as a Bronco moved up too fast
and broke the straight line of defence, Cronulla attacked the gap
furiously. Every team in the competition knew it as the Jack
Gibson trademark left upon Cronulla. The Broncos had never met
Cronulla before. It was all new to the new boys. In reply the
Broncos offered knock-ons, pushed passes, missed tackles,
handovers — the full spectrum of football errors. The final score,
38-8, did not sufficiently humiliate the Broncos for some Cronulla
fans. As Wally signed autographs, surrounded by 200 spectators,
teenagers began chanting "Wally Sucks". He was determined not
to give them the satisfaction of forcing him off. He kept signing

and after a few minutes the chanting waned and died. Then a boy, aged about sixteen, belted Wally heavily on the back. Wally growled at a security guard, "If you blokes don't grab this clown I'll look after him myself." Police nabbed the teenager and asked Wally if he wanted to press charges. He told them he would prefer it if they took the lad outside for an old-fashioned reminder of how to behave.

All the way back to the dressingroom a line of people chanted insults at him. He stopped once or twice to stare an adult in the eye and the crowd in the immediate vicinity would hush, like garden crickets at the approach of footsteps, only to start up again as Wally moved on. Wayne Bennett heard and saw. "I'd hate to be him," he said. "He's had a tough contest, he's got 100 kids lining up for autographs, he's trying to cooperate and he gets bagged." Wally stayed in Sydney overnight to join a television team covering the next day's main game and read the Sunday newspapers: if the Broncos were condemned for their Balmain loss, now the papers said they wouldn't even make the semi-finals.

Wally put the losses behind him as he and Jacqui prepared to dine with the Queen on the royal yacht *Britannia* moored in the Brisbane River for Expo. Jacqui, a former young Labor party member and no royalist, was delighted with the invitation. "You change quick!" noted Wally. Their Mercedes was out of action so they borrowed Jacqui's mother's battered old blue Gemini and drove to Newstead wharf at 7 p.m. Wally had been told, in error, it was not formal and so had worn a dark suit. Jacqui's long cocktail dress was appropriate but, to Wally's embarrassment, every male wore a dinner suit. "This is bloody lovely," he muttered. On board, during aperitifs and savouries, Wally gazed about the two dozen or so distinguished guests until he saw two familar faces, Bob and Hazel Hawke. Hazel chatted with Jacqui who has an easy manner with dignitaries. Jacqui is homespun, straight talking, and without pretence. Hazel is equally down to earth and they were soon swapping stories about the Lewis household and The Lodge. Wally congratulated the prime minister on his recent hole-in-one. At a command they formed a semi-circle to be introduced to the

Queen. "I've met you before haven't I, you're the rugby player," she said. Wally put in a plug for his game, "Yes, Your Majesty, rugby league." He had met her 11 years before when the Australian schoolboys rugby union tourists visited Buckingham Palace. When the Queen passed down the line an elderly English guest remarked jovially, "You must be very famous if Her Majesty knows you." Wally replied, "I think she might have been drummed up on it mate." It is doubtful that any other male guest, not even Bob Hawke, used the great Australian term of comradeship on board *Britannia* that night.

The party moved in to the dining-room and Wally found himself sitting between the Queen's secretary and Pixie Skase, wife of television mogul and Brisbane Bears bankroller, Christopher Skase. Jacqui was at another table with Skase. The royal secretary wanted to tell Wally what a tough life it was looking after the Queen but Wally brushed him as a right royal bore. Apart from Her Majesty he found the most daunting presence to be the personal valet behind every seated guest. Wally's valet moved noiselessly except for the rustle of his starched uniform. Wally felt he had to eat quickly to satisfy the gloved hand of his valet hovering like a chickenhawk to dive for his plate. Since the menu was written in French he was never sure what he was eating anyway. "To top it all," he said, "when the Queen finished her feed, that was it. She up and left, and we, who were only half finished, had to get up and follow her out."

Wally inquired discreetly of his man, "Where do you have a leak around here mate?" The valet blanched, "I beg your pardon?" Wally thought he had been speaking the Queen's English. He explained it more simply, "Where's the toilet?" The valet motioned with his hand, "Follow me, sir." Wally hastened after him, "It's all right, I reckon I can find it, just tell me where it is." But the valet would not be discarded. Wally followed until the fellow lead the way through one door into a bathroom and then propped, held open a second door, and stood aside. There, in front of Wally, was the giant floor phone, as Barry McKenzie so fondly termed it. The valet waited outside and as Wally emerged showed him the soap and handbasin and stood with towel at the ready. Wally gave him a "Turn it up mate" scowl and escaped back to the guests.

The Queen had adjourned to the deck where another 200 guests had joined the exclusive party to listen to a band, while the public gazed up at the spectacle from the wharf. Greg and Judy Chappell provided the Lewises with some friendly company but at 11 p.m. Wally called it a night. As he and Jacqui reached the old blue Gemini they noted a large Rolls Royce, its passenger seats facing each other like a royal carriage, warming up beside them. "This is a bit of a contrast," Wally laughed. Sitting in the Rolls was Christopher Skase. Top Bear peered down at Top Bronco, raised his eyebrows, and cruised off.

The Broncos, who had promised so much, were now performing no better than the hapless Bears. Crisis meetings were the order at the Broncos' Red Hill bunker. The directors were getting twitchy as their $4 million dollar showboat sprang leaks. The first step to protect their investment was to ban Wally from tarrying to sign autographs after matches. The possibility of injury from some brainless youth was too great. Though Wally accepted the ban it saddened him that such a direction was necessary. With the Broncos, Wally had suddenly become accessible as never before to thousands of NSW schoolchildren. He had been the QRL's schools liaison officer and if the Australian captain could not safely sign autographs after club matches in Sydney then rugby league was the ultimate loser.

The Broncos directors had performed well for the players. Of the 53 players on their books only one, a junior, was unemployed. Of the senior players 10 had better jobs than before, largely due to the directors' connections. They had organised bank loans, supplied business advice and were putting some juniors through college. The directors knew only too well they should not interfere with the playing side of the club, but being ex-players they also knew just enough to be dangerous. They were all winners in their own business careers and didn't take kindly to defeat.

The clubhouse provided the directors with their opportunity to meddle. Steve Williams made known to several players his displeasure at consecutive losses. Wally had a mild spat with Gary Balkin, with whom he had been friends for years. Another evening Wally found himself on the receiving end of a Paul

Morgan mouthful. He sensibly excused himself, found Wayne Bennett and the coach intervened. Soon after, general manager John Ribot rang Bennett one Monday morning and said the directors wanted to see him. "You're kidding," Bennett exclaimed. Before signing with the Broncos he had stipulated one inviolable rule to the directors: he wanted sole control, with no interference. He told Ribot, "If the players hear I'm under pressure that's the first thing that will destabilise the club."

Bennett agreed to attend but, like the good coach he is, arrived well prepared. When Paul Morgan began running a player down Bennett stopped him. "Paul, I played with you," he said. "You were never perfect. You made mistakes. I saw days you didn't compete. Days when you didn't run." Morgan countered. "Yeah, but they're getting greater rewards today." Bennett fired back: "It's nothing to do with rewards Paul. You used to play your arse off. You wanted to play well every weekend. But you didn't always do it. You didn't always have a go and what was your problem?" Bennett had him and Morgan knew it, because there was never an athlete who trained longer, never a footballer who played harder than young Paul Morgan. If he couldn't consistently produce his best form — and he didn't — then nobody could. It did not ease the board's collective hatred of losing but every director rolled back through his own football career until he hit an inexplicable off day and recognised the truth of Bennett's argument.

The battle was over. "You've all played the game enough to know what's right," Bennett concluded. "We need your support privately and publicly. If the team thinks you're filthy on a player it's going to put everyone under pressure and we've already got enough of that." Bennett did not hear from the directors again. They too had a learning curve, which embraced the humble art of accepting defeat. Bennett personally likes them all, as does Wally. "They're good blokes really," said Wally. "They occasionally buy you a beer at the club but they're usually busy entertaining their own guests."

Bronco team changes were in the offing. Young Cronulla prop Craig Dimond had prodded a tender Bronco bruise when he said, "The Broncos forwards aren't big and they don't hit hard." Broncos prop Andrew Tessman, Wally's lanky young comrade from Wynnum, was needed to support Dowling. A place also had to be found for Miles-sized centre, Brett Plowman. At team talks Wayne Bennett thought the team's intensity had dropped off markedly. Greg Dowling wondered whether the Broncos were as good as they thought they were. John Ribot said a mental, as much as physical, adjustment was needed for Sydney football. Ribot told me, "In Brisbane, Wally intimidated opponents and worked at his own pace. In Sydney, players were wary of him, but not awed. He had to learn to work that much harder." The team's confidence was ebbing. Attention was focused on the starts the Broncos had been giving their opponents: 12–2 to Parramatta, 14–0 to Balmain, 20–0 to Cronulla. In the Brisbane competition, matches used to develop a momentum as the players warmed to the task. Sydney teams exploded straight into action, revving themselves up with Grand Prix starts the Broncos then had to overtake.

Which made it all the more depressing, and incomprehensible, when the Broncos traipsed off Lang Park at half-time against Easts down 14–0. All Wally could think was that the Broncos would have to score three tries just to draw level. Worse, the crowd roundly booed the Broncos as they walked off. Wally was shocked. "That's the first time in 10 years I'd heard a Lang Park crowd do that," he said. "It affected everyone. We all thought, 'Fancy them booing us off'. And we decided to do something about it." The crowd had every right to voice their disenchantment. Brisbane, with a home crowd average of over 18,000 was second only to Newcastle as the largest in the competition. The Broncos directors needed good crowds to support their investment and the Broncos were not giving full value.

Bennett remained calm during the break. He reinforced what he had said all week. No one could do the job for the Broncos except themselves. He did have a chop at Wally and Allan Langer for not spreading the ball wide. Dynamic Langer at times searched too long for breaks which delayed the ball. Wally, trying to lead by example, was running with the ball more often than normal. Between them they were strangling the flow to the outside backs.

That was the first occasion Bennett specifically criticised Wally's play. It could have been awkward, given Wally's seniority, but to Bennett's relief it was not. "The good part about Wally is that he cops it sweet when he knows he's done wrong," said Bennett. "He handles it as well as anyone. He doesn't like it, nobody does. But equally I don't whack into him unless I'm satisfied, unless I'm sure, he's going wrong."

Easts, with special intelligence from coach Arthur Beetson, seemed to be picking off Wally and Geno with ease. So the two of them made a virtue out of necessity. The try that took the Broncos to an 18–14 lead came through Miles running diagonally in towards the Easts goal posts. As three Easts defenders converged he one-handed a pass to Wally running at the opposite angle. It worked so sweetly Wally crossed without a hand on him. "They followed Gene like lambs," he said. "Just as we planned." A final score of 24–20 eased the pressure on the Broncos as they reverted to equal competition leaders with Canberra.

The Gold Coast Giants, who had yet to win a match, were the competition wooden spooners, but the Broncos had no illusions as they prepared for the local derby. Too many Giants personnel, from coach Bobby McCarthy down, had been overlooked by the Broncos when recruiting staff. Too many egos had been bruised. The Giants would treat this as a grand final. They even hired a psychologist to spend a session with the team. When Wally heard that, he considered it boosted the Broncos' chances considerably. Back in 1985 Wally was heavily criticised for not running with the ball. His passing and kicking games were excellent but as Bobby McCarthy had said, "For some reason he's locked his running game in a drawer." Wally had talked to various coaches about the problem. Though he thought he knew the answer he wanted a second opinion and consulted a psychologist.

In the therapist's office Wally sat down and prepared for a discussion. The psychologist asked him, "What sort of clothes do you wear?" Wally was nonplussed. The psychologist repeated his question. Wally replied, "Same clothes as every other bloke in the street wears. Have a look at them!" The psychologist paused for

30 seconds, looked up and asked, "Do you get satisfaction out of your appearance?" Wally was mystified. "Satisfaction? Pardon me, but I'm not here to talk about how I dress. I'm here to talk to you about why I'm not running with the football in matches. If I was worried about my clobber I'd go and have a look at myself in the mirror before I went out." The psychologist replied, "It's all important in the long run." When the session concluded Wally declined a second appointment. He prefers black-and-white to greys and he'd worked out his problem anyway. With class like Miles, Meninga and Kenny playing outside him, he'd grown used to moving the ball on and become lazy with his own running. Simple as that.

A record crowd — the third ground record established by the presence of the Broncos — packed the Seagulls stadium at Tweed Heads, chanting the Giants warcry, "Fe-fi-fo-fum". Wally broke a 12–12 deadlock when the Broncos received a penalty 10 metres from the Giants line. He wanted to take a quick tap but Giants winger, Ben Gonzales, retrieved the ball and held it behind his back. As referee Graham Annesley was lecturing the Giants, Wally called to the ballboy sotto voce, "Throw the ball on." The lad said, "There's a ball on the field." Wally snarled in a fierce whisper, "Throw...the...ball...on!" The ballboy complied.

Wally caught it about a metre from where Gonzales stood with his ball. Wally hissed urgently to Gene Miles, "Get outside me!" He walked up to referee Annesley with the ball out of Annesley's sight. "This the mark sir?" Annesley nodded. "I'll take a quick tap sir." Wally pulled the ball from behind his back, tapped it with his toe and charged forward. Gonzales was returning to his line with the original ball tucked under his arm, secure in the knowledge no play could occur. Wally raced past an amazed Gonzales 5 metres from the Giants line. Gonzales dropped his ball to chase as Wally plunged forward. About four Giants defenders converged — not enough. A fifth, Chris Close, may have done the trick but instead he covered Miles who would have scored had Wally decided to smuggle the ball to him. Wally dived over. The Giants' surprise turned to angry protest. Hooker Billy Johnstone and Gonzales remonstrated with Annesley. There were two balls on the field, they shouted. Not any more. Greg Conescu had surreptitiously kicked Gonzales's dropped ball to the ballboy. Wally told Annesley, "It's a fair try sir, a fair try." Annesley checked with his touch judges and awarded it. Giants coach Bobby McCarthy laughed about it later, "Full credit to Wally for his ingenuity but it should not have been a try."

The Giants, who had heroically held the Broncos to that point, were now inspired by indignation, none more so than their kamikaze back-rower Ron Gibbs. He hit Wally and then Gene Miles in successive crunching tackles. Wally struck the ground on the point of his shoulder and felt a familiar, sharp pain. Even as he put his hand under his jersey he knew the damage. His fingers touched the raised right collarbone, dislocated from its joint. He folded his jersey into a makeshift sling for his arm and trudged off. Wally's injury was the same acromioclavicular joint he had first sprung in the second Test against France on the 1982 Kangaroos tour. Weakened by successive injury it now required him only to fall heavily at the wrong angle to dislocate.

The Giants' 25–22 upset, their first competition win, induced joyous bedlam in their dressingroom. Champagne flowed, well-wishers crammed every inch of space and manager Peter Muszcat announced, "I don't care who wins the grand final, this will do me." Wayne Bennett felt much the same. "It was their grand final all right. I don't know what they will do for the rest of the season." The Giants won three more matches in 1988 but none more important than that first. The loss returned to haunt the Broncos later when they were mustering every point they could find to stay in the running for the semi-finals. It was the only Broncos loss of which it could be categorically said that on form they should have won.

Wally sat next to Bennett on the sideline, shoulder strapped and iced, until the bitter, losing end of that fateful game and then left for hospital to have his injury examined. He reckoned without the Seagulls stadium's traffic snarl. That record crowd took a record 90 minutes to clear the carpark. Wally sat in his car, shoulder aching, while the sun set and evening fell. Headlights beamed across the carpark and horns sounded irritably as Jacqui Lewis inched the car forward. For Wally and the Broncos the day had been a giant disaster.

After 10 matches, nearly half-way through the season, Wayne Bennett could be happy with the Broncos debut: seven wins and three losses. But he had also lost Wally injured. As Bennett exchanged his Broncos coaching coat for his Queensland coach's cap he contemplated the unthinkable: a state-of-origin without Wally.

10 FIRST BLOOD

At the first meeting of the 1988 Queensland state-of-origin squad Wayne Bennett quietened the players with a raised hand and announced the meeting would last an hour. It was Friday morning, May 13, and the Queenslanders had just begun their traditional camp at the Rushcutters Bay Travelodge Motel in Sydney. Bennett outlined the squad program for the five days leading to the match on Tuesday night. Every detail, day by day, was discussed until at last he said, "And now we'll get down to the two factors which will determine whether we win or lose this game. They are the two single most important factors in our preparation and if these jobs aren't done we're not going to win. In other words it's up to these two factors whether we win or lose. Those two factors are...Sam Backo and Martin Bella."

Bennett opened with a moderate analysis of Sam Backo's form but, as he proceeded, sharpened his words until he began to tear apart Backo's performances that season. How he wasn't giving it 100 per cent, what he should have been doing, where he had let himself down...on and on for 5 minutes. Bennett paused for breath. The room was silent with shock. Fatty Vautin, sitting next to Wally at the back, whispered, "Gees, I think Sam's going to get up and bash him in a minute." Wally glanced at Backo and saw the big Canberra prop's face was flushed with anger. Bennett then turned on Martin Bella and gave him a similar serve, that he was a better footballer than he had shown that year, how he was wasting his talent, that he needed more pride and so forth until the giant North Sydney prop began to shift uneasily in his chair. By now Wally could not bear to look at either Backo or Bella, so scathing had Bennett been. Nor did he want to catch Bennett's eye. It was too embarrassing to hear grown men take such an upbraiding. An army private similarly abused might be excused for belting his sergeant. It was the most humiliating dressing down Wally had ever heard.

The players filed wordlessly out, relieved to escape, and burst into a buzz of amazed chatter at what they had witnessed. As Wally descended the stairs Bennett caught him up and said, for Wally's ears only, "Do you think that was enough?" Wally rolled his eyes, "Oh mate!" From that meeting on, at every training session, Backo and Bella ran with an unmistakable, agitated determination. Whenever it appeared they were calming, Bennett made some half-funny, half-serious remark and the two props would grit their teeth and go harder.

Wally regards Backo as probably Australia's biggest and best ball-running forward. "He uses every part of his body as a weapon," said Wally. "Holds his arms high to fend and keep the ball free, uses his hips well and has a high kneelift." Bella was the perfect foil, a bullocking runner with massive legs, body set low to the ground, who dropped his shoulders into would-be tacklers. Said Wally, "There was no way those two blokes weren't going to be the best two players on the field against NSW."

Bennett's experiences with the Broncos had impressed upon him that all the brave ball skills in the world could not match sheer forward might. Greg Dowling, after 11 Origins and 12 Tests, had retired from representative football and Bryan Niebling, 9 Origins, was beset by injuries. To combat the power of NSW's Steve Roach, Noel Cleal and Les Davidson, Bennett needed forwards of equal size. More than that, Roach and Davidson were naturally aggressive players, whereas Backo's bursts were sporadic and Bella was altogether too civilised. Bennett wanted brawn and he wanted it revving on anger and hostility.

Wally caught the backlash from Bennett's psychological manipulations. That afternoon in a game of touch football Backo, unusually intense, rushed at Wally, knocked him over and fell on him. Wally gasped in pain as his injured shoulder thumped into the ground. "You big, bloody, useless goose," yelled Wally. Backo looked perplexed. "My shoulder, Sam, you just landed on it," winced Wally. After training Backo asked, "Did I really hurt you?" When Wally nodded, Backo apologised, "Mate I'm really sorry, I didn't mean to, I forgot clean about it."

Wally had been telling the media he was a 50–50 chance of playing. After colliding with Backo it was more like 10–90. He had physiotherapy twice a day but the ligaments holding the shoulder in place, once stretched by dislocation, are slow healers. Bennett had given Wally until Monday afternoon for a fitness test but, on Saturday, Bennett suddenly turned and asked, "You're no chance are you?" Wally was surprised into admitting the truth. He wasn't right. A medical test the following night confirmed it. He could do 10 pushups but swinging his arm in an arc across his chest brought a grimace.

Wally was despondent but Bennett had to beware everyone's sentimental wish, including his own, for Wally to play. Apart from his unrivalled importance to Queensland's hopes Wally had never missed a state-of-origin match. The red and black *Courier-Mail* poster for Monday, 16 May 1988, shouted, "WALLY MISSES ORIGIN". That was the magnitude of his omission. Wally was the only player from either state to have played in every Origin since its inception in 1980. With 21 matches he led Greg Conescu, 17 matches, and Mal Meninga, Brett Kenny and Colin Scott on 16. He had captained Queensland 20 times compared with the next highest, Wayne Pearce, who had led NSW seven times. He was leading man-of-the-matches with six awards to Peter Sterling's four awards. The ARL was said to be considering — the moment Wally retires — striking a medal in his name, to be awarded to the best player in future Origin series. Wally was part of the institution of state-of-origin football.

Had it been a third and deciding Origin match Wally would have requested pain-killing injections. For the moment he reluctantly succumbed. His withdrawal set up new pressures and tensions within the Queensland side. Greg Dowling (11 Origins) and Paul Vautin (13 Origins) were the next most senior players. With Dowling out the captaincy logically fell to Vautin. He and Bob Lindner had been sniping at each other in their Sydney newspaper columns about who would be Queensland lock. Vautin criticised Lindner's form under a headline "Mogadon Bob". Lindner had been lock for Australia and Queensland since the 1986 Kangaroo tour. Vautin was Manly's lock and coveted the position for Queensland. The selectors ended speculation by choosing Vautin at lock and Lindner second-row in a pre-Origin trial. Former maroon, Chris Close, was concerned at the public slanging between the two players. It would never have been allowed in his time, he said. Wally, however, carefully noted the pair's interaction in camp and saw that the Queensland ethos overrode all petty bickering.

The Queensland captaincy meant that Vautin was gradually acquiring the honours unjustly denied him in his career. He had replaced injured Ray Price in a 1982 Test but when the Kangaroos were chosen that year the back-rowers were Price, Wayne Pearce and Rod Reddy. He was sidelined for 16 weeks in 1986 with a broken arm and then was overlooked for Wally's Kangaroo tour. Vautin had matured into one of Australia's most reliable players and it was fitting that he captained Manly to their 1987 Sydney premiership. His leadership qualities were later recognised in England when coach Alex Murphy made him captain of the glamour St Helen's side.

Vautin was yet another example of the depth of quality players — among them Mark Murray, Mal Meninga, Greg Dowling and Greg Conescu — who had sublimated their leadership ambitions in the interests of harmony under Wally. "I'm a pretty fierce patriot," said Vautin. "That maroon jumper does something to me." He was delighted to be captain but added, "I'd rather have Wally out there, not in the grandstand." Wally watched his friend assume the captaincy with a mixture of regret and pride. He told me, "Paul's importance is something spectators can't see. When he tops the tackle count you just think, 'Oh yes, as per usual.' What you can't see is the pride he instils in being a Queenslander."

When Wally dislocated his shoulder, even as he sat on the

sideline watching the Giants, Bennett had asked, "Who are we going to put in for you?" Wally replied, "Jacko." Wally's opinion of Peter Jackson was that if you gave him something out of the too-hard basket, he'd handle it twice as easy. The decision was made. Nine days later Bennett officially named Peter Jackson to wear the coveted No. 6 jersey.

New bloke Jackson, upon hearing his selection, lit a cigarette, a habit he had in common with Wally. Apart from that they were a contrast. Where Wally only took calculated risks Jackson was renowned for his impetuosity. Wally stood in deep defence whereas Jackson was a front-line defender. All Jackson's six Origin matches were in the centres but in the Australian off-season he had played half his matches with Leeds at "stand-off" (five-eighth). With Canberra he often positioned himself as second five-eighth. Bennett had coached Jackson with Brisbane Souths and Canberra. He knew and trusted him.

Wally's exit dominated pre-match news but strange rumours were drifting through Sydney pub and club conversations. From the NSW camp came reports of a long standing feud between Peter Sterling and Cliff Lyons, stemming from a Parramatta-Manly match incident. The referee was to be Barry Gomersall, the Queenslander Sydney fans most revile after Wally. He would be refereeing his ninth and last Origin because he was retiring at the end of the season. NSW were about to ensure he controlled his last Origin anyway. For future series NSW demanded Queensland nominate a panel of referees from which NSW could take their choice. NSW would never have selected "The Grasshopper". NSW, 6–4 on favourites before Wally's loss, shortened to 2–1 on. Some betting cards were even giving Queensland 10 points start. The odds were unreal. NSW captain Wayne Pearce identified a danger to his side. "Wally's absence could work to lift their side in that everyone might be trying to do that little bit extra knowing their key player's out," he said. The day before the match NSW manager, Peter Moore, gave a hint of what might come when he admitted he was disappointed by the blues' lack of commitment on the training paddock.

Wally was co-opted by Bennett as honorary assistant coach, offering advice when requested and adopting a role of quasi-team psychologist. He sat down one evening and wrote out telegrams to every team member, including the two reserves, with a special message pertinent to each. Bob Lindner had just learnt that his wife was pregnant so Wally wrote, "Make this game tonight one of which your kid would be proud." To captain Vautin he said, "Tonight you've got the job you've always wanted. Make it one to remember." And his cable to "Action" Jackson said simply, "It's up to you. You're the man."

In the dressingroom Bennett went through his last-minute rundown with the team. The players were steaming and tossing their gelatined joints about like horses at the barrier. Wally sat apart, alone in a corner, head down, listening. Suddenly tears streamed down his face. "That's when it hit me I was going to miss the game," he said. Bennett's gaze lit upon Wally. "Have a look at this bloke," he said loudly. Wally looked up. "He'll show you what it means not to be able to play for Queensland. You blokes have got the opportunity." Bennett called to him. "Get over here." Wally joined them and Bennett made him shake hands with every team member. *Sydney Morning Herald* writer, John MacDonald, asked after the match, "What is this virus that affects expatriate Queenslanders when they pull on a maroon guernsey?"

Wally sat in the stand with Bennett who copes with tension by presenting the face of a sphinx, an imperceptible tightening of the jaw muscles his only concession to emotion. Within minutes Wally was leaping up with excitement. Bennett pulled him down by the shirt. "There's two things I don't like about you sitting up here," he complained. Wally asked, "What's the second one?" Bennett replied, "You smoke." Wally puffed through seven cigarettes before half-time, an inordinate number for such a light smoker, but this was new ground, sitting out an Origin.

Michael O'Connor was the magic act of the first half, dancing past Vautin with an effortless step off his right foot and then off his left to round Gary Belcher, ending with a graceful dive for a try. Only an athlete of O'Connor's class could carry out such choreography. Allan Langer was the prime source of Queensland excitement. NSW played without a second line of defence.

Wally was forever nudging Bennett, "There's a gap over here, they're short on this side." Langer exploited the flaw mercilessly, chipping through and chasing to score two fine individual tries. Wally exclaimed as Langer persistently chipped, "Surely they're going to cover it this time!" Former coach Roy Masters wrote in the *Sydney Morning Herald* that Peter Sterling's club Parramatta played without such cover. It was said a message was sent out to Sterling to stay back to cover Langer's chips, but he would not.

With Queensland leading 12–6 at half-time Wally and Wayne descended the stairs to the dressingroom. In a narrow alleyway a figure barrelled past, knocking people aside, reached the NSW dressingroom door and started yelling even as the door closed. Wally grabbed his coach, "Benny! Look, look!" Bennett, just catching sight of the back of the figure entering the NSW door, asked, "Who was it?" Wally smiled, "Ernie bloody Hammerton." Bennett nodded. Ernie Hammerton, chairman of the NSW selectors, was reportedly in the process of telling the NSW team that, with the exception of Michael O'Connor, they were a disgrace. Wally remembered Hammerton well. As chairman of Australian selectors Hammerton had barged into the Australian dressingroom at half-time in a Test against New Zealand in 1982 and had begun threatening players they would lose their Kangaroo tour berths. It did nothing for the team's morale.

In the Queensland dressingroom Bennett's first words were, "I can tell you it is a very unhappy NSW dressingroom." He predicted that if the team took control in the first 10 minutes of the second half they would win by 15 to 20 points. When Queensland ran to a 26–6 lead 10 minutes from full-time Wally stared at Bennett and wondered, "Is this bloke clairvoyant or something?" The final score, 26–18, flattered NSW who played like a team becalmed. Peter Jackson, working behind a bullock team responding to the names of Backo and Bella, produced a magnificent kicking game. He stamped himself as Wally's heir apparent for the Broncos, Queensland and possibly Australia. Wally hurried Bennett downstairs once more, but the coach would not quicken his unflappable pace. Wally grinned and thought, "Don't tell me you're not happy, you big fake. You're almost jumping out of your shoes."

In the victor's quarters Wally walked straight up to Jackson. They gazed a moment without a word and suddenly wrapped their arms around each other and began laughing and shouting "Queenslanders, you bloody beauty!" Before the match the team had remained a fraction aloof from Wally, determined to show they were worthy without him. Now, with success, they embraced him with relief. They offered Wally their ultimate gift, making him feel part of the win.

Wally sat down beside a cheerful but weary Vautin. "How're you going?" Vautin asked casually.

"Oh, okay," said Wally.

Vautin, with ultra-understatement: "What've you been doing?"

"Just sitting around upstairs watching a footie game."

"How was it?"

"It was a bastard of a feeling!"

Vautin, relenting infinitesimally: "We might have a drink then eh?"

"Can't see any reason why not." And they smiled hugely.

Allan Langer was man-of-the-match with an unprecedented 61 primary votes from 64 media observers. Back at the motel Bennett handed Langer the player's player-of-the-match award as well but really Bennett had just one message. There was another game to go. The players felt the same. Wally too. He felt as washed out as if he had played.

One of the player's girlfriends could not understand. "What's wrong with you blokes?" she asked. "You've just won and you won't come out and celebrate. Let's hit the town and drink until the joint closes." She grabbed a waiter, "C'mon mate, you'll have a drink with us won't you." The waiter got enthusiastic, yeah he would. She suddenly turned nasty, "No you won't! You're nothing but a bloody cockroach!"

The post-mortems that ensued in Sydney were worthy of a full scale civilian disaster. Was it Gomersall? The *Sydney Morning Herald* printed a minute-by-minute annotation of Gomersall's decisions of which the bottom line was: full-time penalties, NSW 5, Queensland 1. Gomersall responded with his usual one-liner, "As regards the Sydney media it's a case of mind over matter. I don't mind and they don't matter." Was it the crowd? Jack Gibson called it a "partial sell-out". It was the smallest for five years, 26,400, compared with the SCG average since 1983 of around 40,000. The blame was sheeted home to the hefty $32 cost of seats in the new Sydney Football Stadium. As Mike Gibson wrote in the *Sydney Morning Herald*, "Rugby league is a working man's game...For $32 a man can take his family out to McDonald's for dinner, pick up the latest Rambo bloodbath at the video store on the way home and toss a carton of beer in his boot as well." Coach John Peard accepted the blame for NSW's apparent lack of enthusiasm.

The one man they could not blame, for once, was Wally Lewis. The headlines, "Yes, There IS Life After King Wally", and "Queensland Dispel The One Man Band Myth" were back-handed compliments to Wally. Mike Gibson, a genuine fan of Wally's, missed him. "He's such a colossus in these games, King Wally, you find it hard to hate Queensland when he's not out there." Never mind. All those addicted to Wally-hating and Wally-busting, all those Einsteins bearing the Wally-wanks and Wally-sucks signs and all the professional apologists for every NSW defeat were about to have a field day with their magnificent obsession.

11 STORM IN A BEER CAN

In the first flush of that Origin win Wally was generous about Peter Jackson's performance. "I might have to get out the head gear and shoulderpads and come back as a fresh reserve forward," he joked. By the time the maroons went into camp for the second Origin in Brisbane he was sick of the pointed questions. He told me, "Jacko had a great game and I suppose there was the unspoken question: do they need me anymore? There was a bit of hurt pride though I was happy in a way because it gave me a challenge." But when the umpteenth Sydney writer asked him if he thought he could perform to Jackson's standards, Wally answered sarcastically, "Mate, I'll just go out there and try my very best to live up to the high standard Jacko set last week."

Wally nearly eliminated Jackson as a pretender to his throne. Taking the wheel of the team bus to drive to the Gold Coast, Wally started off and suddenly hit the brakes, hoping to put everyone standing into the lap of a team-mate or on their backsides. But Jackson, skylarking in the aisle and off balance, sailed through the air and punched two large holes in the windscreen with his head and right hand, showering the bus entrance with crystalline chips. Wally was aghast, fearing Jackson would have concussion or even serious head or neck injuries. Jacko, amazingly unhurt, felt his forehead and brought the bus down with, "That's just to show those NSW bastards how tough I am!" Nothing could stop this Queensland team. Wally put on a pair of sunglasses to protect his eyes from the wind and drove down the coast alfresco.

Martin Bella and Sam Backo, having proved their worth to Bennett, now looked more assured. Bella in particular was a good participant in team talks. A physiotherapist he liked to interpret Bennett's instructions in more intellectual language until, ten words into an explanation, Bennett pulled him up with: "Martin, you're a bonehead. You're a front-rower. You catch the ball, you take it up the middle, you get tackled, fall over, get up, play the ball, go back and start all over again. Got that?" Bennett's problem is that his sarcasm is a close cousin to his humour and the team laughs were at Bella's expense.

Wally had his own irritations. His old coach and friend, Ross Strudwick, had been carping at Queensland and the Broncos to unchain halfback Langer from his master's voice — Lewis. Langer admitted he felt restricted in his game because Wally organised everything. In the first Origin, in Wally's absence, Langer became first receiver and revelled in the responsibility. Wally diplomatically offered to take a lower profile in attack. In addition Bennett had been at him for two seasons to take a higher profile in defence. He wanted Wally in the first line. "He was brought up in the second line of defence and he enjoyed it," said Bennett. "But he's one of the best hitters in football and he had to pull more weight." Langer's speed in cover defence removed that excuse for Wally to stand back. At training Bennett told him, "If you're not fit, you're out," and tested him with 15 tough tackles. With every tackle Wally's confidence grew.

The Queensland captain has the right to a motel room by himself in camp but Wally always opted to room with Gene Miles. Any evening after a few beers their room sounds like a scene from the *Texas Chainsaw Massacre* such is their combined snoring. Usually it's a race to see who nods off first and who stays awake throwing shoes and ashtrays to shut the other up. On match day Wally put on a tracksuit and went for a stroll in the city with Trevor Gillmeister and Paul Vautin and ate lunch at Jimmy's On The Mall. Subconsciously Wally fed on the friendly welcome-backs, good lucks and thumbs-up passersby offered him. He felt content as he walked back to the motel for an afternoon nap. Afterwards he rang Jacqui at home. Her final words are always, "Goodbye, good luck and don't get hurt."

Wally snorted in disgust when he repeated the words. "Don't get hurt! We're not playing netball!"

Wayne Bennett pondered NSW's team for this second Origin. NSW had guillotined eight players from the first match, forcing coach John Peard to frantically forge new partnerships. Noel "Crusher" Cleal, who could run over three players but might not tackle them in return, was gone. His Manly team-mate, young Kangaroo prop, Phil Daley — cautioned repeatedly for new-found, strong-arm play in recent weeks — was in. NSW had lost the 1987 series, had comprehensively lost the first 1988 match. They were under intense media pressure to win. The new Sydney Football Stadium was half-empty for the first match and the third match was back there again. NSW had to win the second Origin to fill the stadium for the third. Said Bennett, "I knew the administration would be desperate to beat us in Brisbane. It was their last throw of the dice. They absolutely had to win."

Bennett remembered Arthur Beetson once describing the first state-of-origins as so violent they were like wars. "Now it's played the way it should be," Beetson had said. "It's fast and tough without any back-alley tactics like the early years." That was it! Bennett suddenly understood. NSW's only hope was a return to the back-alley to throw Queensland off their game. Rough them up, niggle and brawl, take out one of Queensland's top players. Bennett knew the tactic. Phil Daley had developed a head-hunting reputation so Bennett chose him — but he was a symbol, it could have been Steve Roach — and publicly warned NSW, "If Daley injures one of our boys I will request he be cited by the league. He can sit out football for a couple of months if that's what he wants to do." It was an uncharacteristic, but calculated, outburst by Bennett. He told me, "I wanted Daley and the others to know that if they put it on us I wasn't going to stand by and say 'Forget it.' We'd never fought in the two years I'd been coach and I didn't think we had to go back to that level."

Just before the team ran on, Bennett said to Wally, "Are you ready?" Wally, juggling the smooth, cow-hide Steeden football, his mouthguard in place, just looked back. "Go get 'em!" said

Bennett. The roar that shook Lang Park as Wally appeared on the ramp was unmistakable. It lifted and carried him across the grassy threshold. A small smile dimpled his chin. Home again, home again.

Phil Daley immediately exhibited his borderline chest/head high tackles. But it was Steve Roach who fulfilled all Bennett's dire predictions. Five minutes into the match Roach took the ball up, straight into Peter Jackson. Bob Lindner, second tackler, lay on Roach a little, nothing else obvious. Roach played the ball and mouthed off at Lindner who, as marker, turned to watch Benny Elias roof the ball downfield. As the ball passed the half-way mark in the air Lindner too was in the air, felled by a diabolical forearm jolt to the side of his head by Roach. Lindner hit the turf on his back, lifted his head once and then didn't move. With his mouthguard protruding and the whites of his eyes rolling stupidly, he looked like a KO'd fighter. Except this was no prize fight.

When Lindner finally rose Wally checked him out. "I'll be right in a minute," said Lindner. Wally's mind spun back six years to the first Test in France in 1982 when he dislocated his shoulder. Steve Rogers ordered him to get up and get in line. When Wally complained he couldn't, Rogers shouted, "Well get off the field then!" Wally now told Lindner, "Clear your mind, think of what you've got to do, or go off." Neither Tests nor Origins are moments for sympathy. Incredibly referee Mick Stone did not send Roach off, or to the sinbin. He gave Queensland a penalty. It was Lindner, groggy and stumbling, who was helped to the headbin for 10 minutes.

Roach did not learn. Soon after Lindner returned "Block" aimed a stiff left arm at him which, had it connected, would have given Lindner amnesia for a year. Referee Stone atoned and Roach got 10 minutes in the sinbin. Queensland, under instructions from Bennett not to be provoked, simmered but stayed their hands. NSW trooped in at half-time leading 6–4 after Michael O'Connor had repeated his graceful try of the first Origin. This time he drew a different arrow from his quiver, altering his speed, easing then accelerating to utterly confound Queensland's defence. Gasnier, Rogers, Kenny — O'Connor is their peer, four sovereign centres cast in the same mould, blessed with equal gifts of elegance and speed to enthrall two decades of Australian rugby league.

Twenty minutes into the second half Queensland looked down, though not out. Greg Conescu grabbed a scrap ball and fell to tackles by Terry Lamb and Phil Daley. Referee Stone blew a knock-on, Lamb jumped up but Daley purposelessly delayed disengaging. Conescu struggled, Daley held him down. Conescu kicked and struck out, Daley kneeled on him and threw a few peppery punches. The immediate NSW personnel were Paul Langmack, Benny Elias, Steve Folkes, Lamb and Daley. Langmack and Elias made tepid attempts to pull Daley away and Elias broke off to hold up a traffic-cop hand at Sam Backo who was returning at speed.

That's how Channel 9's Andrew Slack saw it too. He said:

> It was as simple as this. Conescu was trying to get up after the whistle had been blown, Daley wouldn't let him, Greg wasn't too enthralled with Daley's performance and away they went, but Daley definitely threw the first punch.

Trouble was Daley still wouldn't let Conescu up. True to his nickname Turtle was flat on his back. He let go of the ball to defend himself. Backo brushed aside Elias but simultaneously a blur of maroon flew in from left stage, hurtled into Daley and dragged him metres away. Wally Lewis thereby achieved what others had not, the rescue of Greg Conescu. Wally quickly rose, clasping Daley who wanted to improve the famous Lewis features with a Liverpool kiss. He held Daley by the lapels and admonished, "Come on Phil, no need for that, don't try and bung it on." In those seconds the cast around Conescu expanded to 19 players plus referee Stone.

The dynamic of the rugby league brawl is that if there is no spite between the teams a one-on-one contest will not escalate. Using that theory Barry Gomersall has successfully isolated such fights by controversially refusing to stop play, thereby centring both team's attention on the ball and not the pugilists. However in this match Roach had already knocked over the powder keg and now Daley struck the flint.

Thus Canterbury team-mates Tony Currie and Terry Lamb held jerseys, Wally Fullerton-Smith singled out Paul Langmack, Roach and Backo waltzed a little and Bella singled out Elias. Others sought to extinguish the scrub fires but the chain reaction only ended when firemen outnumbered brawlers and Stone's whistle was finally heeded.

While Stone heard both linesmen's reports Wally remembered how, years ago, Tom Raudonikis had sunk a likely Queensland win by starting a brawl. He gathered his players and spoke firmly, "These blokes are trying to upset you to take your mind off the game. Don't be sucked in. Concentrate on your job." Stone called Daley, Conescu and Wally over. A linesman accused Conescu of being the instigator, of punching Daley. Wally's eyes widened. "He had the ball," he said incredulously, "He had the ball." So why would he punch Daley? Stone told Wally to shut up and listen. Ten minutes sinbin each for Conescu starting the brawl and Daley for retaliating. A linesman now advised Stone that Wally too had been an instigator, that the brawl was all but over when Lewis ran in and started throwing punches. To Wally this was sheer pantomime. Wally said, "Mick, I never threw a punch, I just ran in to stop it." Stone sentenced Wally to five minutes in the sinbin. "Mick I never threw a punch," protested Wally. "You're off," said Stone and held up his hand for five minutes. Wally argued no further. He did not harangue Stone, he did not gesticulate, he did not hesitate, he did not orchestrate — he turned and ran obediently from the field.

Stone ruled a penalty to NSW and Peter Sterling took the line kick. As Sterling punted, and as Wally reached the gate leading under the Frank Burke grandstand on the opposite side of the field, beer cans began to rain on the field from the Hale Street terraces. Linesmen, television cameramen and newspaper photographers ducked the cans. Lang Park was in uproar. Stone stopped play, three policemen moved around the fence perimeter and the players cleared about 40 cans from the field. Stone restarted play and Elias took the tap.

Wally did not see the cans. He arrived in the dressingroom as Conescu picked up a glass of water. "What are you doing here?" said Turtle, astonished. Wally, disgusted: "He's got me for prolonging the fight. Linesman said it was my fault." Conescu sat back speechless while Wally paced about, silently lamenting his stupidity and cursing the linesman. "They've got 12 men and we've only 11," he thought. "I've let the side down." And then, "No I haven't, it wasn't my fault. That linesman's full of bullshit." After two minutes his blood cooled. "Hang on. All I'm doing is wasting time being filthy on the linesman. What I should be doing is assessing how we're going. Is our plan working? Is our positional play good? We're still behind." Just then a prolonged thunder boomed overhead, rolling on and on. Wally paused in his pacing. He and Turtle exchanged hopeful glances. A white-coated attendant burst in and announced dramatically, "Big Sam's scored! We're in front!" Wally got a warm inner glow. "How'd he score?" he asked. The attendant gave a big smile, "Smashed his way over." Wally thought, "That sounds like him," and imagined how Backo would have scored. He didn't see it until the following night on the television news but it was exactly how he'd pictured.

After the cans were cleared NSW had run three tackles and then faltered. Opportunist Peter Jackson had intercepted and raced to within five metres of the NSW line. That's when the stadium thunder shook three suburbs surrounding Lang Park. Queensland might have scored had not Steve Folkes refused to let Jackson play the ball. Mick Stone unhesitatingly ruled it a professional foul and gave Folkes five minutes in the sinbin. That kept the thunder rolling. Penalty to Queensland. Six tackles later Backo powered his way over and the crowd's roar finally subsided into a satisfied buzz. When Wally ran back on Queensland led 10–6 which became, by full-time, 16–6.

Amid the celebrations in the dressingroom Wally conducted his usual media conference. At the last moment *Daily Mirror* writer Peter Frilingos half turned and inquired, "Oh, one last question mate. What do you reckon, do you think you started that brawl?" Wally, surprised, replied, "Turn it up. I was just standing up for Turtle getting the shit punched out of him." Righto, said Frilingos, good win, and walked away. Wally was puzzled and said to Paul Vautin, "You wouldn't believe what

I've just been asked." Vautin replied, "I bet you haven't heard the last of that."

After the usual post-match function Jacqui Lewis drove Wally, Fatty Vautin and Trevor Gillmeister to join the team at the Ship Inn, the all-night pub in the grounds of Expo. At about 1.30 a.m. the NSW team arrived as well. After a few minutes of awkwardness Wayne Pearce and Steve Folkes walked over and broke the ice. Wally appreciated their action and actually had a chat with Phil Daley, demonstrating that no matter how fierce the war on field, truce is called at full-time. Wally stayed until 5 a.m. then left, but not before he had listened to other NSW players expressing their private dissatisfaction with Daley's actions in the match.

The next morning, Wednesday, 1 June, Wally's phone did not stop ringing. One of the callers was 2GB afternoon drive-time host Stephen O'Doherty in Sydney. Said O'Doherty, "You can't imagine the way they're carrying on down here about the match. They're giving you a real hiding, so do you mind if I get your opinion on it?" Not knowing O'Doherty, Wally thought he wanted a newspaper interview. O'Doherty taped their conversation and it was played that evening on 2GB. It went in part:

O'Doherty: What did you do in relation to the crowd after that incident with the referee?

Wally: What did I do in relation to the crowd?

O'Doherty: Yeah.

Wally: What do you mean? Am I supposed to have run over and got the crowd to do something or other?

O'Doherty: That's the allegation, yes.

Wally: Oh turn it up mate! Don't be a f-*blip*-cking idiot! Jesus Christ! For a start I was running the other way, remember? I don't know whether you know anything about football, obviously you don't, but when I was sent to the sinbin I ran the other way. You didn't happen to see that at all?

O'Doherty: Look, again, it's not me who you should be having this argument with. I'm passing on to you what Ken Arthurson and others have said.

Wally: You just said what did I do to orchestrate the crowd. Isn't that what you just said?

O'Doherty: Did you do anything to orchestrate the crowd, yes?
Wally: Oh mate, don't ask stupid questions. The dressingroom is the other way. Jesus Christ, you're carrying on like a bloody goat. What am I supposed to have done, run over and held up a little conductor's wand and said stand up and make some sort of demonstration?

Wally takes hundreds of media calls per season, more even than Alan Border or the prime minister. He is a very experienced interviewee. As annoyed as he was by O'Doherty's obvious ignorance of the interview topic he would never have dropped the magic word in an interview with the electronic media whether live or taped. He would not have even offended religious folk by taking the Lord's name in vain. That he did both supports his assertion he thought he was talking informally to a newspaper reporter. Radio 2GB, apparently dedicated to true grit newsgathering, edited the tape with microsurgery. They removed only the vowel "u" from Wally's expletive and inserted a milli-second bleep. Thus Wally's obscenity, though edited, was clear and unmistakable. His blasphemy was also left in.

Rugby league straight-shooter Peter "Zorba" Peters replayed that section of the tape on his sports slot in the Mike Carlton breakfast show on 2GB the next morning. Carlton's show was then Sydney's highest rating breakfast program. Peters preceded the recording with his opinion that it was unfair to Wally Lewis and criticised his fellow broadcaster O'Doherty and the station for permitting an announcer with little knowledge of the sport to conduct such a sensitive interview.

Broncos general manager, John Ribot, subsequently wrote a complaint to the Australian Broadcasting Tribunal about 2GB. Ribot accused the station of making a feeble attempt to bleep out Wally's expletive and of not removing the religious exclamation. The then general manager of 2GB Geoffrey Duncan said, "We believe the broadcast was aired with the proper journalistic standards applying." Both O'Doherty and Duncan have since left 2GB. As this book goes to print the Broadcasting Tribunal has still not completed its inquiry.

Maybe Wally should always suffer such interviews patiently,

maybe he should never drop his guard, never trust the media. Peter Peters's comments would have offset the impact of replaying the interview. But anyone who heard the original interview could only conclude that Australia had as its rugby league captain a foul-mouthed, short-tempered blasphemer.

During the season Wally had joined the staff of Channel 10 in Brisbane and consequently was well disposed towards their Sydney news presenter, Steve Leibmann, when he rang that day for a Live Eye interview on the station's 6 p.m. news. Wally stood in the front yard of his home talking with Leibmann off-air via his ear-piece and tie-clip microphone. Leibmann asked Wally if he'd heard about the Sydney reaction. Yeah, he had, bunch of gooses, he said. He'd had a gutful of the can throwing and told Leibmann he didn't want to talk about it. Leibmann said he would ask a few questions about the game.

In his live-to-air interview Leibmann provocatively commented that Wally would have to agree that he was partly responsible for the crowd's behaviour at Lang Park. Wally's first thought was, "You low bastard, you didn't even have the guts to say you were going to put it on me." Wally restrained himself to a polite denial and short explanation. Leibmann suggested also that Wally had set a poor example for children by continually disputing rulings by the referee. Wally kept his cool and denied the allegation. A smooth female voice sounded in his earpiece: "Come on Wally, you don't expect us to believe that do you?"

Wally, staring at a tree in his front yard to give himself something to focus on, thought, "What sheila is this?" and then recognised Ten's news presenter, Geraldine Doogue. What the hell would she know about it? "Yes, I do expect you to believe that," he said. Leibmann persisted and Wally broke the traces. "You're still going on about that — OK it's my fault," he said. And began a long, monotonous and heavily sarcastic rant about how before the game he decided to start this huge brawl, how when he saw his chance he bashed this bloke Daley and got sent off, and straight afterwards — "You wouldn't have seen this" - he sprinted from the dressingroom around the other side of the field, held up a big sign saying, "Please throw cans now", and then raced back in time to finish his five minutes in the sinbin. Wally wouldn't stop even though he could hear Leibmann's distressed, "Oh Wally, mate...!"

Wally concluded, "We did everything incorrectly last night. We apologise for it but we won the game of footy. We just can't believe it that after every game of football Queenslanders have always done something wrong." Leibmann retreated, "Well obviously you don't want to talk about it." Wally replied, "You're right, I don't want to," and pulled his ear-piece out just as Leibmann said, "Well that's Wally Lewis's reaction..." Wally stood in his yard for a few moments, regaining his calm. At Lang Park the previous evening one player had been king hit, a dozen others had wrestled in the Daley-Conescu incident, two players had been sinbinned for 10 minutes and two — one of whom was Wally — had been sinbinned for five minutes. Out of all this, Channel 10 in Sydney had selected him as the scapegoat for the beer-can throwing. He turned and went inside. He was learning. Everybody gets burnt in television.

The day after the match the Lewis phone rang incessantly. On the occasions Wally bothered to answer it, unless it was a bona fide sports reporter he knew, he gave media callers the pro forma reply he had learnt from the *King Wally* book furore: "This is a recording, please check your video tape, I did not throw a punch, I ran in to defend one of my players who was getting the tripe belted out of him, I did not abuse referee Mick Stone, I did not incite the crowd, this is a recording," and hung up.

Those in NSW with a vested interest in burying the actual result of that game hoed in. NSWRL general manager John Quayle gave the hyperbole offical status, accusing Wally of provoking the can throwing by arguing with referee Stone. Quayle said on Sydney radio, "If he hadn't come in and questioned the referee and that sort of thing, it wouldn't have happened. He's got to take a lot of responsibility as far as I'm concerned."

The controversy reached a pitch on Sunday, 5 June. Reports circulated that the NSW clique in the Australian Rugby League board would raise the old chestnut — strip Wally of his national captaincy for the coming Tests against Great Britain. One NSW board member said Wally's language on 2GB did not befit an Australian captain. Fortunately NSW has only three votes on the six-member ARL board. President Ken Arthurson casts the deciding vote and he has never yet buckled to the Wally-busters.

The pressure was enormous. Normally rational editor David Hickie penned a piece in the *Sun-Herald* under the headline, "Prima Donnas Like Wally Have To Go". Hickie wrote:

> Lewis' action in consistently arguing with referee Mick Stone in last week's disgraceful Lang Park fiasco deserved a lot more than five minutes in the sinbin...There is a major — indeed fundamental — issue at stake here. It's the right of the referee to make decisions without being harassed or intimidated by players.

Another experienced commentator, Ian Heads, referred in the *Sydney Morning Herald* to a strutting, shouting Lewis who gave referee Stone no peace. Peter Peters and Greg Hartley wrote in their column, "Lewis ran the game — not Stone — is how some saw it."

The major, indeed fundamental, error by these writers was to continue to believe — several days after the match — that part of Stone's reason for sinbinning Wally was for dissension or backchatting. In the heat of the moment most writers covering the match made the same error — and I was as guilty as any — primarily because it was difficult to understand why else Wally would be marched. His role in the brawl seemed so secondary it appeared that he was arguing Conescu's case — as was his right as captain — and that he got five minutes for arguing too persistently. Wally is adamant Stone made no mention of backchatting. In none of Stone's post-match interviews did he criticise Wally for disputation. It was a non-issue.

For eight years rugby league writers have been watching Wally Lewis in his role as captain of Brisbane Panasonic Cup, Queensland state-of-origin and Test teams as well as the touring Kangaroos and now the Brisbane Broncos. No other contemporary player has been captain so often, for so long. In this age of the television close-up and video replay no other player has been as visible questioning referees as has Wally. He is experienced in that capacity, he knows most of the referees and the limits to which he can go. In his youthful days, to be sure, Wally tried referees on and paid the price. By 1984 he had matured, dropped all that nonsense and, before he was injured, was leading in the 1987 Rothmans Gold Medal judged by Brisbane referees. That his detractors misinterpet on-field interplay was shown by Wally's innocence in the Greg McCallum non-incident in Newcastle. Before he is again convicted of having abused his captain's rights, media prosecutors should take evidence from the referees.

Wally spoke several times to Stone during the beer can Origin, but only once at length, apart from the brawl. He prefaced it with, "Mick, I'm not having a go at you but..." and complained in no uncertain terms about NSW being offside. A study of the match video, however, shows Wally to be innocent of any hectoring charge. Referees have a very simple remedy for vexatious querists: they hold their hand up like a duck's beak, quickly quack it, and penalise the offender. If the player persists in arguing, the referee marches them another 10 metres. In territory-conscious rugby league it is a very effective deterrent.

Hickie quoted Ken Arthurson as saying, "I was disturbed to see Lewis get away with continually disputing the referee's decisions...When referees allow Lewis or anybody else to query their decisions in a manner that is very obvious to the crowd we'll risk incidents like Tuesday night's affair." It is an extraordinary quote from an executive as experienced as the ARL chairman. To Wally, Arthurson denied he said most of the things attributed to him in the media over the storm in a beer can. On 7 June, two days after David Hickie's column, Arthurson was interviewed for the *Courier-Mail* by their chief league writer Paul Malone. He quoted Arthurson:

> Wally had nothing to do with the can throwing and it is unfair that it be levelled at him. Everyone goes around with placards in matches here saying Wally is this and that. He gets punched after matches. It's disgusting and he's under a lot of pressure.

Malone's report comprised a comprehensive defence of Wally by the ARL president. In the modern global village, media statements in Sydney can not be quarantined from Queensland. When conflicting accounts are reported it becomes obvious that the ARL chief has been placed in an intolerable position. Repeatedly he is asked to comment on hearsay complaints; frequently he has to adjudicate on the run; too often he is the victim of selective reporting. Ken Arthurson has paid the price for continuing to defend Wally Lewis.

As always the media campaign against Wally bred its own backlash. In Brisbane, Wayne Bennett was both distressed and furious. He said, "Wally's not perfect but he did no wrong that night. He went in there to protect a player, which I expected him to. I don't care who or where I coach, I expect that. It's a manly game and we help one another." Bennett rang a Queensland team official on Friday, 3 June, and pleaded with him to get the QRL board — meeting that night — to publicly support Wally. The board belatedly complied, releasing a statement that Lewis was being unfairly singled out by NSW administrators and some sections of the media. The board said Lewis had gone to the aid of a team-mate and had not "come in punching". That's where Wally beat his critics hands down. Another player might have rushed in swinging. Not Wally. No one could lay that rap on him.

Reporter Steve Crawley, in the *Sun-Herald*, polled nine former Australian captains and found the majority supported Bennett's view. John Sattler couldn't stop clapping Wally. To Arthur Summons he was a victim of the tall poppy syndrome. Summons said, "I don't think he did a great deal wrong." Arthur Beetson, Graeme Langlands, Ron Coote and Tom Raudonikis echoed that sentiment. Max Krilich, Wally's immediate predecessor, thought Wally maybe deserved a reprimand. Bobby Fulton wondered whether the pressure was getting to Wally. Ian Walsh, once more, urged that Wally lose the captaincy. Worse, Wally was not even worthy of Test selection on form, Walsh said. Wally read Walsh's comments and said, "I've got no time for his opinions."

Arthurson was angry with the Lang Park crowd and questioned the future sales of alcohol at Origin matches but the QRL quashed the idea. Wally and Mal Meninga have been pelted with lemons at Leichhardt Oval, Peter Jackson struck by a cigarette lighter. The NSWRL did so little to protect Wally at Broncos games in Sydney he had to stop signing children's autographs. SCG crowd insults to Wally are notorious.

The great Lang Park storm in a beer can delayed the game less than a minute — 50 seconds to be precise. Nobody was hurt in the brawl or by the cans. Historians harked back to another Lang Park can-throwing match, in 1971. Test halfback-turned-referee Keith Holman sent three maroons and one blue off, prompting a rain of soft drink and beer cans. One spectator even climbed the fence to chase Holman but was hurled back by NSW players. Don Lancashire, now Queensland director of referees, was present at that match and he rated Mick Stone's performance during the opening minutes of the beer can Origin the poorest he had seen at interstate level since Holman's — with precisely the same result. Two incidents, 17 years apart, scarcely constitute a volatile record. In those intervening years Queensland took some fearful hidings from NSW without the crowd objecting. Lang Park patrons know how to lose.

Some suggested that the Origin media promotions had gone overboard. Before the match in question a giant pantomime cane toad inched around the field swallowing radio-controlled cockroaches-on-wheels and belching into the Lang Park public address system. It was harmless stadium theatre. Cans were thrown at blue-jerseyed or blue-flag-bearing supporters parading in the crowd. That sort of tom-foolery may be witnessed any week a New Zealand rugby union team arrives at Ballymore with its flag-waving contingent of Kiwis. Yet all that is spilt on Ballymore's Fourex Hill is beer and nobody has suggested they ban it there.

The good fortune of the state-of-origins is that they are played in cities 900 kilometres apart, in stadiums where the crowds are almost entirely supporters of the home side. Unopposed parochialism does not normally beget violence. If, on the other hand, the SCG was equally divided — with 20,000 NSW and 20,000 Queensland fans — and the Sydney mob set up their Wally's-a-wanker chant, does anyone imagine the maroon fans would turn a deaf ear? Mayhem on an English soccer scale could well ensue.

At Lang Park the die was cast the moment Mick Stone inexplicably thrashed Steve Roach with a feather for flooring Bob Lindner. When Stone later marched Wally, the crowd, like most of us, did not understand why. It appeared he had been dismissed for upholding the principle of fair play for Greg Conescu. To the packed Lang Park terraces Queensland's QC had been ordered from the courtroom. May as well wreck the court.

The subsequent brouhaha engulfing Wally saved Steve Roach. True to his word Wayne Bennett lodged a complaint with the Queensland Rugby League citing Roach for striking Lindner. Roach reacted by claiming that Lindner had elbowed him in the tackle leading to the incident. As Lindner lay prone Wally had asked him, "Who got you — Roach?" Lindner nodded. Wally hissed, "Bloody Block!" He stayed clear of the debate about his Test team-mate. "That's the way Steve plays it," he told me. "He's always going to take a risk and maybe if he didn't play it that way he wouldn't be as successful as he is." Bennett differed. "I know that's how Roach is, but I'm sick and tired of violence going unpunished."

Rugby league bad-boy Les Boyd once remarked that some players, if provoked, counted to 10 before they reacted. "Blocker's probably a bit like I was," said Boyd. "We can't even count to one." Journalist Jeff Wells, in the *Australian*, tore aside Roach's flimsy disguise as the harmless buffoon of rugby league. Wells wrote:

> There is an outbreak of extra-curricular violence, the referee moves in to separate the combatants and Roach moves to one side with a big grin on his face. Then, with an unerring sense of theatre and feel for camera placements, he gives the trademark roguish wink...Roach is indelibly cast in our consciousness as a big overgrown naughty boy who stings people with a peashooter.

In 1983 Les Boyd was suspended for 12 months for breaking Darryl Brohman's jaw in an Origin match. On 23 May 1988, just seven days before the beer can Origin, Easts winger David

French was given 12 weeks for breaking Dale Shearer's jaw. Bob Lindner's ear required six stitches but his jaw remained intact. Perhaps that is why the special Origin sub-committee of the ARL, comprising Arthurson and state chiefs John Quayle and Ross Livermore, took no action against Roach.

The sub-committee decided referee Stone's penalty against NSW was sufficient punishment for Roach. However, according to Sydney reports, the sub-committee also censured Wally Lewis for inflaming the Conescu-Daley incident. Magnanimously, the sub-committee would take no action against Lewis either. No mention was made of the fact that Wally was never cited. The sub-committee admonished him for behaviour about which there had been no formal NSW complaint. It read like Wally had been included in the findings to balance the acquittal of Steve Roach.

QRL managing director Ross Livermore said the sub-committee had conferred by three-way telephone hook-up. Ken Arthurson had later released their findings to the media but Livermore was unaware of his exact words. And what of Wally's supposed harassment of Stone, the allegation which initially so excited Messrs Arthurson, Quayle, Hickie, Leibmann et al? Livermore was adamant the sub-committee had cleared Wally of anything to do with the beer can throwing.

The sub-committee's decision — an attempt to bring peace to their troubled domain — only inflamed Queensland further. The Queensland sports minister, Brian Littleproud, issued an unprecedented statement criticising Roach. He said, "Those first 10 minutes, in which high tackles were a feature, seemed to spark the whole ugly affair." The Brisbane *Sun* was moved to editorialise:

> If this sort of thing continues and the authorities condone it, maybe the law will have to become involved because, whichever way you look at it, on or off the field, violence is breaking the law.

The sub-committee's decision upset Wayne Bennett. "This will open a Pandora's box," he told me. "They're saying that if you belt somebody in an interstate game but don't get sent off, you won't be cited. I have no doubt in my mind that NSW players are given protection." Bennett suddenly ceased to become easily accessible to the media. "Yeah, I spat the dummy real bad," he recalled. "To suggest Wally started the can throwing business was ridiculous. The media didn't stick up for Wally, the administrators didn't stick up for the game. They could have stopped it dead. I expected them all to show some balls and they showed nothing."

Lost in the welter of wailing was Queensland's retention of the Origin interstate shield. Wally read a NSW player's comment that when the cans flew he feared for his life. And that Benny Elias said he felt a change come over the NSW team after the incident. "The only thing that put them off," said Wally, "was Jacko intercepting Terry Lamb's pass to Garry Jack." Wally wrote in his Brisbane *Sunday Mail* column on 5 June:

> I have heard some poor excuses in my time but blaming a fight for losing a rugby league match is about as weak as you can get.

It seemed impossible that out of this calumny and acrimony Australia could produce a harmonious Test team, yet it was an imperative. Landed on our shores was Great Britain's most serious challenge in a decade. Australia had just eleven days to heal its deep, self-inflicted wounds before the first Test.

12 BLACK POWER

The British Lions to tour Australia in 1988 included three of the most exhilarating ball runners in international rugby league. Captain Ellery Hanley was Britain's costliest player with a transfer fee on the open market estimated at half a million dollars. He was in the van of the new wealthy class of English players whose clubs had ridden the crest of the nation's economic resurgence under prime minister Margaret Thatcher. Son of middle-class Jamaican immigrants to Britain, Hanley's lifestyle ran to a $200,000 villa in Leeds, a $20,000 car courtesy of his Wigan club, a Puma sponsorship and $2,000 a match. He displayed a proud, Vivian Richards-type bearing, clashed with Wigan's disciplinarian coach, Kiwi Graham Lowe, and generally became known as the *enfant terrible* of English football.

Above all he was a class footballer. Playing everywhere from wing to lock he had combined great strength with speed to score 15 tries in 22 Tests. He came to Australia with the 1984 Lions as a young winger but few impressed in that losing side. Wally diagnosed Hanley as an individualist and wondered about his team commitment. Before the 1986 first Test in England, Wally advised Gene Miles to test Hanley's enthusiasm. Miles ran straight over Hanley who disappeared as a force in the series. By making Hanley captain the English Rugby League thrust responsibility upon him.

Henderson Gill, another Wigan star, was the most flamboyant winger in rugby league anywhere. He exhibited all the showmanship of American gridiron players, swivelling his hips Elvisfashion after scoring a try, yet he was no show pony. Incredibly strong and elusive he had been scoring for England since 1981. Said Wally, "He runs sideways, then back, then a little way forward then sideways again...runs 100 yards and ends up making two." Wally would rather have a winger who ran five metres straight ahead, but added drolly, "He'd probably be handy if you were trying to run down the clock. You'd never catch him." Wally was ambivalent about Gill's antics. "You tackle him, he gets up and pushes you and carries on," said Wally. "But you know he's not going to blue, he just does it for the crowd. And then after the game he says, 'Sorry about that.' It cuts no ice with me."

The third flash was the fastest of them all, indeed of any footballer in England or Australia as sprint contests subsequently proved. Martin Offiah, a rugby union convert, was Britain's top try scorer in 1987–88 with 44 touchdowns. That feat broke the Widnes club try-scoring record which had stood since 1959. In early matches on the 1988 tour he simply burnt off provincial wingers. His speed, though, was not quite matched by his experience and Wally's theory that a stout, flat defensive line would drive Offiah over the sideline subsequently proved correct.

The three players were all black, all quick and all strong and wore their hair short-back-and-sides in the fearsome style of Mike Tyson, or even Grace Jones. Black power had come to rugby league.

After the 1982 Kangaroo Invincibles swept all before them the English Rugby League promised changes. In the third Test against Wally's 1986 Kangaroos it showed. The Britons edged to 12–12 before Wally led the Roos to safety. With the massive influx of Australian and New Zealand coaches and players to British clubs the standard had improved further by 1988. Test candidates Wally, Garry Jack, Andrew Ettinghausen, Tony Currie, Peter Jackson, Peter Sterling, Bob Lindner and Wally Fullerton-Smith had all played with English clubs. Wally knew that the Poms, coached by Malcolm Reilly, a dual premiership winner when he played with Manly in Bobby Fulton's days, would be competitive.

He had gleaned little intelligence about the black brigade but he respected other tourists he knew: half Andy Gregory — "A really hard nosed little fellow"; centre Garry Schofield — "A good bloke, rates with Terry Lamb as the best support player around"; and prop Kevin Ward — "A hard man, strong, honest. I used to have a drink with him when I was with Wakefield Trinity."

Early in the tour Britain looked ominous, knocking over the capable New Guinea Kumuls 42–22, North Queensland 66–16 and Newcastle 28–12. Offiah was an immediate sensation scoring six tries in his first two matches in Australia. Andy Gregory, asked if Offiah was the fastest player he had ever seen, replied, "I don't know, I've only ever seen his back." The British witnessed the controversial second state-of-origin and were mightily impressed by the defence, their own weak suit. Six days before the first Test the British collapsed against NSW northern division 32–12 and then their second stringers were flogged 30–0 by Manly in a dispiriting midweek walkover. Unless Malcolm Reilly was foxing, the British were still outclassed.

The Australian team was chosen on state-of-origin form and Queensland was gratified to find unfashionable Greg Conescu, the players' player, returned as Test hooker. Dropped were stalwarts Gene Miles and Wayne Pearce, both of whom conceded their form was not 100 per cent. The team met general approval apart from a bizarre interview former British hooker Mike Stephenson reported with Malcolm Reilly. It read in part:

> I get the impression Reilly feels the Queensland maestro, Lewis, has lost some of his glitter...When superstars begin to lose speed, anticipation and temper, you can guarantee they are on the slide. No one can deny that Lewis is one of the greats but Father Time seems to be catching up with him.

Wally no longer ignited at such comments. After 25 Tests, 17 as captain, it was inevitable that the moment he consolidated his leadership the rumour would begin that he was past his best. Wally concentrated on helping to blend the two Origin states into an Aussie side. The two players at the epicentre of the recent Origin earthquake, Greg Conescu and Phil Daley, were now packing down as hooker and prop forward. Australian coach Don Furner's great strength is creating accord. He set about giving this team a sense of history.

It was the 100th Test between the two great rival nations — a centenary Test in Australia's bicentenary year — with Britain leading 49–46, and four Tests drawn. The first ever Test, in London in 1908, was a 22–22 draw. England won the next and have led ever since. Furner took the Aussies out to Fairfield where the 1908 Kangaroos worked out before leaving for England. It was a long, tiring drive to Sydney's western suburbs and once there they were engulfed by thousands of schoolchildren seeking autographs. Not the best physical preparation but even in discomfort Furner was establishing a unifying experience. He replayed a video of their narrow win in the 1986 third Test in England and reminded the team how New Zealand had exploited the Origin series the year before to score an upset victory.

Wally watched the team attitude change day by day. The esprit of the new boys, Andrew Ettinghausen, Tony Currie, Peter Jackson, Sam Backo and Phil Daley drew the team together. No player wanted to be part of the first Aussies to lose a Test to Great Britain in a decade. Wally watched Sam Backo try on his green and gold jersey. Backo growled, "Fits good, feels great," pure pride glowing in his face. In the end Wally declared it one of the closest knit Australian teams he had known.

All the same he felt a tinge of sadness as he retired in the evenings to his room in the Camperdown Travelodge. After so many years sharing with Gene Miles it was strange to be alone, without the human diesel snoring into the night. He rang Gene one morning.

"What're you doing?" asked Wally.

"Oh not much," said Gene.

"I'm in Sydney."

"Yeah?"

"Here with the Australian team, you know."

"Mmm."

"What're you doing Saturday?"

"Don't know, why?"

"Oh, we're playing a Test match down here." Gene finally had to laugh.

A crowd of nearly 25,000 failed to fill Sydney's new football stadium but a British lion's head and the Australian coat of arms stencilled on the field, and Union Jacks draped in the stands, gave the match a sense of occasion. Wally was one of the few who knew all the words of his national anthem, Peter Jackson's eyes brimmed, Backo stared intensely. The British team, psyched up by team meetings that morning, looked distinctly unawed.

Wally's first problem was comprehending the directions of French referee, Francis Deplas, a 34-year-old camping store manager from Toulouse. His English was confined to "Yes, no, inside the five," a few other common rulings plus a fairly good suspicion of when he was being sworn at. He whistled 28 stoppages in the first half, 18 penalties and 10 scrums, most of which were so atrocious Greg Conescu lost four tightheads. It would be easy to blame Deplas but in fact ferocious defence by Britain jolted Australia and returned the British 58 per cent of possession.

Footballers study opponents' attacking styles like bowlers study batsmen's techniques in cricket. The Australians knew Ellery Hanley to be at his most dangerous running to the right and fending with his left hand — a right field runner. Hanley did just that, cruising outside Peter Jackson to score the first try of the series. BBC commentator Ray French said of his country's 6–0 half-time lead, "This Test team has never played together on tour. Malcolm Reilly had kept them back and they've come out fighting."

The Australians filed thoughtfully off the field and Wally heard the Poms, as they ran up the race at half-time, whooping and hollering, "We've got these bloody Aussies!" He found a strange relief in their ebullience. "It made me feel good because we'd bombed four tries, we'd played like mugs and they thought the game was over."

Whatever Furner does at training it is Wally who directs the team mid-match. Wally calmed the agitated Australian room.

"We're playing with plenty of enthusiasm but no brains," he said. "Now let's talk about it." He hammered the theme of back to basics. "When we get out there let's control the ball. They kick off, it's our ball, we'll work it for five, kick, we've got the wind behind us, I want a good chase. We'll see how they go and when we get the ball back we'll hold it again. If we do that we're going to end up down near their line. Once we get there we can start worrying about being flash."

For 10 minutes the match teetered. Australia pressed and Sam Backo, who has a long and proud Islander history in his blood, produced Australia's black power, shunting over for a try. Six points all. British fullback Paul Loughlin topped the English goalkicking charts in 1986–87. He lined up a penalty almost in front. It would put Britain back in the lead and rejuvenate tiring British limbs. He missed. The British watched the ball sail wide and saw victory disappearing over the horizon. Peter Jackson scored to put Australia ahead 12–6. Wally wanted to push Australia into a safety zone. Backo worked the ball close to the British quarterline. Dummy half Conescu raised his eyebrows at Wally: D'you want it? Wally nodded and slotted over a field goal, extending the lead to 13–6. That hurt the British. Now they would have to score twice.

As Wally ran back to half-way he grabbed Vautin and said, "We've got to really consolidate here, Fatty. You're the most experienced forward on the paddock." Vautin responded with inspirational forward play, bullocking forward, shedding tackles. Few commentators could understand when coach Furner replaced him with Steve Folkes. Vautin was angry and disappointed. "This bloke's got to be kidding," he muttered as he trudged off. Vautin believed, rightly or wrongly, Furner had a set against him. Wally turned to applaud Vautin off and the crowd followed his lead. Vautin's slumped shoulders straightened, his chin lifted and his trot acquired a new purpose.

Jackson sealed the match with a second try and charged about leaping and shouting at peak volume. Wally caught him and said, "Mate, I think you've made history. I don't know anybody else who's scored two tries in their first Test." In fact Jim Morgan scored the double in 1970 at Lang Park. The final score

-- 17–6 — was unjust to Britain. Pugnacious bantam Andy Gregory stood broken, wondering how Britain had let the match slip. Kevin Ward was so down he could scarcely accept his cheque as man-of-the-match. Australia were simply more used to pressure, more used to winning.

In normal circumstances the third state-of-origin, a dead rubber, would have been an anti-climax for Queensland. NSW fans treated it as such with the second smallest crowd in Origin history, less than 17,000, turning out in Sydney. But Queensland had various scores to settle. Allan Langer, who outplayed Peter Sterling in the first Origin, had a quiet game in the second. Test selector Ernie Hammerton was reported as saying, "Sterlo put the kid in his place tonight." Less than 48 hours later Langer was in hospital with acute tonsillitis. Martin Bella remembered that before the series the media had given Queensland little hope. He said, "We got together after the second match and decided we wanted to embarrass them for what they wrote." Bob Lindner sensed the southern push to replace him with Wayne Pearce for the second Test. Wayne Bennett wanted his Origin ledger, standing at 4–4, to finish in the black. And then there was the fiasco of NSW's alleged fourth Origin win in Los Angeles. Remembering NSW's 1986 winning treble, Wally said, "We all had about two pounds of salt to rub into NSW's wounds."

Their task was made immeasurably easier with an act of numbing small-mindedness by the NSW team management. Phil Daley was sacked for breaking the team camp, without permission, to visit his pregnant wife. Before issuing his fiat, NSW manager Peter Moore asked Australian chairman of selectors Ernie Hammerton if sacking Daley would diminish his chances of second Test selection. Hammerton confirmed it would not. That conversation alone deserved an inquiry into the machinations of the NSW and ARL selection processes. Wally read it all and said, "It could never, ever, happen in a Queensland side. It's a totally different spirit, we're a family."

Yet the family trailed NSW 18–10 at half-time due to some brilliant crossfield running by Cliff Lyons to open gaps for his outside backs. On a broader note Wally felt that Queensland wanted a result without having to work for it. Bennett caught the same scent and ripped into Backo. Did he want to be a one-Test wonder? That's all Backo needed. "You look and see how often Queensland scored after a Backo bust," NSW coach John Peard lamented as Queensland crushed his team 38–22. Backo was man-of-the-match but Martin Bella won his second consecutive players' player award. John MacDonald saw yet a further dimension of the game. He wrote in the *Sydney Morning Herald*:

...Lewis' contribution was monumental. The sobriquet King Wally was never more deserved. He played NSW virtually on his own for much of the first half...When NSW were stopped on the flanks, in the centre, anywhere...it was invariably Lewis. His anticipation, determination and ability to read a game were never more apparent...There may have been better players over the years, but you wouldn't need many fingers to count them.

NSW recriminations were immediate. Chairman Hammerton was reported as saying, "Better team, better coach." He denied saying it. Coach John Peard replied, "Maybe he picked the wrong players." Wally heard about the sniping and thanked Lord Dally Messenger he was not born in NSW. "Even when Queensland lost badly we never started bitching about players or coaches," he said. Journalist Andrew Slack coined it nicely: "Hammerton's utterances do for diplomacy what AIDS has for promiscuity."

Wally accepted the Origin shield to cat-calls from cats in the crowd and retreated to the Queensland dressingroom where for 10 minutes, without the media or officials, pandemonium reigned. The entire team stood in the showers, screaming choruses to Peter Jackson's tuneless compositions — derogatory doggerel — about NSW football, beer, crowds...anything. A clean sweep against NSW was another jewel in the Emperor's crown.

The team arrived back at their Rushcutters Bay Travelodge motel at about 10.30 p.m. in fine form, expecting to add to the eight Queenslanders of the first Test team. At 11 p.m. team manager, Dick "Tossa" Turner, arrived with the Test list. He walked past Wally and delivered a bitter aside, "They've dropped Bobby." Wally managed one word. "Martin?" Turner morosely shook his head. For having downed NSW 3-0, Bob Lindner, Australia's best forward in the first Test, who had topped the maroon tackle count only hours ago, had been dropped for Wayne Pearce. Phil Daley, having fortuitously escaped NSW's mauling, retained his place ahead of Bella. The mood in the motel turned from celebration to black frustration.

Lindner harboured no personal animosity towards Wayne Pearce yet felt cheated. "Have I been his fill-in for the past two years?" he asked. Lindner's move to Sydney had not been as happy as other Queenslanders'. He had joined Parramatta past their peak and was playing out of position — second-row — to patch up the Eels' shortcomings. The Sydney experience was souring on him. An optometrist, he drove a BMW to training which attracted the ire of his predecessor Ray Price who thought it unsuited to a workingman's club. Lindner's wife was badly frightened by a break-in and was once attacked as she returned to their apartment. It was no surprise when Lindner returned to Queensland in 1989.

Martin Bella was so upset by his omission he could not speak. An Australian under-18 representative he had worked long and hard to graduate to the nation's senior team. He finally said emotionally, "Obviously you don't have to perform in Origin games to play Test football." Word spread that Ken Arthurson was not required to cast a deciding vote on any position, which meant the Queenslanders on the selection board had not fought for Lindner or Bella. Though those worthy officials were at the Queensland celebrations the players addressed not a word to them that evening. Wally, in his traditional speech, concluded, "Martin, you might not be good enough for the selectors to put in the Test team but you can be in my team any day of the week," and looked pointedly at the selectors.

A 5-1 record in the 1987-88 Origins exactly reversed the NSW wins in 1985-86 and the NSW players were beginning to examine their system. Several senior players filed a letter of complaint to the NSWRL about their treatment during the Origin series. NSW had dropped Daley for visiting his wife whereas the Queensland management flew players' wives down to watch the Sydney Origins. In selecting 25 players in the series compared to Queensland's 17, NSW had shown less confidence in their team.

The Queenslanders received a record bonus of $7,500 each for their clean sweep and at the end-of-series formal dinner — no wives — at a riverside restaurant Wally glanced about the tables. Dinner suits and starched flyaway collars sat majestically on broad shoulders. With their crooked noses, caulied ears and scarred eyebrows, the diners could have been prohibition leaders at the Cotton Club. Sam Backo, sipping port and smoking a cigar, presided like Al Capone; Wayne Bennett looked a deadly, poker-faced hit-man; and Fatty Vautin could have been a dangerous, smiling, Irish syndicate chief. Vautin has the untidy habit of pushing food he does not like off his plate on to the tablecloth. When the waiter removes his plate a large, clear circle results. If there is no circle Wally knows Fatty has enjoyed the meal. At 11 p.m. the Mob adjourned to Expo, still in their monkey suits, but who would dare razz them! Wally resumed his attempts to induce liquor to pass Wayne Bennett's lips. "If you don't have a drink tonight you're impossible to please," Wally told him. Maybe Bennett was holding out for a Winfield premiership.

The Broncos seemed too brittle to be a threat to Bennett's teetotalism. After dislocating his shoulder against the Gold Coast Giants, Wally was unfit for the next match, against Canberra, the first Broncos match he had missed. He fidgeted about the Lang Park dressingroom before the game telling anyone who would listen, "This is Wayne's old club, they'll be out to belt us to show him he shouldn't have left Canberra. You've got to win this for Wayne."

New realities had been faced by Bennett. Before the season Bennett had warned Gene Miles to stay out of the forwards. He wanted Gene's strength saved for breaks out wide, not busting up the centre of rucks. Ten weeks later Bennett conceded the Broncos lacked steel up front and, against Canberra, Miles began his long anticipated career in the second-row. Manager John Ribot reduced it to figures: "Most of our forwards were between 90–95 kilos," he said. "Balmain had several forwards averaging over 100 kilos." Ten kilograms in imperial weights is 1 stone 8 lbs. The Broncos' heavyweights were being flattened by Sydney's super-heavies.

While Geno made the move, other old mates of Wally's were not faring so well. Just as Wally thought that former Australian fullback Colin Scott was picking up form, Scott, aged 28, lost his place to Shane Duffy, aged 20. Bryan Neibling, though a 1986 Kangaroo, could not find a first-grade place. Wally took the liberty of pleading Niebling's case with Bennett. Since moving to the front-row Niebling had ignored his ball-playing skills to concentrate on power running, said Wally. "Then he'll have to change," said Bennett. Wally felt his loyalties wrung by the harshness of Sydney football.

Raider Sam Backo turned on his Origin pals in the Broncos to lead Canberra home 36–16. Lang Park fans adhered to their greater Origin loyalties and cheered Backo from the ground. Their motion was seconded by Wayne Bennett who immediately set about signing Sam for 1989. Coach turned journalist, Roy Masters, examined the Broncos personnel and pinpointed a damaging lack of Young Veterans — the three to five-year men who had played 60 to 100 first-grade games. Brisbane had Veterans: Wally and Co.; and Youth: Michael Hancock et al; but few Young Veterans, like expatriates, Jackson, Lindner, Belcher and Currie, who buttressed the Origin team. Wally listened to the theory and sighed, "Yeah, there wasn't much we could do about it." The Broncos, though still second in the premiership table, had lost four of their last five matches. Wally saw how hard the rest of the season would be. "All the facts were in front of us," he said. "Easy Street had ended. We knew we were going to have to work."

Bennett had the dubious pleasure of telling the media, "I told you so." He had preached gloom and doom even when the Broncos were on their winning streak. "A lot of our blokes are great ad lib footballers with natural ability," he said. "But in Sydney, with tight defence, that's not enough. We have to work for things on the field."

The Broncos flew south and stayed overnight in Wollongong for their match against Illawarra. Wally had a laugh when Gene

Miles, tape wound around his ears for his second stint in the forwards, complained about his head throbbing — before the match even began. Torrential rain nearly postponed the game and the Broncos opening form was nearly as miserable as the weather. Veteran Illawarra centre Brian Hetherington sold inexperienced young fullback Shane Duffy a huge dummy for the Steelers' first try. Duffy chose to leave Hetherington and cover the winger instead. Wally spoke patiently with Duffy under the posts, "In a dry game Duff, that's good. But in a wet game always take the bloke with the ball because then he has to pass and with a wet ball the support is 50–50 to drop it."

The Broncos trailed 10–6 at half-time. The Steelers were coached by Terry Fearnley, the Australian coach who alienated Wally and his Queenslanders on the 1985 tour of New Zealand. Though he had intended to keep the memory to himself, Wally turned before the team ran out for the second half and said earnestly, "Listen, if we never win another game all year, win this one for me, because of all people, I don't want to lose to this bloke." The Broncos, led by noted mudlark Greg Dowling, granted Wally his wish, overrunning the tiring Steelers 32–10.

The Broncos stayed on the second rung of the ladder by squeezing home against St George 26–22 at Lang Park, but other events overshadowed the result. Bennett told the team to stay on the field at half-time and a 30-metre-long plastic banner proclaiming "Power Brewing" was pegged at four corners to form a corral in the centre of the field. This became their dressing-room before the prying eyes of the television cameras and an astonished crowd of 20,000.

Wally, used to staying on field from his rugby union days, was quite happy to plonk down instead of taking the long walk to the changingroom through back-slapping wellwishers. He noticed that a few players were more interested in peering over the top of the banner at the gyrations of the nearby Broncettes, than listening to coach Bennett. The idea, to give Power value for their sponsor dollar, was John Ribot's. He confided his plan to Wayne Bennett without fully informing the Broncos directors. The experiment took the Broncos into a head-on confrontation with the Lang Park Trust and the NSWRL.

The crux of the problem was that Bond Brewing, previously Castlemaine Perkins, had a 10-year exclusive advertising contract for alcohol at Lang Park. Power Brewing, after outlaying $3 million to sponsor the Broncos for three years, saw their opportunities for brand exposure dramatically reduced. They had planned advertising placards and hoardings to be placed strategically around Lang Park to be caught by the television cameras, even the commercial-free lens of the ABC. Power were now limited to displaying their name on the players' jerseys. The Broncos threatened to take their home games to the Gabba or the local showgrounds but the NSWRL replied that the premiership agreement stipulated the Broncos play at Lang Park.

The chairman of the Lang Park Trust was Ron McAuliffe, still smarting from having backed the wrong syndicate to put a team into Sydney. McAuliffe could never resist having digs at the Maranta syndicate, publicly and privately. Broncos general manager John Ribot, coach Wayne Bennett and captain, Wally, all of whom had worked for McAuliffe at the QRL, were pained by Senator Ron's opposition. Wally, for nearly a decade McAuliffe's favourite son, had to disown his patron's antagonism.

Broncos director Paul Morgan told me, "McAuliffe made one mistake. He should have come with us. It's an absolute travesty that with his knowledge, experience and charisma, we don't have him on the board of the Broncos. He deserves a better fate." I relayed those sentiments to McAuliffe one day and he hesitated a moment, perhaps hoping an opening still existed to realise a life's ambition, to direct a Brisbane club into Sydney. But the pride — obstinacy — of the old war-horse reasserted itself. Since the consortium fall out he hadn't spoken three words to Maranta, he said. "And I'm not likely to." These words became sadly prophetic when, eight weeks later, McAuliffe died suddenly at the age of 70.

The Broncos-Lang Park Trust impasse may have been overcome had goodwill existed between the two sides. As it was Maranta and Ribot apologised to ARL and NSWRL chiefs Arthurson and Quayle for the corral ploy, and an uneasy peace descended.

The seeds of the next Broncos disaster were sown when coach Bennett, Wally, Geno, "Turtle" Conescu and "Alf" Langer went into camp in Sydney one Thursday morning for the third state-of-origin and then, almost immediately, quit camp to join the other Broncos who flew down on Friday for their night match against South Sydney. That kind of unavoidable neglect of the Broncos eventually influenced Bennett to withdraw from state-of-origin coaching. Manager John Ribot, chaperoning the rest of the Broncos to Sydney, picked up disturbing vibrations from the players. They were talking about playing golf on Saturday morning, the races in the afternoon and hitting Kings Cross Saturday night. Ribot later confided to promotions manager, Kev Keliher, "That's the worst atmosphere I've ever felt in a dressingroom. This is going to be bad." And so it was, 22 dropped balls and a 16–4 drubbing. Wally went nearly hoarse screaming out, "For Christ's sake, just once, let's hold the ball for four tackles and kick it...have you got that?" Yeah, yeah, they said, and dropped the ball on the second tackle. Wally joined Souths players, Mario Fenech, Craig Coleman and Bronco Djura for a drink afterwards. Wally gets on well with Fenech, has always found him pleasant natured and had no hesitation in admitting that the Broncos didn't deserve to win. Mario told him, "Mate, if it's any consolation, that's the best we've played in two years."

With the second Test at Lang Park on Tuesday, 28 June, Wally was in camp when the Broncos took on Canterbury. The rookie Broncos held a brave lead until, midway through the second half, Canterbury coach Phil Gould sent veteran Steve Mortimer on, returning him to the scene of his 1985 state-of-origin glory. Mortimer laid on two tries and whisked the subsequent premiers to a 25–10 win.

Two consecutive losses, to Souths and the Bulldogs, plummeted the Broncos to sixth place on the ladder. Wayne Bennett arrived grim-faced at the next Broncos training with a plan to improve the Broncos' performance. Wally listened attentively. He and Bennett had already shared the triumph of the Origin wins and he was midway through defending the Ashes against Great Britain. His loyalty and commitment to the Broncos was unquestioned but in those weeks, although he ran on wearing the Broncos maroon and yellow, his heart was probably swathed in the green-and-gold.

13 BULLDOG SPIRIT

The French expression for headhunter is *coupeur de tetes* — cutter of heads. Had Wally spoken the lingo he might have been able to gesticulate, draw a finger across his throat and enlighten French referee Francis Deplas what Great Britain were about in the second Test in Brisbane. For a period in each half the tourists reverted to their worst habits, equating hard play with illegal tackles, swinging their arms in roundhouse fashion at Australian heads. Wally decided not to bother confronting Deplas because as the evening wore on it was obvious to him, as it was to the Lang Park crowd, that Britain's flailing arms were flinging away the series as well.

The Australian Test squad had spent that afternoon at Festival Hall watching Michael Spinks's capitulation to Mike Tyson in the cable-televised world title fight. It was an apt preparation though it must be said the Australians hunted first and hunted highest and the culprit was Wally Lewis. His first tackle, for which he was penalised, was a thumping, chest-high, legal hit on his opposite, David Hulme. His second offence, which went unpunished, was a head-high, full body slam on Roy Powell which snuffed a threatening British move.

The British did not retaliate, at least not until they started to lose and then they went at it with a vengeance. Andy Gregory was eventually sinbinned for 10 minutes, Phil Ford was lucky not to go and Deplas apparently could not see Kevin Ward's scything elbows and arms. Ford, a winger chosen as centre, was all at sea in his new position and it showed the first time Michael

O'Connor ran at him. In a man-on-man backline confrontation
Ford pawed untidily at O'Connor and then, clinging with his
left hand, swung a wild right-arm haymaker at O'Connor's
head. If boxers failed to see such punches fights would not last
a round. O'Connor ducked and accelerated away to score. As
the Australians ran back past Ford several called sarcastically,
"Nice tackle mate." Later, when Ford aimed a similar blow at
Garry Jack, Wally rushed in, pinioned Ford's arms and admonished him, "You're a bloody lunatic pal." However much Ford
was a menace to Australia he was a worse threat to Britain,
giving away penalties and letting in tries.

Wally was eventually flattened in a head-high hit by British
fullback Paul Loughlin. Peter Jackson quickly removed Wally's
mouthguard as he lay motionless, arms outstretched. "I saw a
few stars," said Wally. "I was hurt, but not too badly. It just
made me determined that if I was ever going to play a good
game it was against these headhunters." Jack Gibson observed
sagely, "They're getting all wired up, they'll get beat." Mick
Cronin agreed, "They're trying to outmuscle Australia. They
can't win that way." Four minutes before half-time Wally
handled twice in a sweeping 40-metre try to give Australia an
18–4 lead.

Australia had monopolised 60 per cent of possession and,
with every six tackles, consistently made more ground than
Great Britain. Wally eyed the team, wondering how best to sew
up this Test and the series. The British were bound to mount a
last ditch counter-attack. He remembered Bennett's master-
stroke in the Origins, took a deep breath and launched
into...Sam Backo. The big prop's eyes lit up and Wally suddenly saw how strong-willed Bennett must have been to continue his criticism in the face of Backo's angry glare. Wally took
fright, carefully backed off and concluded mildly, "Now c'mon
Sam, you know your job, let's get out there and do it."

Malcolm Reilly's half-time address was reflected in the British
play. No high tackles, no dropped ball and sound kicking. They
recovered to trail only 18–10 and for 20 minutes had much the
better of the game. The tourists' fourth black player, unfashionable second-rower Roy Powell, led the way. "He wasn't a thug,

didn't try to belt our blokes, just played it straight up and down," said Wally. "We gave him plenty and he kept having a go. I admired him."

Tension mounted in the Australian side, especially when Britain won two tight heads after Deplas's apologies-for-scrums. After several fruitless non-conversations Peter Sterling had abandoned trying to explain to referee Deplas the scrum problems. Wally approved the idea of a neutral referee but if it was at the expense of clear communication he would rather have a Pom referee and put up with the bias. After another hopeless scrum and another bout of Deplas hooting "Nor! Nor! Nor!" Wally walked over with a fixed grin and announced to Deplas pleasantly, "Excuse me you Frog goose, do you have any idea what you're doing? No? I thought not, well I just want to say you're as much use here as an ashtray on a motorbike, OK, thank you." Deplas looked perplexed. He could not understand the speech, had not detected any obscenities and Wally's demeanour seemed non-threatening. Deplas waved him away. At least it enabled Wally to vent his frustration.

Sam Backo vindicated Wally's stern words at half-time, and ended all doubt about the result, by charging over from dummy half. It was identical to his try in the first Test. Wally heard the British players yelling, "Watch out! He'll go himself." But as Wally observed, stopping Backo close to the line was like stopping a freight train. Wayne Pearce, a lighter class engine, then emulated Backo's try and the first person to plant his feet beside Pearce and lift him bodily from the ground was Wally. They looked at each other with matching massive grins, their joyous faces dispelling any thought of a schism between these old Origin foes. Pearce returned the affection after Wally galloped over himself making the full-time score 34–14.

In the dressingroom Wally was just relaxing when several reporters began asking whether a series win was a fine way to wind up his representative career. Wally replied, "Listen, I'm not retiring. The day I retire will be when the Australian selectors think I'm not good enough to play for Australia any more. In other words I'll always consider playing for Australia as the ultimate."

From the moment his form could be observed each week in the Sydney premiership, Wally became the yardstick for the performances of other players. Whenever any of Sydney's dynamic runners — Michael O'Connor, Garry Jack and later Ellery Hanley — turned in a good game, the question was posed whether they were better than Wally. The prime contender was Peter Sterling. With Ray Price and Mick Cronin retired to the commentary boxes and Brett Kenny injured, Sterling was like Atlas, carrying the Parramatta team. His club secretary Denis Fitzgerald said, "Sterlo is not as explosive as Wally but...Peter takes a bigger role, being involved in every ruck. He dictates a match more than Wally, as good as Wally is." *Sydney Morning Herald* writer, Ian Heads, agreed. He wrote:

> I have no hesitation in ranking him (Sterling) ahead of "King" Wally Lewis, whom he outpoints comprehensively in the score of involvement in any game. Sterling is a restless, tireless worker, never off the ball; Lewis at times has the tendency to fade out of matches.

The *Sydney Morning Herald*'s most experienced league writer, Alan Clarkson, reduced the field to three, Wally, Sterlo and Mick O'Connor. He wrote:

> Lewis is a maestro in attack, capable of winning a match with one pass or an astute kick or perhaps a body-jarring tackle. He is a powerhouse who has repeatedly made the difference between a team's winning and losing...Lewis, Sterling and O'Connor are great footballers, genuine match-winners in more than one area of their games. But of the trio I rate Lewis the best — a player who would be great in any era of the game.

Wally was man-of-the-match in the Brisbane headhunting Test and the Great Britain manager, David Howes, joined the band who place him at the top of world rankings. Said Howes, "He's a class act and we've really rated him No 1 player for a while now."

Great Britain coach Malcolm Reilly had no doubt Wally was the best. More important, he said, when Lewis was paired with Sterling they constituted the heart and soul of the Australian team, having played 12 Tests for just one loss. "They are not only great individuals in their own right," said Reilly. "They are natural leaders and use the players around them magnificently. When they have moved on, Australia will be eminently beatable."

The Australians were due to go into camp on Thursday, 7 July 1988, for Saturday's third Test. Wally rang Don Furner and pleaded with him, "Donny, get us into camp Monday morning. Don't treat this any different. We've got to be there, the whole lot of us." Furner explained that he and the Australian managers would be in Canberra for a President's XIII match against Great Britain. Wally said, "If you're worried about the discipline leave one manager in Sydney. Get whoever you like to do the conditioning, we can still do the ballwork. Just get us there." Furner became convinced. He would call the ARL and see it was done. Wally rang the ARL himself and gave secretary Bob Abbott the same lecture. "Get on to somebody and make sure we're in there on Monday otherwise the attitude's going to be different," he said.

It was no use. A return call reported the bad news. They would go into camp on Thursday afternoon. The team had just two training sessions for a Test match. If the ARL would not take the British seriously, what could they expect of their players? It should never have been Wally's job to whip the ARL into action. But he had never lost a Test to Great Britain and could not understand the ARL's insouciance. Apart from that he knew what it was to struggle to motivate a complacent team, knew how frustrating 80 minutes of second-rate football could be, knew how bad he would feel if they lost.

Instead of preparation the Australian management was strong on congratulations, issuing ringing endorsements of Wally on the eve of his 27th Test. Team manager Peter Moore and coach Furner told him he was still at his peak and asked him to continue in representative football in 1989. "As far as I'm concerned he is the greatest footballer to ever play the game," said Moore. "He is also a brilliant captain and all the players would be saddened to see him go." At the Australians' motel in Sydney hundreds of British camp followers daily gave the headquarters a carnival atmosphere, overjoyed to run into Australian players in the lift, eager to be photographed with them in the foyer.

Meanwhile a new spirit had entered the British camp. They had thrown away their lead in the first Test and virtually disqualified themselves in the second. So far they had not done themselves justice on this tour. Now the team was imbued with a fierce "pride in the jersey" which had their camp corridors vibrating like a tuning fork. Kevin Ward ignored an injured ankle to declare he would play. "I'll have to, there's no one else," he said.

When Australia lost Peter Sterling 34 minutes into the first half of the Test they were already behind 10-nil. Wally looked at the scoreline and thought, "We're a better side than they are, but that's a lot of points to peg back." Wally had his own theories. Players who had stood tall in the first two Tests suddenly went missing. Some looked as though they were thinking more about the approaching Winfield Cup semi-finals. One player piped up midway through the second half, with Australia well behind, "Gees, if we don't pull our fingers out we're going to lose this." Wally looked around sourly and said, "It's a little late to be thinking about that."

Twice Australia looked like recovering and each time Britain drew away. Minutes into the second half Wally fought, twisted and levered himself through four British tacklers to stretch out for a fingertip touch-down. Any feat of strength, speed or skill on an international level is an inspiring sight. Wally's try reduced England's lead to just four points. "We thought, 'This happened in the first Test, we'll be right now'," said Wally. "But then they scored again and we were back where we started from." He gathered the team beneath the posts and said, "OK, we all got overconfident, thought we were home and hosed because we scored one try. We've got to put some pressure on them, they're the ones who have been coughing up the the ball this series, not us." Sam Backo responded with his third try in three Tests to again cut Britain's lead to four points, 16–12.

But inexplicably, from then on, experienced Australian Test players began committing elementary mistakes — Jack ran over the sideline with the ball, Jackson turned the ball over to Britain instead of kicking, Ettinghausen kicked no matter what the tackle count, Vautin was dispossessed looking to throw a late pass. On it went. The final indignity came when second-rower Mike Gregory broke through on a 60-metre dash to the Australian line. Screaming in support was "Chariots" Offiah and illegally tugging on Offiah's jersey was Wally. "I knew if Offiah got it we wouldn't catch him in a plane," he said. He and Wayne Pearce, two never-say-die Aussies, chased the two Brits right to the line with no other green-and-gold jersey within cooee.

Delirium overtook the British team as the siren sounded on a winning scoreline of 26–12. Malcolm Reilly, chaired from the field, called out, "Bulldog spirit. Beware the Englishman with his back to the wall." It was their first win over Australia in 16 Tests, their first in Australia in 14 years. Absurdly, in Great Britain's moment of victory, Wally was called upon to accept the Harry Sunderland medal as the Australian player-of-the-series. He dolefully accepted the medal, uttered the obligatory congratulations to Great Britain and then spoke his mind, "I think everybody in our team will admit we were absolutely disgraceful out there today." Previously Australia could get away with it. Not any more. International rugby league was alive and well again.

Wally accepted the Ashes trophy for Australia and stood with David Hulme's exchanged white jersey slung around his neck, blood trickling from a cut cheek, red velvet medal box in one hand, silver trophy in the other. He lifted the trophy above his shoulder but barked at photographers who asked him to crack a smile, "I've got nothing to smile about." He braved the singing and bonhomie in the British dressingroom to shake Malcolm Reilly's hand. In London the popular papers were already pasting up their headlines — "True Brit" said the *News of the World*, "Glory Be" exclaimed the *Sunday Mirror* and "Reilly's Heroes" cried the *Sunday Express*.

After three Origins and three Tests — six matches where Wally was expected to give his all — he was only two-thirds through his 1988 representative duties, not to mention the Broncos matches to come. Wayne Bennett, who had as much to lose as any coach with Wally, Langer, Conescu and later Gene Miles summoned from the Broncos ranks, asked how much a player had to give to his country. "Sam Backo is expected to cart the ball up and take hard tackles 20 times and make 20 or 30 hard tackles a match," said Bennett. "Sports scientists say the body needs a certain regeneration period after body-contact sport. The players are not being allowed the necessary recovery time."

Fortunately the next Test was against Papua New Guinea, a romp which did not require Wally to lay down body and soul. Scarred and broken-nosed Gavin Miller and unmarked Allan Langer were two new and contrasting faces in the Australian team. Wally phoned Langer with the news of his selection one Sunday night. Langer, exhausted from a weekend away, thanked him politely for the call. Wally, who regards Test jumpers as the equivalent of knighthoods, said, "Well don't go overboard eh, are you happy or what? You've just been picked to play for your country." Langer solemnly agreed it was a terrific thing. Wally, exasperated, concluded, "Well I'll just leave you to have the party you're obviously just about to throw, cop you later." The next morning at the team gathering Langer, refreshed, slipped on his first green-and-gold jersey and Wally got the response he expected, a self-conscious grin as Langer stared happily into a mirror.

The Test was transferred to Wagga and the Australians spent several days spreading rugby league goodwill in the Riverina's Australian rules territory. The country people responded with a handsome crowd of nearly 12,000 to watch Australia, world champions, play the code's newest football nation. The Papua New Guineans had beaten New Zealand in 1986 and more recently, in May 1988, defeated a second-string Brisbane side 44–24 in sweltering humidity in Port Moresby. The Kumuls were outclassed against Australia, not the least because they were in such awe of their opponents. Many of their team had nicknames after Australian players: captain Bal Numapo, a centre, was Mal Meninga — "the man himself" - and others were called Crusher (Noel Cleal) and Guru (Eric Grothe). At a Wagga welcome the night before the Test the Kumuls spent the evening chasing autographs and posing for photographs with their much-admired opponents. "We were their heroes," said Wally. "They looked at us like we were Gods, it made their night just to shake hands. The next day when they tackled you they'd just as likely help you up and say 'Hello'. Funny little blokes, few of them over six foot, but very tough, very hard."

Mal Meninga, perhaps conscious of his weakened left arm, played quietly until the Kumuls tested him out. "This little forward put a genius hit on Mal and I started laughing right away," said Wally. As Meninga sucked in air Wally called out, "Gees these blokes can hit can't they Mal." Wally saw Meninga's determination and suddenly remembered, many years before, being elbowed in the head by Mal in a Brisbane club match. Being young and uncool Wally had exclaimed, "You dirty big black bastard!" Meninga's eyes had blazed in disgust and next ruck he called "My ball!" and ran straight at Wally, crashed through him and everyone else for a 50-metre try. As he returned he had grinned sarcastically at Wally, "Thanks a lot, Honky!" When Wally saw Meninga angry again he knew what was in store for the unsuspecting Kumul. "Next ball the same Kumul tried to hit Mal again," said Wally. "Mal went Bang! and ran straight over him, just like a car running over a cat."

The final score was 70–8, the biggest cheer being reserved for the Kumuls' single try. At match end, the players swapped jumpers but the Kumuls' halfback and a second-rower missed out. Allan Langer and Gavin Miller weren't giving away their first Aussie jerseys for anything. Champagne flowed in the Kumuls' dressingroom as though they had won instead of suffering the worst defeat in Test history. Wally felt sorry for the Kumuls who had played their hearts out. "They'd acquit themselves well in the Queensland state league competition," he said. "Losing by such margins in a Test can set them back." Kumuls' captain Bal Numapo had the last word. "Just playing a Test in Australia is an honour," he said.

Wally's final representative match in Australia in 1988 pitted the home side against the Rest of the World — a Bicentenary afterthought foisted on a satiated Sydney public. Rest of the World coach, Graham Lowe, rang Wally and warned him, "I'm going to stir things up a bit. I'll have a go at you and get a few people interested in this game." Fine by me, said Wally. In an interview with Roy Masters in the *Sydney Morning Herald*, Lowe said:

> Australian footballers are overpaid, overbearing, overexposed and generally up themselves overall. I'll be reminding my boys that between the ages of 8 and 20 they played in mud and slush and never got a cracker from the game. Australians have grown up on firm fields and are waited on. They're given blazers, jackets and new boots to wear and they even send their under-eight teams on end of season trips to Surfers Paradise.

Great Britain had lost a gladiatorial battle to New Zealand only a week earlier. Now the opponents were expected to unite against Australia. Envy of the Aussies was part of Lowe's drive to meld the Poms, Kiwis, one Frenchman and one Kumul into a cohesive force. The Australian selectors tacitly admitted that motivation mattered as much as form and made five changes to the team that lost to Great Britain. A new-look side — Gavin Miller and Gene Miles in the second-row, Steve Roach at prop and Mal Meninga welcomed back in the centres — ensured they regained the enthusiasm missing in the third Test.

By their very nature such matches are exhibitions of attack. Five of the six tries were scored by backs and the fact that Australia ran out 22–10 winners reflected their better combination. After the mystery of Francis Deplas, Wally was delighted with the refereeing of Papua New Guinean, Graham Ainui. He penalised as readily for a crooked scrum feed in the last minute as in the first and he maintained a firm five metres on both sides. "When he spoke quietly he was clear," said Wally. "When he got nervous he shouted and spoke too quickly." Wally stored that knowledge away for the World Cup final in New Zealand in October, his last football match of the year.

The Rest of the World match produced one of the saddest sights in modern rugby league when Mal Meninga fractured his left arm for the fourth time in 14 months. Although protected by an arm-sheath the size of a stormwater drain-pipe the weakened arm fractured in a simple tackle. As Meninga walked past gingerly holding his arm, Wally asked, "You all right?" Meninga shook his head. After a few minutes he reluctantly left the field, a tragic figure, shrouded in a blanket, condemned to another season out of the game. Wally went into the city for a beer with Geno, Turtle and Alf but sympathy for Meninga's fate took the shine off any victory glow. Wally read medical opinions, subsequently canvassed in the press, that an arm break takes 6 to 13 weeks to heal and up to two years to regain full strength. Not that it had anything to do with him — or so he thought.

14 THE GREAT ADVENTURE

With seven rounds left in the Winfield Cup the Broncos stood equal sixth, with Balmain, on the premiership table. In the rundown to the semi-finals they had to play three of the top seven — Manly, Penrith and Balmain. It was a daunting task considering the Broncos had lost six of their last nine matches. Statistics were starting to expose their failings. They were scoring an average of 22 points a game but conceding 19. Their defence was like a sieve compared with the stonewalls of the leading clubs, Penrith and Canterbury, who were conceding a meagre 11.7 and 12.6 points per game respectively.

In 15 matches penalties had favoured the Broncos only four times. It was evident the Broncos were sliding because of poor defence and discipline. The pathetic loss to Souths was the last straw. Wayne Bennett addressed the players at the next training session. He waited until his deadly serious mien quelled the chat, and began. He had warned them if they did not reduce their errors and penalties he would fine offenders. He had tried to get his message through, exhorted them, coached them, toughened training drills on suspect areas, but everything failed. So now he was responding the only other way he knew, hurting them in their pockets. He had devised a system of fines for errors and stupid penalties. He would allow each player two mistakes per game: two missed tackles; or one missed tackle and one dropped ball; or one bad pass and one failure to chase from marker. Only two unpunished mistakes per game and after that $50 per error. For a stupid penalty from which opponents kicked a goal the fine was $100. The scheme was to be kept secret. It would not do for other teams to be baiting Broncos with, "That's a $50 fumble Geno!"

One of the great incentives to join the Broncos had been the generous win bonuses. Though docking players for mistakes wasn't in the fine print the players could not morally dispute Bennett's words. But the fines were bound to be hard on the team's playmakers, Wally, Geno, Dowling and Langer. The difference between a brilliant or bungled pass was often a fine line, most obviously with Miles's one-handers. As compensation Bennett applied a $50 reward for players who worked hard at the essentials — making three tackles in a row from marker, trapping the opposition in their in-goal and so on.

Wally listened to Bennett's plans and could see immediately how hard it would be to offset a $50 fine. Making two tackles from marker was noteworthy. Making three could be thwarted simply by the opposition deciding to move the ball wide to the wing. "Hard to make three tackles from marker?" echoed Bennett. "Hard when you're as lazy as Wally!" Maybe, but Wally saw other inconsistencies. A forward who knocked on taking the ball up conceded 10 metres. The fullback doing the same conceded 50 metres. An equitable fines system would have to reduce the entire game of rugby league to a set of careful equations, checked and balanced for every position and every occasion.

As Wally suspected, he was the player to suffer most. In three consecutive weeks he was fined $400, $200 and $300. He even set a record one match of $500, from a dozen match mistakes. Miles reached $400 once and Langer clocked up $250–300 a couple of times. "I'm not a miser but after a while it was whacking me in the pocket," said Wally. "It was really annoying. I'm what I would call an adventurous player. I don't believe in playing safe all the time. I'll play safe a fair majority of the time but if the opportunity is there I believe I have to do something with it. Same with Alf and Geno, we take more risks than others."

Wally pondered his position. Did he curb his game, save himself fines and not accept opportunities which might lead to tries?

Yet if the main playmakers all became over-cautious the team might well not win which would cost them the largest financial loss of all, their $1,500 win bonus. Wally remembered Wally Fullerton-Smith, in a *Rugby League Week* profile, light-heartedly listing as his Pet Hate: "Wingers, overpaid imposters who look flash running down the sidelines to score tries but do little else." Wally mused, "He's half right there. They're not called on to make tackles left, right and centre so they don't miss as many." He was not reflecting upon Joe Kilroy and Michael Hancock, two of the best and most involved wingers in the premiership.

Bennett's eyes glinted at these arguments. Every player was becoming a bush lawyer to explain away errors. "Wally's justification was 'I'm creative, I'm going to make mistakes,'" said Bennett. "I can't handle that. He is creative, and I don't want him not to be. What I'm saying is he has to create at the right time and at the right place. That's what we're paying him for out there, to take the right options. He can't play five balls, we score off two and they score off three going the other way. Wally and Geno played that way for 10 years in Brisbane and got away with it. We couldn't win in Sydney if we didn't get the errors out of our system. We were giving other teams more opportunities than they were giving us. A Sydney grand final is just minimised mistakes."

Bennett examined a video after every game, judged the players and at training on Tuesday, numbering up by jerseys, 1–13, read out the fines. With a trace of sarcasm in his voice he would read, "Lewis, two missed tackles, three bad passes, didn't chase from marker twice, one dropped ball, eight mistakes, less two (permitted mistakes), $300." Those who had no fines would giggle while Bennett looked pointedly at the player in the dock. Some of the younger players actually made money under the system, competing for bonuses through exploits above the call of duty.

Wally decided to wear the system and make it work. He went from 7 mistakes to 5, to 3 and in one game actually made no mistakes — not a dropped ball or missed tackle, nothing. At training Bennett cried "Halleluja!" but Wally went up to 5 again next match. The worst of it was that the players could not tote up their fines at the end of the season and deduct it from their bonuses. Having been fined Tuesday they had to fish into their wallets and pay by Thursday. Bennett collected up to $1,000 every week, extracted from the players as painfully as wisdom teeth. Wally asked facetiously one Thursday, "How's that new fence going?" What fence? asked Bennett, curious. "The one you're building with all the cabbage we're paying you every Thursday night!"

Did it work? The Broncos headed for a showdown with Manly at Brookvale Oval. If proof was ever needed of the toll Sydney football takes of teams it was here. Of the 26 players who had run on to Lang Park for that memorable opening match 16 weeks earlier, only 7 of the Broncos survived and 6 Sea Eagles. Bennett used the occasion to run a selection of scenes from a video of that founding victory. He introduced it with, "I want to show you a film of a team I really admire. They are a great team but occasionally have lapses of concentration which cost them dearly." The film provoked wonder in Wally. "Sitting there you got a comparison of what it was like then and how it was last week," he said. "You couldn't help but think, 'Gees, we were keen then.' "

Bennett reinforced his new system of fines with a simple strategy. No more squandering possession. The Broncos were to aim for 85 per cent ball retention — about five of the six tackles. And they were to stop Manly crossing their line in the first half. Mick Stone called Wally and Fatty Vautin into the referees' room to toss and was amused to see them greet each other with their Three Stooges handshake. He shook his head and said, "Well I don't have to tell you two the rules, looks like you're having enough fun anyway. Let's have a hard, clean game, OK?" The captains nodded, righto Mick. Stone moved to the door, looked back and saw them begin chatting. He laughed, "Oh well, I'll be going then, will I?" Wally and Fatty yacked for a further five minutes and then parted with their inimitable au revoir, "Guess I'll see you around," and "Yeah, catch up with you." Wally immediately had to forget friendship and focus on the game because, as he put it, "Fatty wanted to beat us, he wanted to beat us bad."

After the Broncos rolled Manly in the first round Greg Dowling had accused the Sea Eagles forwards of going missing in action. The Brookvale Oval crowd of 17,000 remembered and booed both GD and Wally when they ran on. Unfortunately for Manly it rained and Dowling, Australia's best wet-weather forward, threw himself about on the soft pitch without a care for his chronically painful shoulder. Paul Vautin may have been desperate but his Manly team-mates seemed to want victory too easily. They set out with a flourish, reverse flick passes, overhead lobs, scissor movements, the lot. It was tailormade for the Broncos' new percentage plan and when they changed ends Brisbane led 16–4. As they walked towards the gates Dowling said to Wally, "Have a listen to that?" After a pause Wally said, "I can't hear anything." Dowling smiled back, "No, doesn't it sound beautiful."

The 28–10 result kept the Broncos near the top of the table as they rounded to their next hurdle, Penrith. The Broncos watched the third Test in Sydney and saw Greg Conescu walk off injured and Wally bruise his suspect shoulder in the dying minutes. The Broncos had that evening to readjust to playing the next day without their Test trumps. Conescu was no chance and Wally went for a kilometre jog that morning to loosen up. Wayne Bennett delayed a decision as late as possible, until half-time in the reserve grade match. Watched by the club doctor Wally completed some sit-ups but struggled through push-ups. He insisted, "I can play." Bennett inquired, "Are you 100 per cent?" Wally shook his head. Bennett: "You're out."

Part of Bennett's necessary readjustment to losing his champion was to assume a cold impersonality, as though to say, "You're nothing special, get out of the way." No bad lucks or sympathetic gestures. Necessary for Bennett, deflating for Wally. It was becoming his worst season for injury: four missed matches, one through knee surgery, the rest through shoulder dislocations. Being ruled out was no small thing for Wally. Footballers are like actors or musicians, rehearsing all week for their 80 minutes upon the stage. To be deprived of that performance leaves them fidgeting, frustrated spectators. Wally had certainly performed the day before, in the third Test. But his mental commitment to helping the Broncos remained unquenched.

The Penrith Park mob still got their money's worth. As Wally walked to the Broncos sideline bench they razzed him, "Too scared to play eh, you big sheila!" It was probably as well Wally did not subject his tender shoulder socket to Penrith's massive pack. Andrew Tessmann retired to the headbin with a smashed nose, Shane Duffy was carried off with his neck in a brace, Dowling stayed on only because Bennett had no front-rowers to replace him. Yet the Broncos won 8–6 because, as John MacDonald wrote in the *Sydney Morning Herald*, "Brisbane didn't do anything great, they just didn't do anything wrong...it was that simple, no flair, no flamboyance." From an average of four tries a match the Broncos were down to two. But for the second week the Broncos line was not crossed before half-time. Bennett's fines were working fine.

Wally watched that match with the Broncos auxiliaries sitting in a low shed in front of the main Penrith Park grandstand. With a row of Broncos extras standing behind the main bench, Wally was not visible to the crowd. *Sydney Morning Herald* photographer Mark Baker, cruising the sideline, snapped the tense Broncos camp and caught Wally nervously puffing on a cigarette. The incriminating scene — Wally in the act of taking a draw — became a large, back-page sports photograph in the *Herald* next day.

Tobacco's link with sport is rapidly becoming a taboo as the medical lobby in Australia pressures the federal government to outlaw tobacco companies sponsoring sport or using sport in cigarette advertising. The *Herald* received calls expressing disapproval of Wally's habit. The *Herald*'s Tony Sarno, wrote, "There he was, a man whose talent and position should have made him a monument to the virtues of sport, exercise, and healthy living, the idol of thousands of children, caught flagrante delicto with a cigarette." Sarno canvassed other sportsmen and found that Commonwealth Games pole vaulter Neil Honey smoked, as did cricketers Allan Border, David Boon and Greg Matthews. Ian Botham was once suspended for smoking something else.

Wally smoked until he was 22 then stopped for four years. On a long boring bus trip midway through the 1986 Kangaroo tour, Greg Dowling, who had given up, and Geno, who still smoked, ganged up on Wally in a wrestle. They'd let him up if he had a cigarette, they said. Wally didn't want one but went along with the game. Even though next morning his throat was sore he had another cigarette three days later. This time they didn't need to put him in a headlock. After a week he was smoking again. Ironically his father, Jim Lewis, who smoked for 30 years, gave up on that same tour.

Wally can be genuinely classed as a light smoker. He does not smoke at home, he never smokes in front of his own children or anyone else's if he is at a party where children are present. "I never smoke during the day," he said. "The first would be at 6 p.m." Sometimes he goes a week without, as though he had forgotten the habit, but picks up again when relaxing. He smokes so little it does not affect his training. He does not recommend smoking, doesn't want his children to smoke and has never personally appeared in a cigarette advertisement. However he plays in the Winfield Cup and all the Australian players wore the Winfield cigarette logo on their shorts during the Test series against Great Britain.

Wally is aware of his public image and of his responsibilities as a national sporting identity to set a good example. He knew he was not visible to the public at Penrith Park and did not know he was being photographed. Three months later, at the World Cup final in New Zealand, a television cameraman focused on him smoking after the match and Wally waved him away with, "If you're going to film me I'll put the smoke down." Wally has been unlucky that he only feels the need to smoke in public when he's watching a football match in which he should be playing or has come off injured. He's been caught twice that way. But, like it or not, a sporting figure of his stature smoking in public is now news.

Downing Penrith and Manly lifted the Broncos into a select seven at the top of the premiership table, all within two points of each other. The Broncos were equal second, with Manly and Balmain, on 22 points. Canberra, Penrith, Cronulla and

Canterbury led on 24 points. The table was so crowded and competitive that even after the Broncos dispatched Wests and North Sydney in their next two matches, they did not improve their position.

Wally had mixed fortunes against Norths. With young Terry Matterson injured, Wally took over as goalkicker. In the pre-season he had taken part in a goalkicking contest organised by the Illawarra Steelers. Every Sydney club entered their specialist kickers — Balmain's Ross Conlon, Terry Lamb from Canterbury, Mal Meninga from Canberra. Wally slotted five kicks over from six to tie for the lead with Wayne Portlock from Easts. "I couldn't believe how well I was hitting them," he recalled. It didn't last. In a kick-off Portlock succeeded with his second shot from the sideline for outright victory. Wally is so good at ball skills Bennett's choice seemed sound. Wally lands the ball on a postage stamp from kick-offs yet he managed only two goals from six attempts against Norths and those in front.

He made up for it by scoring two tries, both from loitering near Gene Miles close to the Norths line and catching the ingenious one-handed basketball passes Geno threw him. In Wally's second try no fewer than four Norths defenders surrounded Miles, leaping like kids in a schoolyard for the ball Geno held in his upraised arms. But Geno gave it to his favourite schoolmate. Miles's move to the forwards meant he and Wally were more often able to exploit their almost telepathic understanding.

Wally had always been a target for big hits — Ron Gibbs nailed him for the Giants, Paul Loughlin for Great Britain, and now Paul Conlon for Norths. Conlan drove into Wally with a right elbow jolt under the heart and Wally went down. Referee Mick Stone urgently summoned the Broncos strapper and after treatment Wally stood up, gingerly holding his ribs. Play resumed, Norths won a scrum and spent four tackles. Wally half doubled over, coughed into his hand and the blood-stained spittle gave him a fright. He sat down and called to winger Michael Hancock, "Mate grab the linesman, grab the ref, grab a doc, quick." He had trouble breathing and feared his lungs were punctured. Hancock yelled back, "I'll wait for a break in play." Wally gasped back, "Michael, call the bloody doctor!"

Hancock drew Stone's attention who signalled for the clock to stop and trotted over. "You want assistance?" he asked. "Mick, look," said Wally and coughed into his hand. Stone was taken aback, put a sympathetic hand on Wally's shoulder and signalled for help.

The Broncos doctor, Dr Peter Friis, examined Wally but could find nothing amiss with his ribs or chest. It might be burst blood vessels at the back of his throat. Friis advised him to come off. Wally said, "I'll go off and come back on." Referee Stone, who had remained beside Wally, shook his head. "It's a headbin," he said, reminding them of the law which permits temporary replacements only for head injuries. Why a chest or throat injury should be considered any less dangerous than concussion only the ARL knows. Wally looked up at Stone and, trying his luck, said to Friis, "Leave me on the track then doc, I'll make one more tackle and accidentally bump my head." Stone quickly knocked that plan on the head. Wally elected to stay on. The match had been delayed two minutes.

The incident drew guarded criticism of Stone for the length of the stoppage and league writers the next day pointed out that the usual procedure was to let play continue unless the injured player was interfering with the game. But under the laws of the game if a referee believes an injury is serious he can stop the game. Mick Stone considered Wally's symptoms sufficiently worrying to warrant such a stoppage.

Brisbane's third last match of the season was against Parramatta who had lost six matches on the trot. Footytab gave the Eels 9.5 points start and just one of the *Sydney Morning Herald*'s ten tipsters favoured Parramatta. Of the Eels' half dozen champions in the 1982 Kangaroo Invincibles only Steve Ella remained.

Wally, Gene Miles and Allan Langer were backing up from Australia's match against the Rest of the World four days earlier. On Wally's admission his first-half form was not much better than some of the veterans who played in a Golden Oldies preliminary match. As the Broncos came in at half-time, fortunate to be tied 10–10, Bennett looked at Wally with mock surprise and said, "Oh, you were out there, were you? I didn't see you for the first half hour." Wally didn't need to be told. "I was one of the blokes waiting for somebody else to do something," he confessed later. With hindsight, Bennett, had he possessed a capable replacement, would have pulled Wally off. "He was tired," he said. "He and Geno, they're both getting older now. But, you know, even late in the game Wally still generated a few things for us."

Parramatta changed up three gears in the second half and stormed in winners 22–14 to the rapture of their success-starved hometown crowd. Exuberant spectators shocked Wayne Bennett by hurling insults and abuse at him. Wally gave a bitter laugh when he heard. "Benny will learn," he said. "It's the same old story. If you're half a chance to beat the Broncos you can hear the crowd from Sydney to Parramatta."

Balmain coach Warren Ryan, analysing the semi-final contenders, named Wally, Langer and Miles as the Broncos gamebreakers. He wrote in the *Sydney Morning Herald*:

Wally could roll a cigarette while the defence closes in on him. He camouflages problems and carries teams through tough patches. On days when he appears to have done very little he has usually spent the afternoon salvaging, with his smart kicking game, the forwards' failure to advance the football.

Brett Kenny came away from Parramatta Stadium feeling sympathy for Wally and Gene. "A lot of people expect them to play great football all the time," he said. "But they get watched very closely. It's been hard for the representative players from Brisbane lately, especially with all their travelling." Peter Jackson observed that the Broncos never looked like making a break unless it came from the top trio. Wayne Bennett had already taken steps to rectify that by inviting Jackson to join the Broncos in 1989. Jackson challenged Wally one day, "Give me three reasons why I should join you blokes?" Wally replied, "Jacko that's easy. First you're mates with everybody in the team, second you love the coach and third you want to come home."

The Broncos, though equal third with Balmain and Canberra, on averages were now last of the top seven. Another loss and their dream of a coveted spot in the semi-finals would be over. The team's confidence was once more shaken. Bennett tested the water at training, asking each player how he felt. "They'd speak positively," said Wally. "But in the back of everybody's mind there was a wavering — 'Gees, Gold Coast beat us, Parramatta beat us...' "

But not Newcastle, the Broncos' last home game of the season. A week's rest enabled Wally to answer critics of his running game as he sparked the Broncos to a 24–8 win. Rival coaches who tagged Wally as no danger outside his opponent's quarter were relying on Wally's apparent lack of sustained speed. Wally scored two tries against Newcastle, the first a 60-metre marathon, the furthest I have ever seen him travel at full gallop. Six minutes later he was in again, after a dash of 40 metres. In each case he reached top speed after only 15 metres and then hung on as Newcastle's defenders tried to run him down. Wally is deceptively quick. Though not a long strider he accelerates through straight line defences with a burst of leg speed and then looks for his supports. "I was a shot duck," he laughed after his solo efforts. "I drank 13 glasses of water at half-time." With one match to go he seemed fresh and ready to lead the Brisbane novices into the final five, a feat never achieved by a team in its first year in the Sydney premiership.

It was fitting that the Broncos, one of the new clubs, should have to battle one of the premiership's oldest clubs, Balmain, for the last position in the semi-finals. If Parramatta is the new heartland of rugby league, Balmain is its venerable soul. For days before the match the watering holes down Balmain's narrow, winding terraces were alive with debates about the merits of Wally versus Balmain's new acquisition Ellery Hanley, who seemed more dangerous as a Tiger than a Lion. Wally had heard through the underground that several Balmain reserve graders were not happy at being turfed aside to make way for Hanley. Wally had nothing against Hanley but he believed the ARL should have introduced a minimum matchplay rule before imports could play in semi-finals. He said, "The last thing the game needs is a premiership being decided because a club is rich enough to throw in a few overseas pinch-hitters."

Wally's presence tempered the loyalties of the Tigers' most famous supporter, Laurie Nicholls, renowned for wearing a singlet and no shirt whatever the weather, even at Test matches in England's wintry north. He admired Wally and hated to hear crowds abuse him. "The man is a great player, a great Australian captain and a friend of mine and they boo him," he said. "That breaks my heart."

It did not require a psychic to divine that the Broncos were faltering on their run to the semi-finals. They lost Greg Conescu and Greg Dowling at Tuesday training. The Broncos did not have the reinforcements to counter the Balmain heavy artillery of Roach and Sironen or cavalrymen Pearce and Elias. Bennett bravely selected 19-year-old rookie Brett Plowman, a 100 kilo centre, for his first match as a forward. Plowman, a year out of school, was the talk of the club early in the season when, in the wee hours and fortified by strong spirit, he walked up to Gene Miles at a night club and announced, "I'm after your spot." Geno smiled and replied, "That bloody right eh? Well good luck to you." Now Plowman was joining Geno, but neither was in the centres. Despite their patched up team the Broncos were rumoured to have laid $10,000 on themselves to win. Betting on football matches by players is illegal and Wally declined to comment on the reports.

It was an extraordinary match. Balmain were superior and yet did not easily climb clear of the tenacious Broncos. Indeed had Wally produced his normal form they might have won. But he could not find new centres, Grant Rix and Rohan Teevan, with the long passes which used to hit Gene Miles half-way through a gap. Wally was uninvolved, shunted the ball on and scarcely went for a run. Inevitably he paid dearly as Balmain applied pressure. After one fifth-tackle play Wally took dummy half's pass standing only five metres back from the ruck, easy pickings for Benny Elias running from second marker. Harassed by Elias, Wally could not get his kick away. It became a handover to Balmain and from that possession the Tigers ran in their first try. Elias and Steve Mortimer had muzzled Wally's kicking game in NSW's memorable state-of-origin triumphs in 1985. Now Elias had crowded him again with the same result.

At full-time the Tigers had won 20–10 and Wally moved quickly to congratulate Wayne Pearce before they were engulfed by spectators. He made his way to the Balmain quarters, wished them well for the semi-finals and was grabbed by their coach Warren Ryan, who shook Wally's hand and said earnestly, "Mate you're the greatest player in the game, I mean that. I hated you out there today but that's because you were the opposition." Wally thanked Ryan and escaped, in no mood for compliments. In his own dressingroom he took off his boots and sat on the floor, his hand shielding his eyes.

Wayne Bennett, applying Origin lessons, was determinedly cheerful in defeat, praising his team to the media. Wally decided Bennett's sunny performance was just that, an act. "I looked across and I knew he was about as happy as I was," he said. "He had a nice mask on but I thought, 'You're full of bull Wayne.' " Wally felt he had let himself and the team down. He couldn't explain his own patchy game. Bennett had his theory. "He's human like the rest of us," he said. "The season was catching up with him and he had more responsibility than anybody else. We all had to play well against Balmain and he was the only player who didn't. He wasn't strong against Parramatta or Balmain and we lost both of them. That's how important he is to us. Against Balmain he didn't have a dig. I don't know why. But it was a bastard of a day for it to happen."

And so the great adventure of the Broncos' first season was over. Wally left the Leichhardt Oval dressingrooms and stood in the shadows watching the remnants of the crowd wend their way home. He had given himself two goals for 1988, the Sydney semi-finals and the World Cup. The first was lost, the second yet to come. A coach walked by, leading a dozen or so junior footballers. As they disappeared down the street Wally heard him organising the kids to walk in some order, "Come on now boys, let's hear it, all together in time, Wally's a wanker, Wally's a wanker." Wally did not smile again until he walked in the front door of his Brisbane home that evening. His two-year-old son, Mitchell, greeted him brightly with, "Did you have a good game today Dad?"

15 BEST IN THE WORLD

Impossible as it might seem Wally's fame in Queensland actually increased with the Broncos' elimination. Midway through the season the Broncos sponsors, Power Brewing, filmed a television commercial, featuring Wally and several Broncos, to launch their beer in September 1988. The film company looked at several old colonial houses as possible settings and then Wally suggested his former house at Norman Park. Filming got under way at 6.30 a.m. and Wally began sweating over a genuine barbecue plate. There was no script. Greg Dowling and Greg Conescu were told to ad lib and hassle Wally with orders and complain about the meat being underdone. Barbecues are second nature to footballers and they joined in the spirit of the shoot. Wally made up his own line which a keen ear could pick up. While asking the blokes about their steaks he spotted a girl standing in the backround under a small paw-paw tree and called out, "What about you with the paw-paw on your head!"

The commercial concluded with Wally wiping his brow, taking a long swig from a can of Power's Bitter and exclaiming, "Ahh, that's better." Then, turning towards the camera, he says with a good natured grin, "Sorry Bondy." The words were directed at Perth magnate, Alan Bond, who had taken over Castlemaine Perkins, brewers of Queensland's major beer, Fourex. Wally appeared in a Fourex commercial four years earlier and his friendly apology sent the clever, subtle message that if it was okay for Wally to switch allegiances it was good enough for the rest of Queensland. After half a dozen "Sorry

198 Best in the World

Bondy" takes, each requiring Wally to skoal half a can of beer, his head started to spin and he told the producers, "You'd better fill the next can with soft drink otherwise I'm going to be pissed in your commercial!"

The Power ad was an instant hit on Queensland television. Customers flocked to hotels ordering a dozen "Wallies" or "Sorry Bondies". Power Brewing were unable to meet demand and hotels sold out within hours of deliveries. People who saw Power delivery trucks would follow them and publicans nailed up signs saying either, "The Power Is With Us" or "We're Powerless." Like the Broncos, Power Beer became a Queensland phenomenon almost overnight and Power had soon grabbed 10 per cent of the southeast Queensland beer market. But the cheekiest part of the campaign was to come. After a few weeks Power varied the television commercial. Instead of Wally saying "Sorry Bondy" as he turned towards the camera, Greg Dowling's voice was heard warning him, "Don't say it, Wally," and the ad ended. The impression was that Bond Brewing had complained about the original commercial, perhaps even taken legal action, and that Power Brewing had changed the commercial to conform. Nothing of the sort occurred. Several variations of the "Don't say it, Wally" theme were shot the morning of the original commercial. It was a master stroke, a brilliant advertising gimmick that struck a chord with loyal Queenslanders.

This was the second time Wally had become the star of television commercials which entered the folklore. The first had been the 1984 Fourex beer jingle which began, "Here's to Wally Lewis, for lacing on a boot..." While both commercials were commissioned from advertising agencies there was little doubt that the subject, Wally Lewis, helped inspire the huge public response. Wally was getting maximum television exposure but it wasn't leading him anywhere. Though it didn't provide him with a new career, it did give him an idea.

When the Broncos were formed, stockbroker director Paul Morgan told me Wally had all the qualities to succeed in business. Wally was a natural leader, a motivator and performed at his best under pressure. "There has to be something for the guy after football," said Morgan. "I'll find it for him. I've just got to stop him thinking football all the time and get it down to only 90 per cent of the time."

Wally didn't wait for Morgan to find him a future, he grabbed it himself. Sport, which had dominated his days since childhood, was being challenged by his media life. He had enjoyed his guest spots as a football commentator on television and admired Mike Gibson's work on Channel 9's *Wide World of Sports*. He set himself to combine the two spheres he knew best, sport and the media, to become a television sportscaster. He had several talks with Nine's sports chief David Hill but eventually joined Channel 10 in Brisbane which had a team covering the Broncos' Winfield Cup matches. The station sent him to Sydney for screen tests and tuition under a talent coordinator. Wally plunged into his new career, learnt how to follow autocues, to read ahead of what he was saying and to acquire newsreading word emphasis which gives television newsreading its sing-song cadence.

He practised daily at Ten's Expo newsroom which resembled a goldfish bowl with hundreds of visitors staring in through glass walls, all trying to attract his attention as he read. He rehearsed so often fellow staffers began to understand the concentration that Wally applies in a football match. And when the auditioner deliberately jammed the autocue Wally responded by coolly ad libbing without breaking stride. It was good experience and necessary for the nerve-wracking countdown to his first newsreading night. He had a small sports spot in the main news, soon after the bulletin began, and it was over before his nerves could dry his mouth. He looked a fraction wooden and was caught unawares once when he returned live after a film sequence, but otherwise he had adapted to his new public role as Wally Lewis, newsreader.

Conscious he was still a rookie on air he studied videos of his reading for flaws and flounced home one evening disgusted with himself. "They rang with about 10 seconds to go and said I'd have to go straight into this extra script I hadn't even read," he said. "I'd never done it before but all I could do was agree." As he read the second last item he reminded himself to say, "And finally tonight..." but when he finished he sat back for a second

— which on screen seems longer — suddenly remembered and with just the hint of a sheepish smile, read the unscheduled item. His style improved so quickly Ten soon signed him on a healthy contract and decided to send him to Seoul with their Olympic Games crew.

He was in elite company there with Mike Gibson, Bruce McAvaney, David Fordham, Rex Mossop, Billy J. Smith and former Canterbury-Bankstown star Graeme Hughes. Equipped with their team blazers and distinctive baggage, Wally found it not unlike a football tour. The team was soon inventing nick-names (Wally's was Danny de Vito) and planning practical jokes. South Korean students were still rioting and the television team obtained a tape of rifle fire and exploding grenades to play outside "Moose" Mossop's bedroom door but he quit the cramped press village accommodation before they had a chance to run it. On the work front Wally was embarrassed to find himself superfluous. Mike Gibson told him, "I hear you're dis-appointed you've got nothing to do? Don't complain. You're over here watching the greatest sporting event of all time. Get out and watch how the other blokes work. It's the chance of a lifetime. I wish I had your brief." Wally's attitude changed and he began to enjoy the Olympics.

He attached himself to old friend Laurie Lawrence and the Australian swimming squad but mercifully avoided Lawrence's emotional reaction to Duncan Armstrong's 200-metre gold medal swim. Such was the crush after the race Wally couldn't get near Armstrong but yelled out "Dunc!". Armstrong looked across and shouted," Wal!". Wally's heart was full of Aussie pride and he called back, "Mate, bloody great swim." Armstrong waved. Wally managed one more word, "Thirsty?" Armstrong grinned and nodded. Wally knew Armstrong had not touched alcohol for six months and had another race in four days, but he also knew swimmers didn't mind a beer. He told 1984 butterfly gold medallist, Jon Sieben, "Get Dunc, 7.30 at the Press village." So the three Queenslanders — two Olympic gold medallists and the rugby league bloke — enjoyed a quiet ale together and Wally, for once, was the minor celebrity.

He watched the Australians at tennis practice, had a soft

drink with Liz Smiley, John Fitzgerald and Darren Cahill and took photographs of Chris Evert, Pam Shriver and Zina Garrison. Strolling past the practice courts with Australian diver Stephen Foley, Wally espied the beautiful Argentinian Gabriella Sabatini and raised his camera. As he touched the shutter Sabatini suddenly bent over to pick up a ball. Laughed Foley, "Wal, I'll give you five hundred bucks for that photo." On his way to Seoul, waiting for a connecting flight in Tokyo, Wally sat near several Canadian women sprinters, one of whom was stretched on a seat. He looked again and saw it was bald Ben Johnson using the women to hide from photographers. And that was before Johnson's disqualification for taking muscle-building steroids. Wally was shocked that Johnson should risk his athletic career and bring his nation's name into disrepute by taking drugs. Wally adheres to the Laurie Lawrence philosophy that talent, dedication and good old Aussie guts are the essential ingredients of sporting success.

Another evening, back at the swimming pool, Wally watched Julie McDonald in her 800 m heat and Lawrence asked him, "How do you think she's going? Give me your ideas on what she's doing right and wrong." Wally squinted into his field glasses. "She's doing it pretty easily." Why? said Lawrence — in a way that reminded Wally of Wayne Bennett. Wally peered into his binoculars again and said, "Well I'm looking at her face and she's not straining, and she's not shortening stroke. Ah, her kicking is still strong and I reckon that would be the first to go." Lawrence grunted a non-committal "Mmm." Now Wally was certain Lawrence was from the same school of stonewallers as Bennett. They only reacted if you were wrong.

During his 10 days in Seoul, Wally went for several long runs around the Olympic village streets. Through eating the local low-fat food he gained only a few pounds by the time he flew home to join the Australian team for the World Cup final against New Zealand in Auckland. He had not played for eight weeks and wrote in his newspaper column with unconscious prescience, "Mal Meninga's broken arm was a tragic illustration of how players can be left high and dry if they are injured playing representative football." Wally was referring to the

absence of any ARL compensation fund, an inconceivable over-
sight for a supposedly professional sports administration. Wally
was glad the Cup final was scheduled for October 9 — after the
Olympics ended — but anyone who suggested he might not be
available because of Seoul did not know his priorities.

The Australian side was selected with a bias towards players
from the Sydney semi-finals — those who had the least break
from the playing season. Consequently the only survivors from
the team which played Great Britain in the first Test four
months earlier were Wally, Garry Jack and Michael O'Connor.
Yet such is the enormous depth of Australian rugby league that
there was never a suggestion the Cup final team was not the
equal of those selected against Great Britain. In fact, away from
the interstate politics which always govern Australian selections
in the wake of the state-of-origin series, this new squad looked
stronger than its predecessors. Dale Shearer and Andrew Farrar
stiffened the backline defence, Gavin Miller and Benny Elias
introduced imagination to the forwards.

A warm-up match against a Wellington Invitation XIII
showed how rusty the Australians had become. Down 8–0 they
recovered as soon as they remembered how to tackle and to
string more than three passes together and ran out 24–12 winners. They flew back from Wellington that evening, jumped
into hot springs to ease the aches and settled into their water-
front motel in Auckland. It was then they discoverd that rugby
league madness had overtaken the city. Newspapers had been
running advertisements, "Six weeks to go", "Five weeks to go"
and posters plastered everywhere declared it "The Final Test".
The World Cup — the Courtney Goodwill Trophy — was on
display in a store window in the main street and shops had sold
thousands of cup T-shirts and souvenirs. Television ran constant replays of past Kiwi triumphs and the radio was thick with
the voices of Kiwi players pledging their all for their country.

Rugby league, the weak brother to rugby union in New
Zealand, had been pumping iron. Interest in the final was so
great the match was transferred from league's traditional
Carlaw Park to the 50,000 capacity Eden Park, home of the All
Blacks. For the professional game to appear at the Mecca of

rugby union was unprecedented; for the ground to be sold out a week in advance was unbelievable. It was proof, said Kiwi coach Tony Gordon, that rugby league had crossed the class barrier in New Zealand. One third of the country had sat up until 10.30 p.m. in 1987 to watch the Kiwis defeat Australia and the Cup sell-out was an extension of that.

The mania had spread to the New Zealand players and officials. On radio, Clayton Friend threatened to break rival Allan Langer in half. The NZRL took one look at Eden Park's 20-metre deep in-goal area and ordered it reduced to seven metres to nullify Wally's bombs and chip kicks. "I was terrified at what Lewis could do with that much room," said NZRL president George Rainey. Criticism by Wally about the timing of the final — so many weeks after the end of the Australian season — was interpreted as an Aussie whinge. Wally listened, read and made his plans. If the New Zealanders wanted hype, why not send them overboard? From then on he practised media disinformation, labelling the Kiwis as the natural favourites...the best Kiwi team he had ever seen...playing at home before a big crowd...we might be a bit short of matchplay. "I heard myself and thought, 'What a load of bull I'm talking here'," said Wally. "But they lapped it up."

The crowning motivation for Wally came from an unpleasant play on his own name. In Britain, but not in Australia, a common usage for "wally" is a fool, usually in the context of a mild insult as in, "You'd be a right wally, wouldn't you?" When Wally arrived he was asked by reporters if he knew what "wally" meant in New Zealand. He replied, "Well you blokes are half-pint Pommies and if it means the same thing as it means in England it won't particularly upset me." Auckland's radio 91FM breakfast hosts Mike Regal and Danny Watson picked up that Wally, whatever its English derivations, also meant controversy and that meant ratings. In the week leading to the match they ridiculed his name and then, tiring of that game, interviewed a fake Lewis whingeing about everything New Zealand. Finally they pretended to ring Australia where, of course, the fake Australians answered, "Wally who?" Since Wally's manager in Brisbane, Wayne Roberts, runs a madcap breakfast program Wally is used to breakfast radio idiocy but, as with the earlier Wally-buster T-shirts, he reacted angrily to abuse of his name. The Australian camp closed ranks around their captain and developed a siege mentality, concentrating their minds more than coach Don Furner could have hoped.

Part of Wally's campaign of disinformation was to hint that, to make up for Australia's lack of match fitness, their big forwards, Steve Roach and Paul Sironen, would act as enforcers on the Kiwi pack. At a team meeting Wally, the Australians' most experienced Test player and the victim of two previous Kiwi Test ambushes, proposed a strategy: "No fighting in the first 20 minutes, no matter what the provocation, and no mistakes during that period." Afterwards Steve Roach cracked good humouredly, "Boy are we going to stick it to these Kiwis." Wally turned on him sharply and said, "Block, you've got to promise me you won't bash anybody. Just cop it. You can do what you like in the last five minutes."

Wally led the Australians on to the magnificent ground to the mixed applause and derision of the biggest crowd most of them had ever experienced. The home team kept them waiting in a biting wind and 50,000 New Zealanders peered curiously at the Aussies as though they were seeing 13 aliens close up. A roar greeted the Kiwis and a glance at their line-up showed why they were favourites. All but three of them played in either the Sydney or English leagues and their players outranked Australia in aggregate Test experience by 134 matches to 104. They were so strong that Newcastle captain Sam Stewart and Shane Cooper, the half-back Wally regarded as New Zealand's best, were relegated to the reserves bench. But it was a wonder the New Zealand team could stagger onto the field at all such was the burden of New Zealand hopes. The All Blacks had won the rugby union World Cup and the Kiwis were to make this the double. It was reported that as part of their motivational build-up each Kiwi team member had been given a tape on which former Test prop Kevin Tamati, one of the toughest forwards ever to wear the black and white, spoke emotionally of the pride of playing for his country. As Tamati spoke, strains of the New Zealand national anthem and Maori hymns played in the backround.

Kiwi captain Dean Bell introduced the New Zealand prime minister, David Lange, to his players and then Wally stepped forward to introduce the visitors. But Lange swept down the Aussie ranks so quickly that Wally ended up several paces behind, mouthing "Arpity, Arpity and Arpity." The prime minister of the opposing nation was the last bloke Wally wanted to meet before a big match. Another of his pet hates is the Maori haka which all New Zealand football teams perform before kick-off. His prosaic response to the haka is, "Why the hell would you want to prance and jump around before the game?" Whatever it did for New Zealand's spirits he didn't want the Kiwi antics diverting his players' minds from their task. He ordered them into a semi-circle facing away from the haka and, as with Lot's wife, warned them not to look over their shoulders. Dale Shearer risked a peep and was rewarded with a snarled, "Rowdy!"

The promotional theme was Anzacs at war but Eden Park was not Flanders Field and the Kiwis' opening play resembled the waste of going over the top. Wally exhorted his players to fall over when tackled to deprive the Kiwis of targets for headhunting and gang hits. "Our blokes got the hang of it after five minutes," said Wally. "They were running up and diving through tackles which frustrated the Kiwis trying to belt us. They'd only get half a hold and we'd jump and play the ball quickly."

Having set out with battle intensity, the New Zealanders abruptly fell into temporary adrenalin debt. Eight minutes after the start Australia were awarded a penalty inside the Kiwi quarter and Wally saw New Zealand had only one defender guarding the 10-metre blind side. He thought, "They must be going to put another bloke there surely," but the Kiwis were slow to re-form and Wally glimpsed the opening. It was the left blind, his favourite side for passing and stepping. He yelled the codeword "Hooch!" and the green and golds drifted into a three-quarter pace, mesmerising chain of passing towards the open side of the field — Elias to Langer, to Roach and back to Langer again. The Kiwi defence moved out to smother them. Wally suddenly accelerated, scissored diagonally behind Langer, accepted a hand-off pass at top speed and swerved down that gaping blindside. Only wily Mark Graham — 28 Tests, same as Wally — guessed the caper. He veered across in cover but Wally fed Wayne Pearce and Allan Langer was on hand to scoot over. So neat, so easy, their jerseys were still clean.

"Hooch" was an old move Wally developed with Wynnum in 1984 and Queensland used it to score the match-winning try against NSW in the third Origin in 1987. The execution of the try, as much as the points on the board, turned the Aussies on. Surfboarders have their hollow waves, runners have endorphin highs, but the footballer savours his moment as a chess player would: to see an opening, to hope it doesn't close, to know how to exploit it and then to grasp it. Rugby league players slam themselves and each other about hard grounds for the money and the love of it but in every match they look for the footballer's buzz, the closed-fist, sky-punching, pre-planned move that comes off.

In the 16th minute Wally went for a simple tackle on winger Tony Iro who ducked his head into the Australian captain's right arm. Wally heard a sound like a golf stick snapping and felt a sharp pain. He twisted his wrist and felt his forearm bones grating and rasping together. Broken. He retreated behind the Australian defensive line, rolled his sleeve up and held his arm. But New Zealand were mounting a furious offensive and Wally grimaced as he used both arms to stop huge forward Adrian Shelford. In the ruck he stood at second marker whose job it is to chase the ball. He told Andrew Farrar, who was first marker, "Mate, I'm gone, I've broken my arm, you chase him." Farrar did and also took the kick downfield when Australia regained possession. Wally ran across to trainer Larry Britton, called for strapping for his arm and returned and told Allan Langer, "Alfie I'm busted, don't give me the ball." With the crowd noise Langer didn't understand and from the next scrum threw the ball straight at his captain. Wally caught it, went down and gave Langer a fierce glare. "Eh, what did you say?" said Langer.

Still unsure how much he was restricted Wally moved to dummy half but his attempted pass dribbled out of his right arm and rolled along the ground. Now he knew. Next ruck Langer had caught on and cut out Wally with a long pass. Wally went to the sideline to have his arm strapped and told anxious coach, Don Furner, "It's broken, just let me play on, I'll give you a yell when I'm gone." Furner's confidence in Wally, established on the 1986 Kangaroo tour, was such that he patted him on the head and nodded. Said Furner later, "He wanted to stay on and that was good enough for me."

Back in play Wally made three ineffectual attempts at tackles and it became questionable whether staying on was any advantage to the team or himself. Australia led 11–0 but Wally did not want to leave until the team had a safe margin — ideally 19 points, which meant the Kiwis would have to score four times to win. Yet Australia had Terry Lamb ready to run on, a replacement so capable that only a player of Wally's stature kept him from Test selection. "No disrespect to Ba (Lamb), but I just felt I could still organise the game a little longer," said Wally.

In support of his decision the Australian team was combining smoothly and Wally's understanding with Langer had sorted out the ball distribution. While he stayed the Australians felt confident they could repel the Kiwis' best efforts. Wally's presence was a psychological security.

New Zealand did not seem aware of his incapacity or, if they were, did not take advantage of it. They gave away so many penalties and dropped the ball so much in the first half that while the Australians kicked 11 times in general play the Kiwis only kicked once. Yet towards half-time they rallied and once again attacked the Australian line, only to be denied through sensational last-ditch tackles by Garry Jack and Allan Langer. Australia looked rattled. Wally sensed that if the Kiwis scored they might undergo a charismatic revival and be rewarded with a miracle. Paul Dunn was sent off for a professional foul, leaving Australia a man down, defending, metres from their line.

Wally acted swiftly. New Zealand were awarded a tap penalty. Wally grabbed the ball and disputed the decision with Papua New Guinean referee Graham Ainui. Kiwi fullback Gary Mercer tried to snatch the ball back. Wally held him off. Kurt Sorensen, always on a short fuse, joined in and next moment they were struggling on the ground. Wally, forgetting his bad arm, hugged the ball. Ainui separated them but Wally kept talking to Ainui and Ainui kept answering. From the time Ainui awarded the penalty, to when New Zealand finally took it, 45 seconds had elapsed. Long enough to bank New Zealand's fire. The Kiwis lost momentum and the Cup.

Wally's ploy wasn't an underarm but it was definitely underhand. It did not set a good example for the junior footballers of Australasia and it took advantage of an inexperienced referee. But it was as old as Methuselah and it helped seal the match. As a lad, at Lang Park, Wally had seen NSW's Tom Raudonikis con Queensland with it and in 1986, at Headingley, Leeds, Wally had pulled it on fiery Great Britain forward Chris Burton and French referee Julian Rascagneres with equal success. That's why Don Furner left Wally on the field carrying a broken arm. Wally did not buy his experience or invent his wisdom, he acquired it over hundreds of matches, with as many referees and thousands more players. Not much occurs on a football field that is new to him and because he is smart, and concentrates, he retains the knowledge and uses it to rescue Australia.

Arm dangling, Wally was good for one more pass, second handler in a seven-man passing rush covering 50 metres, ending with Allan Langer scampering in for his second try. He fooled Kiwi fullback Gary Mercer so cruelly that Mercer stumbled giving chase and sprawled flat on his face. No sooner had Langer touched down than there was Wally, using his good left arm to lift Langer up by the jersey to congratulate him. Wally doesn't spend his life rushing ahead of everyone to hug try-scorers, he's there because he either set up the try, was part of the movement or was in close support if needed.

That made it 15–0 and Wally was content. With only minutes to half-time Wally signalled to coach Furner and walked off. The massive Eden Park crowd, with an inkling now of the nature of the injury, momentarily forgot their misery and recognised his courage with prolonged applause. He had played for 20 minutes with a broken arm, recalling the exploit of Great Britain captain Allan Prescott, who carried a broken arm to victory in a Test in Brisbane 30 years earlier. Wally wrapped a blanket around his shoulders, watched to the final score of 25–12 and single-handedly accepted the World Cup from prime minister Lange in the grandstand. In the dressingroom Wally stopped celebrations briefly to thank coach Don Furner, who was retiring after being with him since the 1986 Kangaroos. "We couldn't have sent you out any better," he said. Furner disclosed his secret pact with his captain. "I never worry how Wally trains," said Furner. "Just as long as he plays well and he's never let me down." But the most apt tribute to Wally came from opposing coach Tony Gordon, "The greatest footballer to pull on a boot."

NZRL officials moaned that in 80 minutes the Australians had set back New Zealand rugby league 10 years. Wally agreed it was a shame but told me, "If I'd had my way I'd have beaten them by another 20 points." He was unforgiving because of the bagging he had received over the radio that week. On Monday morning, the day after the Test, he rang Auckland's radio 91FM and asked to talk to the breakfast show hosts who had maligned him. When they declined Wally told the producer, "What a couple of gutless wonders, they hand it out all week and now they won't answer the phone." The *Auckland Star* newspaper ran a front-page photograph of Wally phoning the station and their sports section reported his anger at their jibes. "I don't think sportsmen should have to put up with that," he said. "I love it when people like them make jerks of themselves publicly. I just wish they were big enough to admit it."

After the combined euphoria of victory and pain killing tablets wore off Wally became acutely aware of his aching arm. He caught a plane home that day and was with orthopedic surgeon Dr Peter Myers at Holy Spirit Hospital in Brisbane that evening. Wally was sitting, facing Myers, when the radiologist walked in behind him. Wally did not see the radiologist's face but Myers looked up and said, "Bad eh?" Wally swivelled around and the radiologist said, "Sorry mate." It was no more than Wally had been expecting but he wasn't prepared for Myers's next comment. Holding the x-rays against a lighted screen the surgeon said, "What are your plans next year?" Wally blinked and

Myers said, "Put it this way, I know you're a headstrong bloke and if I tell you that you can't play, will you take any notice?" Wally replied that if it was that bad, he would retire. Myers told him to present himself the next day for surgery. He had an idea.

The bone broken in Wally's arm was the radius, the bone on the thumb side of the arm. In a normal adult the standard procedure would have been to insert a stainless steel plate over the break to immobilise the bone while it knitted. But orthopedic surgeons operating on sportsmen have studied reports of Mal Meninga's arm which, having been repaired with such a plate, has fractured again several times during matches. A plate is attached to the bone by screws inserted in drill holes which, in a body-impact sport like rugby league, can themselves create points of weakness in the bone. Myers had a steel plate on hand when Wally went under the anesthetic on 11 October, two days after the Cup final. If there were any problems aligning the break accurately Myers intended using the plate. Instead he inserted a 20 cm long, curving stainless-steel nail, threaded through the centre of the bone — through the marrow — from the wrist almost to the elbow. It had a hook on the end near the wrist to stop it sliding out of sight and to enable Myers to fetch it out again, probably at the end of the 1989 football season. Next day Myers told Wally that after the nail was inserted he had tested the fracture and found no movement in the bones. Myers was delighted with the results.

About six weeks later, soon after the protective cast was removed from his arm, Wally was back indulging in his new recreation, speedway driving at the Brisbane Exhibition ground. He and Gene Miles had begun as celebrity drivers but quickly advanced to rookie races in sprint cars which can reach 100 kph in the short straight. One night Wally won his heat and was in mid-field in the 15-lap sprint feature when his front wheel touched the wall coming off the main straight. Wally's car flew into the air, did a 360 degree spin and dumped heavily on its roof. Despite his safety harness, helmet and steel roll bars, Wally crashed around inside his cabin, bruising himself, banging his arm and dislocating a little finger which he popped back in himself. "Oh no! Lewis has shot 15 ft into the air," yelled the race caller. Jacqui Lewis was on her feet stumbling down the grandstand stairs with Gene Miles's wife Debbie behind her. But Jacqui was so shocked her legs gave way and Debbie caught her and helped her to a seat. "I couldn't talk," said Jacqui. "It was terrifying. I've seen him take knocks in football, dislocate his shoulder and break his arm but this was a bit different. I told the Broncos to put a halt to it. Maybe after football, but first things first."

Wally's arm ached that night and next morning he went straight to hospital to have it x-rayed. No apparent harm was done but a few weeks later Wally noticed a small lump between his wrist and where the nail was inserted. It hurt if he bumped it and he feared the speedway accident was causing the nail to reverse out of the bone. Dr Peter Myers diagnosed a small ganglion — a soft tissue cyst — where the nail hook was irritating the wrist. He gave Wally the option of removing the nail for the season or playing with it in. Wally chose to leave it in, Myers's recommendation. On 23 January 1989, Wally reentered hospital and in a brief operation Myers hammered the nail further into the bone to clear Wally's wrist. That afternoon Wally surprised the duty nurse with, "I'm off, I've got to read the news tonight." The operation had been kept secret and when he turned up at Channel 10 that evening staff stared at him. Was he all right, he looked pale and dopey, they said. I'm fine, said Wally, serene in the aftermath of the hospital's anesthetic. "Everyone was expecting me to screw up," laughed Wally. "The camera went bang, lights went on and I read right through. Afterwards they said, 'Gee, that's the best you've ever read,' and I looked at the tape and it was."

16 THE ONCE AND FUTURE KING

Patricia Millar taught English at Brisbane State High and, in 1977, Wally and Chris Roche walked into her class as repeating seniors. Both were stars of the school's first XV and Roche went on to represent Australia in rugby union. Both had a reputation for being less than conscientious students although Roche reformed sufficently to later graduate in law. The publication of *King Wally* inspired Patricia Millar to write a short article, subsequently published in the Brisbane *Courier-Mail*, about her year teaching Wally. She wrote:

I wasn't exactly delighted to get him. He and Chris Roche came into a class that might have been put together to gratify someone's sense of irony. Bright kids jostling self-consciously against plodders, strugglers and renegades. I aimed my lessons somewhere at the middle, and I kept order. And that last bit wasn't as easy as it sounds. So I was fairly glum at first about Wally.

There was one thing, though, that made me wonder about him. He had a bad reputation. But one day, the year before, I had seen him with some little kid who had hurt his arm at sport. They were near one of the staffrooms as I walked by. The little kid was sitting down, nursing his arm and trying not to cry. Wally was kneeling alongside him and he was just talking to him. You know, quietly, nicely, the way you talk to a little kid when he's upset or hurt. It was just a little thing but I liked it.

Anyway there he was in grade 12 English, studying the same stuff he'd done the year before and probably bored out of his mind. Then he fell in love. She was a lovely girl. She was in that class and she could write. I had taught her for a couple of years and we were sort of friends. One night I drove her home from a play and she told me Wally had been showing some interest. She had chosen to be in the school hockey squad to tour New Zealand in the May holidays. When this information circulated one of the boys made a remark about her figure, which was very nice and, she told me, "Wally spat on him". A true gallant!

I liked them both. They were as different as chalk and cheese and no one saw any future in their romance. She was bound for university. All he wanted to do was play football. But they were in love. I remember the first day they came into class together. He absolutely glowed.

And he tried. He handed in decent stuff. He could write quite entertainingly. I don't have to tell you what his favourite topic was. He lived for football. A couple of times his girlfriend brought him over to my place and she and I were spellbound listening to him. He loved it. The love of it shone out of him. I liked him for that too.

Lots of the boys loved football. I knew Roche was very talented too. But the others weren't talented enough, not to make a living out of it. I urged them to take their work seriously, try to get a reasonable tertiary entrance score, look for a good job. And they dreamed on about football.

So I started to turn up to watch them play. They were good. Even I could see that. They dominated play, they swept up and down that field and made it all look easy, and there was a joyousness in the way they played. It did you good to watch them. They were the conquering heroes all season long. Then came the final game. It was against Gregory Terrace and they were undefeated too. There were hundreds and hundreds of people there to watch. And we lost.

I can still see Wally, standing behind the try line with the others, as the Terrace boy kicked that final goal. His hands were on his hips, defeat was staring him in the face and there wasn't a thing he could do about it. I felt sorry for them. It wasn't that I was devastated or anything that State High had lost. But you know how it is. I wanted my kids to win.

The following week they had a creative essay to do. One of the topics was a quote from Shakespeare, "If we should fail..." They could use it as they liked and write a story on the theme. I put it there for Wally. And he did write on it. He wrote about the week leading up to the game, the expectations and optimism. He wrote about coming to terms with failure. It was mature and rather moving.

I had been wondering how his English studies would cope with the hype of the football season but, oddly enough, it wasn't until after it ended that his work went off. He just wasn't interested. I tended to take it personally — I always do — and we had a minor skirmish or two. "I got the death look," I told his girlfriend as we laughed about one of these disagreements later. He looked sheepish then. I suppose it was for her sake that he generally behaved himself in my class but he could recognise good motives and he knew I cared about my boring English literature and about his work and he humoured me, most of the time anyway.

Towards the end of the year he and Chris Roche made the Australian Schoolboys team bound for Europe in the Christmas holidays. I drove to Perth that Christmas and whenever I found something in the interstate papers about the schoolboys' tour I cut it out to give to Wally's girlfriend. But when I saw her again everything had changed. She had met someone else and she was now in love with him.

She was a nice girl and it must have been very difficult for her, when Wally came back, telling him. And for him, it must have been the most depressing time of his life. He came from the heady victories of the tour, home to a broken romance and a future that didn't seem anywhere near ready to happen. He had to go down to the dole office and register for work. I saw him at school a couple of months later. He seemed dispirited. He was driving a smallgoods van. He asked me if I had seen her. I said no. I thought it was all very sad.

Wally never let go of his dream. He put his trust in the thing he loved, in football, and it was good to him, in the end, it was. Probably there was never any doubt about the way it would turn out. He is gifted.

But I'm sure he had worked for his success too and I have been proud of him, these ten years since he left school.

The qualities which so endeared that youth to Patricia Millar, and prompted her to write that sensitive and moving portrait, remain intact in Wally today. He was kind to the tearful lad in the schoolyard then; today he receives 500 fan letters a year, mostly from schoolchildren, and he tries to answer them all. One letter reached him marked simply, "King Wally, Footballer, Brisbane." Another came from an eight-year-old Toowoomba boy who wrote that he loved football and practised with an old shoe in his backyard because his family could not afford to buy him a football. Wally organised for a stretched limousine to collect the boy and his family and bring them to the Broncos' end-of-season presentation night to meet all his heroes.

The disappointment Patricia Millar saw in Wally's face when Brisbane State High lost to Gregory Terrace was just as evident, and as genuine, many years later when Australia lost to Great Britain and the Broncos lost to Balmain. Wally's greatest asset is his ability to concentrate. When he wants to, he learns quickly. In her English classes, Patricia Millar saw glimpses of the intelligence which Wally most fully expresses during matches. He did put his trust into football. He has given 10 years of his life to it and has been rewarded handsomely. But at a cost.

One Sydney season has made Wally fitter than ever — 92 kilos compared with his normal playing weight of 95 kilos. "I can't wear half the trousers in my wardrobe," he said. "I've lost about three inches around the waist." But his year with the Broncos was the most injury prone of his career with a knee cartilage operation, a dislocated shoulder and a broken arm, as well as countless other minor knocks and bruises. In eight months, from January to August 1988, Wally made over 60 visits to the physiotherapist for heat and ultra-sound treatment, traction, massage and manipulation of his neck, shoulder and knee joints. Injuries which an 18-year-old throws off in a few days, linger in the 28-year-old for a week.

His football obligations — to the Broncos, state-of-origins, Tests and television commentaries — required Wally to fly to Sydney 50 times in 1988. Football trips and camps, television, his trip to Seoul and his hospitalisations took him away from home for nearly 100 nights of the eight-month football season — over one night out of three. Annotating these absences, Wally said, "It's really hard on Jacqui and the kids. We were that far from d-i-v-o-r-c-e one week," he said holding his forefinger and thumb fractionally apart. "She was just fed up with me being away."

Jacqui has noticed the step up from Brisbane to Sydney football. "In Brisbane they played a game and relaxed," she said. "In Sydney they're thinking about the next match an hour after the last. I'm not used to Wally getting cranky two days before a game as he does now."

Wally's commitments have severely reduced the time he spends with his children. When his eldest son, Mitchell, now aged three, sees Wally on television, he cuddles the screen and says, "Hurry home Dad." His favourite time with Dad is in the evening before bedtime. Unfortunately this coincided with when I used to arrive to begin the long series of interviews necessary for this new book on Wally. One evening I sat down and normally shy, gentle Mitchell ambushed me — whacking me over the head with his plastic golf stick. He was letting me know in no uncertain terms that I was encroaching on his time with Dad. I won him over next visit by arriving with a clown's red plastic ball on my nose.

Mitchell also had to contend with the arrival of a brother, Lincoln Clay, on 24 October 1987. Wally was convinced the baby would be a girl and had Jaimie Lee (Curtis) on his short list until Grant and Lisa Kenny got in first. Lincoln caught them by surprise. They had spent 16 hours moving house and Wally, exhausted and covered with grime and sweat, had just put his feet up, cold drink in hand, when Jacqui said, "Wally..." in a portentous voice. It was 23 October, 10 p.m. What? he said, with mock irritation, knowing full well what was to come. Said Jacqui, "I think it's time to go." Wally warned her, "No it's not. I've been shifting all day, I've had it, you better not be serious," and then, accepting the inevitable, "If it comes while I'm having a shower, bad luck." At the Mater Hospital, Wally lay in a bean bag on the floor beside Jacqui's bed, tried the chairs in the fathers' waiting room, dozed in the bean bag once more and at midday the next day was still on hand to watch his second son being born.

The expanding Lewis family meant lifestyle changes. He traded in his sleek black, Nissan 300ZX sports car on a second-hand family Mercedes which now features children's seat harnesses as well as the famous WJL-06 number plate. Wally and Jacqui helped design their palatial new, ranch-style home on an acre at exclusive St James Park, Birkdale, an outer suburb of Brisbane. While Wally was away — in Seoul, various Sydney trips and the World Cup in New Zealand — Jacqui supervised the concreting of their sweeping driveway, the building of a pergola and the purchases of carpets, furniture and drapery. She established the house with a confidence and certainty which belies her effervescent, amiable personality. Like most sporting widows she has learnt to cope with being alone. No wonder then she chose as "Her Favourite Room" for a magazine article, the master bedroom — the only place she can be guaranteed to have privacy with Wally from football, business, media, family and even the children.

When Wally is at home Jacqui acts as his unofficial manager, taking telephone messages, making appointments, keeping a blackboard on the kitchen bench to remind her of family and other important dates. Any hour of the evening in the Lewis household during the football season used to be an experience in manic living. The telephone rang every five minutes. In between cooking meals for the children, hushing their pet poodle and keeping an eye on the television news, Jacqui smoothly vetted the incoming calls. They now have two silent telephone numbers. A machine answers one and only their parents know the other number.

The faster the pace in the house, the more laid-back Jacqui becomes, a deliberate counter to the non-stop pressure of being married to possibly Australia's most sought-after sportsman. Yet she still finds time to play netball and one evening arrived home seething about an opposing player who had long fingernails. Jacqui couldn't get any satisfaction in her complaints to the umpire and so reported the matter to the match committee. If you're married to Wally Lewis you're not awed by referees.

Rugby league continues to confer honours upon Wally. In 1987 he was made a Member of the Order of Australia (AM) for his services to the game. He won the Queensland Sports Star of the Year and was inducted into the Australian Sports Hall of Fame in Melbourne. In 1988 Rugby League Week conducted a poll of 100 first grade players and Wally, with a vote of 57 per cent, was chosen by his peers as the top five-eighth in the Sydney premiership. In the same season's Dally M awards, Wally was named leading five-eighth against an impressive array of talent. Accepting his award, Wally smiled at Terry Lamb in the audience and said, "I didn't play against Canterbury so Ba (Lamb) didn't get the chance to play all over me. But I remember the day we played Cronulla. Michael Speechley wasn't a bloke I'd heard too much about and he gave me as hard a game as I've ever had."

Wally was then among the nominations for Representative Player of the Year. The list included Michael O'Connor, Garry Jack, Sam Backo and Allan Langer, all of whom had dominated nearly every match they played that season. But who could deny the words of former Australian lock Johnny Raper when he announced, "I'm very particular about rating players of the past with players of the present...but this guy could rub shoulders with the greats of the past...Wally Lewis would you please step forward to receive your award."

Wally was the Broncos' top try-scorer and was voted the Broncos' best back at the club's first annual awards. But the achievement which gave him as much pleasure as any award was his placing in the Rothman's Gold medal. Though 14 points behind the winner he was the Broncos' leading player in the competition which is judged by Sydney's referees.

The Broncos missed out on a semi-final berth but they could take satisfaction from knowing they were the league's biggest crowd-pulling club. Their average home crowd of 16,000 was second only to Newcastle's amazing average of 20,600. But the Broncos drew almost as well when they played away — averaging over 14,000 — which made them easily the competition's most popular side. Their seventh placing in the Sydney premiership disappointed all those, including Wally, who hoped they would make the final five. But their first season win-loss record of 14–8 was achieved against teams who treated their round against the Broncos as though it was a grand final. Wayne Bennett wrote, "I got sick and tired of coaches saying how their team had turned in their best game against us since Adam played in bare feet."

While the Broncos as a team were a drawcard there seems little doubt that many in the crowd came specifically to see captain Lewis. Rugby league writer Ian Heads wrote:

> "Sydney rugby league teams preparing to play host to the Brisbane Broncos could do worse than flood their district with posters saying simply, "He's playing". If they did that they would at the very least double their gates every time."

Heads dubbed it the "Lewis Factor" and likened Wally's impact to the way Bradman used to excite cricket crowds in his day. Another journalist, Roy Masters, estimated that Wally's advertised inclusion in the Broncos team for their second match against Penrith was responsible for 3,000 of the sellout crowd of 17,000 at Penrith Park.

Wally's performance in the Sydney competition fulfilled all the expectations of the man who, for so long, did most to stop him going there. Ron McAuliffe and Wally worked in tandem, on and off the field, for 10 years to restore Queensland's rugby league pride. When the former Labor senator died it was almost a sign to Wally that his task, too, might be nearing completion.

McAuliffe's death particularly saddened Wally because they had just begun to repair the schism that occurred when Wally was employed by the Maranta consortium. McAuliffe, who had backed the losing consortium, thereafter pressed Wally to retire and enter politics or television — preferably politics. Wally is friendly with Prime Minister Hawke. It is not just sport which they have in common. The character trait in Wally which makes him so proud of captaining Australia is reflected in Hawke's prime ministership, and appeals so much to the electorate. Wally is interested in politics, but is inexperienced and for the moment is concentrating on his television career.

McAuliffe was president of the Lang Park Trust and the more the Broncos clashed with the Trust, the greater the strain placed on Wally's friendship with his venerable mentor. McAuliffe stepped up his pressure on Wally to retire and head into politics. When Wally refused they had their first falling out in a decade's close and friendly association. The real reason eventually emerged one evening over a drink. "Ron thought that my joining the Broncos turned me against him, though of course it didn't," said Wally. "He tore strips off me and I told him that the Broncos were my employers now and I had to give them my best. I said, 'I'm playing football and they're paying the bills.' "

They parted company on unhappy terms. Wally scarcely spoke to McAuliffe all season but, the week before he died, McAuliffe twice rang the Lewis home. Wally was in Sydney with the Broncos preparing for their crunch match against Balmain. McAuliffe told Jacqui, "Tell Wally that we'll always be best mates. Tell him I understand why he has to stick with the Broncos." Jacqui reassured McAuliffe that Wally had never harboured any ill-feeling and would be glad of the calls.

Five days before he died, McAuliffe, drinking with the manager of the QRL club, Dick Breen, recalled how he had been inspired to enlist in the army when he saw a brass band marching down the street and he had stepped in behind. He said to Breen, "When I go make sure I have a brass band and a huge wake. If I forget to give you the money I'm sure the QRL will give it the tap on the head. They'll spend a few bucks on me. I want everybody to have a good time." McAuliffe died from a cerebral hemorrhage on 16 August 1988.

I spoke to Wally at the funeral and we marvelled at the remarkable cross-section of people among the hundreds who packed the Fortitude Valley church for the Requiem Mass funeral. Among the pews knelt the deputy prime minister Lionel Bowen; the former governor of NSW Sir Roden Cutler; the chief justice of Queensland Sir Dormer Andrews; cricketers Alan Davidson and Tom Veivers; Bob Templeton and Chris Handy from rugby union; his two former QRL officers Wayne Bennett and John Ribot; Brian Kerle from basketball; bookmakers, police commissioners, and McAuliffe's old mates from the Rats of Tobruk.

McAuliffe never wore the green-and-gold of Australia but deserved to, such was his contribution to rugby league. So, as the coffin bearing the late QRL chief was wheeled from the church, his old friend and erstwhile Sydney sparring partner, ARL president Ken Arthurson, stepped forward and draped the casket with a 1988 Australian jumper bearing the number 7. Arthurson had hoped to find a number 6 — Wally's number — but time had not permitted. Then, back at the QRL club, they had the biggest wake ever seen in rugby league in Queensland and a brass band cheerfully oompahed on for hours.

McAuliffe's bequest to rugby league was the state-of-origin series, which in turn gave us Wally Lewis, whose Broncos and Queensland teams extracted grudging respect from Sydney — the political and playing power base of rugby league. Between them, Senator Ron and Wally turned rugby league into a booming two-state game, virtually doubling the game's popularity in Australia.

Although Wally signed a three-year contract with the Broncos his agreement enables him to retire at the end of 1989. If he decides to play in 1990 he has agreed to make himself available for an unprecedented second term as captain of a Kangaroo tour to Great Britain. He would turn 31 on 1 December 1990, midway through this tour. Newly appointed Australian coach Bobby Fulton was 31 when he captained the 1978 Kangaroos and Max Krilich was 32 when he led the 1982 Invincibles. Wally seems to have been around a long time because he has captained Queensland and played for Australia since he was 21. Of the 26 players who ran on for the first state-of-origin in 1980, only Wally, Chris Close and Graeme Wynn remain in first-grade football. The rest have retired, become coaches, retreated to less strenuous country divisions or are out to pasture in English clubs. Of the 1981 Australian team, in which he made his Test debut, Wally is the only player still in active service.

The man who may well decide Wally's future is Wayne Bennett. His only doubts about Wally's ability to play for another two seasons revolve around his heavy representative duties. "He has 22 weeks in a row to go, every Sunday," said Bennett. "Last season it was catching up with him and 1989 will be no different." The Broncos have introduced more quality players into their team which should reduce the pressure on Wally. Towards the end of 1988 he was captaining the Broncos, taking line and field kicks, calling moves, making breaks, setting up tries, scoring himself and then taking the conversions. "Wally's a big match player," said Bennett. "It would be nice if we could just play him in the rep matches and the final five."

Bennett will not put Wally into reserve grade — not without advising him to retire first. "I'll be the first bloke telling him to go if he stays too long," he said. "If he's enjoying his football and regards the money as a bonus, that's fine, he shouldn't give it away, because you're retired an awful long time. If he keeps going just for the money then he's in trouble."

With every new season Wally is compared with the greats of the past — Johnny Raper, Reg Gasnier and Bobby Fulton. Wally is more than a player. His career has spanned the renaissance of rugby league not only in NSW and Queensland, but in England and New Zealand. Through Queensland's revival, Wally, more than any other single player, has contributed to rugby league's international resurgence. As a result he has become the player-statesman of Australian rugby league, a respected spokesman and advocate for the game.

The marvellous fact about Wally Lewis is that he is still playing. Week after week he can be seen, rocking rugby league matches with calculated moves which make the rest of the players look as though they are three steps behind. It is as though time had played a trick and we could still see Don Bradman striding out to bat, or Herb Elliot bursting into the straight. Wally is up there with them.

It is a fortunate generation which produces a champion whose greatness is acknowledged and widely appreciated during the span of his own playing career. One day — sooner now than later — Australian rugby league won't have Wally Lewis and fans will have only their memories of him to compare with the great players of the future. In 1989 rugby league fans have one of their last opportunities to be able to say, "I saw him play."

INDEX